CHINESE
ENTERTAINING

CHINESE
ENTERTAINING
SPECTACULAR FOOD FOR PARTIES
COCKTAILS ◆ BUFFETS ◆ DINNERS

LISA KINSMAN

with photographs by Christine Hanscomb

Conran Octopus

To Rodney

This edition published 1986 by
Conran Octopus Limited
37 Shelton Street
London WC2H 9HN

This paperback edition published in 1992 by
Conran Octopus Limited

Art Director Douglas Wilson
Art Editor Clive Hayball
Photographic Stylist Antonia Gaunt
House Editor Susie Ward

ISBN 1 85029 419 4

The publishers would like to thank the following for
their assistance: Neal Street East, 5 Neal Street,
London WC2;
Heal's, 196 Tottenham Court Road, London W1;
The Conran Shop, Fulham Road, London SW3;
Mark J. West, 39 High Street, Wimbledon Village,
London SW19.

HALF TITLE PAGE Gift-wrapped Mango and Strawberry
(p. 125), Lattice Layers with Fruit (p. 129),
Caramelized Fruit.
TITLE PAGE Fancy Fish Cakes with Asparagus (p. 83),
Pomegranate Duck (p. 93), Stuffed Tofu Puffs (p. 102).

Typeset by Servis Filmsetting
Printed and Bound in China

CONTENTS

I could never have imagined myself becoming a cook. During my childhood in Hong Kong family meals were lengthy affairs, involving a great variety of dishes, all of which I was made to taste, even if only in small amounts. I vividly recall family discussion relating to the food we were served – the Chinese are very concerned with all aspects of gastronomy and can truly be said to live to eat! – but I do not remember expressing any interest of my own. Indirectly, however, I must have gained a basic grasp of culinary practice, but without any real knowledge or practical experience.

In England, after I married, I found myself doing a great deal of entertaining, and discovered that I enjoyed it enormously, although at that time I had to limit myself to a fairly tight budget. It was from entertaining that I developed a real interest in cooking. Entirely self-taught, I found increasing pleasure in creating dishes different from those served in restaurants, adapting and developing classical ones to make them into more flamboyant party pieces. Business entertaining for my husband's company brought requests for me to cook professionally for various events, and necessarily larger numbers. I rapidly progressed to buffets for 200, and even tackled an anniversary celebration for no fewer than 700 guests!

I found catering on this scale highly stimulating and a rewarding means of self-expression, requiring a great deal of mental and physical discipline. I was trained in interior design and had developed a career as a freelance designer. Now I discovered that there are many parallels between cooking and design. In both one needs to be conscious of materials and surroundings, to make the end result aesthetically pleasing. In fact arranging a successful menu is not unlike interpreting a client's requirements. It is an exercise in design – very subjective – with the finished whole the result of individual effort.

In the East, to be invited to share a meal in someone's house, and thus to participate in the family's life, is a great compliment, and a truly memorable meal reflects credit on the person who prepares and serves it. Even after living in England for a long time, I still subscribe to the Oriental idea of service, and believe that serving your guests with food on which you have lavished time and care is one of life's greatest pleasures. This book invites you to share that pleasure.

My food is essentially Chinese, and although adapted to the Western style of life by the use of ingredients familiar and acceptable to European tastes, it is in no way Europeanized. Some of the dishes in this book, such as Peking Duck, are actually very traditional. However, I avoid such classic Chinese delicacies as sinews and duck's feet, neither of which is to be recommended by either association or taste. Even so, I have been pleasantly surprised to find myself coming to enjoy some of the more unusual ingredients I disliked as a child, which proves that one's palate may be educated, even if not immediately receptive. Many specifically Chinese ingredients can be bought in preserved form by mail order.

The Chinese diet is an exceptionally healthy and well-balanced one. A Chinese meal involves a variety

6

of dishes in which the quantities tend to be small – a very healthy way of eating. A well-balanced meal includes food which the Chinese think of as being strong and 'masculine' in character, such as meat and poultry, served in conjunction with more 'feminine' vegetable dishes, and fish, which belongs somewhere between the two ends of the scale. As a non-vegetarian I like to combine the flavour of meat with vegetables, but vegetable dishes also stand very much in their own right, and you will find plenty of them in this book.

The Chinese cook is concerned with texture, determined by the method of preparation and cooking (pp. 136–137) and the subtle blending of ingredients so that none is too assertive, with emphasis on colour, appearance and presentation as well. All the dishes in this book reflect these concerns, to which of course today's culinary climate is also particularly favourable. It is unfortunate that the uninitiated should regard Chinese cooking as something of a mystery. After all, cooks worldwide use the favourite Chinese methods of frying, steaming and braising, so why should Chinese cuisine be expected to pose more problems than any other? The truth is, anyone can become proficient. I wrote my first book, *Chinese Delights*, in an attempt to dispel the mystique and remove some of the misconceptions. Still bearing entertaining and parties in mind, I continued trying out and testing recipes, embarking on a few flights of fancy without, I hope, losing sight of practical considerations, and decided to write this book to record the results.

It is a book intended to be read for pleasure as well as practical use, to be dipped into as a book at bedtime, as well as coming into its own in the kitchen. All the recipes will be entirely accessible, even to the novice cook, and the photographs are designed to show what you should be aiming at. Don't be put off by the lengthy recipes – some of the longest are actually easiest to prepare.

Chinese food is designed for sharing and is therefore ideal for parties. It stimulates conversation, and the numerous dishes which go to make up a meal ensure that interest is maintained throughout.

I give menu suggestions for different types of parties on pp. 138–139, but you will have no difficulty – and a great deal of fun – in making your own selection of dishes, appropriate to your own style of entertaining. You will find recipes to suit every season and occasion, some surprisingly low-budget, some more extravagant. They are arranged for easy reference in sections based principally on courses. In planning your menus, feel free to dip into all of these, mixing and matching to suit your preference. Explore and improvise to serve food in your own special style, and aim to produce dishes that will win appreciation – and stimulate you to further experiment.

Lisa Kinsman

7

8

HORS D'OEUVRES

Hors d'oeuvres are designed to create a relaxed mood before embarking on the main meal to follow. I have chosen casual, informal dishes, but some of them are substantial enough to satisfy the hungriest guests. All can be served either as dinner party starters or as finger food at a drinks party. Personally I never offer nuts, crisps, or dips with crudités at my parties. I find that Chinese food is so much more interesting – in taste, texture and appearance.

Hors d'oeuvres may be served in a variety of ways at a drinks party. Traditional serving platters need to be large enough to avoid overcrowding and display the food to best advantage. Anything pretty to set off the food can be used: lacquered trays, wickerwork baskets, glass cake stands. Fresh lotus, Savoy cabbage or radicchio leaves also make very attractive natural receptacles. Starched napkins, casually twisted so that the food can nestle in the folds, are a particular favourite of mine for offering hors d'oeuvres.

When hors d'oeuvres appear as a first course, I prefer plates to the traditional individual serving bowls favoured by Chinese. It seems a pity to spoil the appearance of the food by piling one helping on top of another and covering everything with the accompanying sauce: given more space, and the sauce served in a separate bowl, it looks so much more appetizing.

Clockwise, from left: Carrot Hearts *(p. 29)*, Crispy Crab Claws *(p. 15)*, Pea and Chilli Prawn Bundles *(p. 12)*, Pacific Prawn and French Bean Bales *(p. 13)*, Salmon on Display *(p. 18)*, Lychee Satellites *(p. 25)*.

NESTS OF SPICY PRAWNS

The impact of these nests is quite striking. They are guaranteed to generate conversation at the dinner table as guests speculate on their construction. Some have actually imagined them to be handwoven, never guessing how simple they are to produce! They may be served hot or cold so may be prepared in advance. The filling can be reheated, though this must be done quickly to prevent further cooking. The nests should then be filled immediately before serving to preserve their crispy texture. The nests can be stored, stacked, in an airtight tin.

◆

MAKES 12

for the nests
2 oz (60 g) thin Chinese egg noodles, in one cake
1 teaspoon (5 ml) salt

for deep-frying
1 pint (600 ml) corn oil

for the filling
3 oz (90 g) raw peeled prawns (if unavailable, cooked prawns
may be substituted)
½ teaspoon cornflour
salt and white pepper
1 tablespoon (15 ml) corn oil
2 oz (60 g) Spanish onion, diced
1 tablespoon (15 ml) Shaoshing wine
1 tablespoon (15 ml) Sweet and Chilli Sauce (p. 130)
½ teaspoon sugar (optional)
2 tablespoons (30 ml) chopped coriander

◆

10

To make the nests, cook the noodles in boiling water with the salt for 1 minute. Use a fork to separate the strands during cooking. Drain, then refresh under cold running water until firm and springy. Drain again and leave to rest in a wire sieve for several hours. (Covered with clingfilm, the noodles can be kept quite successfully for use a day or two later.)

Heat the oil for deep-frying in a wok or deep-fryer to 275°F (140°C). Take a few strands of the drained noodles and arrange them loosely in a wire strainer, taking care not to overfill it. Press a second wire strainer into the first so that the 'nest' formed by the noodles is kept firmly in shape.

Holding the two strainers together, plunge the 'nest' into the hot oil and fry at an even temperature just until light golden but not browned. (If the oil becomes too hot during cooking, reduce the heat, or remove the pan from the heat altogether for a short time if necessary.) When cooking is complete, remove from the oil, invert the strainer and tap gently to release the 'nest'. Drain on kitchen paper. Use the remaining noodles to make nests in the same way.

To make the filling, dry the prawns thoroughly and cut them into fairly small pieces. Mix with the cornflour, seasoned with a little salt and pepper.

Heat the oil in a pre-heated wok or frying pan with a pinch of salt. Add the onion and stir-fry over a moderate heat for 30 seconds until softened but not browned.

Add the prawns to the pan, turn up the heat and stir-fry for about 1 minute. Add the wine, sweet and chilli sauce, ¼ teaspoon salt, pepper to taste and the sugar, if used, and stir-fry for a further 30 seconds. Turn off the heat and mix in the coriander.

Drain any excess liquid from the prawn mixture and use to fill the 'nests' just before serving.

───────── ❖ ─────────

Above: Nests of Spicy Prawns

SESAME PRAWN TOAST

In this recipe I use a food processor rather than the cleaver characteristic of Chinese cooking because the texture here is not of prime importance. The toast may be prepared 15 minutes in advance and kept warm in the oven (375°F/190°C/gas mark 5).

◆

MAKES 32

9 oz (270 g) small raw peeled prawns (if unavailable, cooked prawns may be substituted)
1 oz (30 g) white sesame seeds
2 oz (60 g) pork fat, very finely diced
1 egg white
$\frac{1}{2}$ teaspoon cornflour
$\frac{3}{4}$ teaspoon salt
$\frac{1}{2}$ teaspoon white pepper
1 teaspoon (5 ml) sugar
4 slices medium-sliced white bread, crusts removed

for deep-frying
$1\frac{3}{4}$ pints (1 litre) corn oil

Dry the prawns with kitchen paper. Put the pork fat into a food processor with the egg white, cornflour, salt, pepper and sugar. Add $1\frac{1}{2}$ teaspoons (7.5 ml) water and mix lightly.

Add the prawns and process until they are chopped but not reduced to a paste. Check the seasoning by taking a small quantity of the mixture and frying it in a little oil. Adjust the seasoning if necessary.

Spread the bread slices evenly with the prawn mixture. Spread the sesame seeds out on a plate. Press each bread slice, spread side down, on to the sesame seeds, to coat evenly.

Heat the oil in a wok or deep-fryer to 300°F (150°C), add the bread slices, coated side down, and deep-fry for 4–5 minutes. Turn and fry for 1 further minute or until golden-brown. Take care to maintain a steady temperature so that the bread does not brown too quickly.

Remove the toast and drain on kitchen paper. Cut each slice in half and then crossways into 4 strips. (Small triangles or other shapes would also look attractive.) Serve hot.

❖

PEA AND CHILLI PRAWN BUNDLES
illustrated on pages 8–9

The cooked bundles may be reheated in a microwave oven or in a conventional oven (375°F/190°C/gas mark 5) for 10–15 minutes.

◆

MAKES 8–10

3 oz (90 g) split peas
8–10 raw peeled prawns, preferably 2 in (5 cm) long
$\frac{1}{4}$ teaspoon salt
white pepper
1 teaspoon (5 ml) sugar
light soy sauce
$\frac{1}{4}$ teaspoon cornflour
$\frac{1}{8}$ teaspoon chilli powder
1 egg, beaten
spring roll paper

for deep-frying
$1\frac{3}{4}$ pints (1 litre) corn oil

◆

Place the split peas in a saucepan with 18 fl oz (500 ml) water, the salt, 2 pinches of pepper and half the sugar. Bring to the boil then simmer uncovered for about 1 hour, until the water evaporates and the peas are pulpy.

Wash and dry the prawns. Put them into a bowl with the remaining sugar, the soy sauce, cornflour and chilli powder. Stir lightly to mix and set aside.

From the spring roll paper cut 8 3-in (7.5-cm) squares and 8 10-in long strips $\frac{1}{2}$ in (1 cm) wide. Return remaining sealed spring roll paper to the refrigerator.

Place 1 teaspoon (5 ml) of the pulpy peas and a prawn in the centre of a spring roll paper square. Draw the edges of the paper gently together to form a bundle. Around it place a spring roll paper strip and carefully tie this into a knot, taking care not to break it. Make the remaining bundles.

Heat the oil to 275°F (140°C) in a wok or deep-fryer. Add the bundles in 2 batches (the oil should cover them comfortably), with their tops spread slightly to resemble flowers. Deep-fry for 1–2 minutes, until golden-brown, then drain on kitchen paper. Serve hot.

❖

PRAWN FINGERS
illustrated on page 37

These can be kept hot in a conventional oven (375°F/190°C/gas mark 5) for about 10–15 minutes. Strips of boneless chicken could be used instead.

◆

MAKES 10

10 large prawns in the shell, about 3 in (7.5 cm) long (if
unavailable, smaller prawns can be used to make up the
required length)
white sesame seeds
½ teaspoon cornflour
phyllo pastry sheets
¼ teaspoon salt
white pepper
2–3 drops sesame oil
1 egg, beaten

for deep-frying
1 pint (600 ml) corn oil

◆

To roast the sesame seeds, put them into a pre-heated wok or frying pan and stir-fry without oil over a moderate heat until they are golden and their nutty flavour becomes more pronounced. Remove from the heat and allow to cool.

Peel the prawns, devein them but leave the tails intact. Wash and dry the prawns with kitchen paper before mixing them with the cornflour, seasoning and sesame oil. Make crossways cuts at intervals along the length of each body, without cutting through, to prevent the prawns from curling when they are cooked.

Cut the phyllo pastry into 20 × 4-in (10-cm) squares.

Sprinkle the prawns lightly with sesame seeds. Place a prawn diagonally on each phyllo square, leaving the tail exposed. Fold the corner of the square diagonally opposite over the top of the prawn and roll up neatly and securely. Roll this in a second phyllo square to make a perfectly secure finger. Brush the edges with egg to seal them.

Heat the oil to 275°F (140°C) in a wok or deep-fryer. Add the prawn fingers and deep-fry for about 1 minute, until a light golden-brown. Drain the prawn fingers in a sieve, then on kitchen paper.

PACIFIC PRAWNS WITH FRENCH BEAN BALES
illustrated on pages 8–9

These require virtually no cooking and may be prepared several hours in advance. They should be covered with clingfilm until needed. They look particularly good presented on a dark tray or serving dish. A thin spaghetti, often sold as spaghettini, is the best pasta to use to tie up the bundles.

◆

SERVES 12–16

12–16 large raw prawns, about 3–4 in (7.5–10 cm) long
4 oz (120 g) French beans
8 oz (240 g) broccoli
salt
2 teaspoons (10 ml) sugar
about 30 strands spaghettini

for dipping
Sweet and Chilli Sauce (p. 130), or
Spring Onion and Ginger Sauce (p. 131), or
Ginger and Vinegar Sauce (p. 132)

◆

Cut the broccoli into florets. Top and tail the French beans and cut them into 1½-in (3.5-cm) lengths. Cook the vegetables together in boiling salted water for about 1 minute, removing them while still firm and crunchy. Drain and refresh immediately under cold running water, then drain again.

In the same saucepan cook the prawns in boiling salted water, together with the sugar, for approximately 2–3 minutes. Drain, refresh under cold running water, then drain and peel.

Cook the spaghettini in boiling salted water for about 3 minutes, until the strands are flexible, and then drain well.

Take 4 pieces of bean and tie them into a bundle with a strand of spaghettini, using a double knot. Keep as close as possible to the beans so that the spaghettini does not break as you tie it. Arrange the French bean bales, prawns and broccoli on a serving dish as shown in the photograph and serve with one of the suggested dips.

13

HALF MOONS AND BUTTERFLIES
illustrated on pages 26–27

◆

These charming pastry crescents and bows with a prawn filling may be prepared several hours in advance, then reheated in a microwave oven, or in a conventional oven (325°F/160°C/gas mark 3) for 10–15 minutes.

◆

HALF MOONS · MAKES ABOUT 20

for the filling

4 oz (120 g) small raw prawns (if unavailable, cooked prawns may be substituted)
$\frac{1}{2}$ teaspoon cornflour
$\frac{1}{4}$ teaspoon salt
white pepper
$\frac{1}{2}$ teaspoon sugar
2 tablespoons (30 ml) corn oil
1 oz (30 g) Spanish onion, finely chopped
$\frac{1}{4}$ teaspoon 5-spice powder
$1\frac{1}{2}$ teaspoons (7.5 ml) cornflour mixed with 3–4 tablespoons (45–60 ml) water
$7\frac{1}{2}$-oz (215-g) packet frozen shortcrust pastry, thawed
1 egg, beaten

for deep-frying
$1\frac{3}{4}$ pints (1 litre) corn oil

BUTTERFLIES · MAKES ABOUT 20

filling as for half moons (above)
spring roll paper
1 egg, beaten

for deep-frying
$1\frac{3}{4}$ pints (1 litre) corn oil

◆

Half moons: to make the filling, place the prawns in a bowl with the cornflour, salt, pepper to taste and sugar. Mix together and leave to marinate for about 20 minutes.

Heat 1 tablespoon (15 ml) of the oil to a moderate temperature in a pre-heated wok or frying pan. Add the onion with a pinch of salt and fry until softened but not coloured. Transfer the onion to a dish.

In the same pan, heat another tablespoon (15 ml) oil to a very high temperature. Add the prawns and stir-fry for approximately 1 minute, then add the onion, 5-spice powder and cornflour mixture. Stir-fry for a further 30 seconds. Transfer the mixture to a bowl and chill in the refrigerator for several hours.

Roll out the pastry about $\frac{1}{8}$ in (3 mm) thick. Using a 3-in (7.5-cm) biscuit cutter, cut out rounds until all the pastry is used up. Using a teaspoon, spoon a portion of the filling over half each round. Brush the edges with egg, fold over and press lightly to seal.

Heat the oil to 275°F (140°C) in a wok or deep-fryer, add the half moons and deep-fry for 30 seconds to 1 minute, until golden. Remove with a slotted spoon and drain on kitchen paper.

Butterflies: Cut 4 equal-sized triangles from a 9-in (22-cm) square of spring roll paper. Place a teaspoonful of the filling in the centre of each. Brush the edges with egg. Fold the nearest corner of the triangle across to meet the centre of the opposite side.

Seal the edges with egg. Gently bring half of the long edge towards you, to close the opening, then brush with egg (see diagram). Hold this between finger and thumb and do the same with the opposite side. (Do not worry if there are some variations in shape. The folding process is simply to prevent oil from spoiling the filling by making contact with it.)

Heat the oil to 260°F (130°C) in a wok or deep-fryer. Add the butterflies and deep-fry until light golden. Remove with a slotted spoon and drain on kitchen paper. Serve hot or cold.

14

CRABMEAT AND RICE BALLS

Although I have never seen these on a Chinese menu, they make use of staple Chinese ingredients and are perfect to nibble with drinks. They may be prepared and cooked several hours in advance, then reheated in a microwave oven or in a conventional oven (325°F/160°C/gas mark 3) for 10–15 minutes

◆

MAKES 20

6 oz (180 g) fresh crabmeat, or 8 oz (240 g) frozen crabmeat, thoroughly thawed
8 oz (240 g) cooked, long-grain rice
1 tablespoon (15 ml) corn oil
¼ teaspoon salt
white pepper
2 tablespoons (30 ml) oyster sauce
2 teaspoons (10 ml) cornflour mixed with
2 tablespoons (30 ml) water
1 spring onion, finely chopped
1 oz (30 g) fresh coriander, finely chopped
1 large egg, beaten
2 oz (60 g) dry white breadcrumbs

for deep-frying
1 pint (600 ml) corn oil

◆

If you are using frozen crabmeat, drain it thoroughly and pat dry with kitchen paper.

Heat 1 tablespoon (15 ml) oil to a high temperature in a pre-heated wok or frying pan, add the crabmeat, season with salt and pepper to taste and stir-fry for just over 1 minute. Add the rice and stir well to mix, then add the oyster sauce and cornflour mixture and stir-fry for about 1 further minute. Stir in the spring onion and coriander, transfer to a bowl and cool slightly.

Form the mixture into balls about the size of walnuts. Place each ball on a fork and dip in beaten egg. Shake off any excess, then roll in breadcrumbs.

Heat the oil to 325°F (160°C) in a wok or deep-fryer. Add the balls in batches and deep-fry for 1 minute. Drain in a wire sieve, then on kitchen paper. Serve hot.

❖

CRISPY CRAB CLAWS
illustrated on pages 8–9

This exotic looking dish will win high approval for the delicious flavour concealed beneath the crab claws' crusty exteriors. To save any last-minute rush, everything can be prepared the previous day and kept in the refrigerator so that only the cooking remains to be done. They may be cooked 30 minutes in advance and kept warm in a low oven. Worcestershire sauce goes well with them.

◆

SERVES 15

15 medium crab claws
9 oz (270 g) small peeled prawns, preferably raw
2 oz (60 g) pork fat, very finely diced
1 egg white
½ teaspoon cornflour
1¼ teaspoons (6.5 ml) salt
¼–½ teaspoon white pepper
1 teaspoon (5 ml) sugar
½ large loaf medium-sliced white bread
2 eggs, beaten

for deep-frying
1 pint (600 ml) corn oil

◆

Dry the crab claws thoroughly with kitchen paper. Put the pork fat into a food processor with the egg white. Add the cornflour, salt, pepper and sugar and 1½ teaspoons (7.5 ml) water and mix together lightly. Add the prawns and blend in the mixture to a paste.

Cut the bread into ¼-in (5-mm) cubes. Coat each crab claw with the prawn mixture, pressing it on lightly to make sure that it remains in place, but leaving the claw end exposed. Dip each claw into the beaten egg, then roll in the bread cubes so that the surface is covered. There should be a little space between the bread through which the prawn mixture shows a contrasting colour.

Heat the oil to 300°F (150°C) in a wok or deep-frying pan, add the claws in batches and deep-fry for about 2 minutes, until golden-brown all over. (Do not let them brown too quickly or the prawn mixture inside will not have a chance to cook.) Drain in a wire sieve, then on kitchen paper.

15

❖

SPINACH-BEDDED CORAL MUSSELS

Crisp lettuce or mustard and cress could be used instead of spinach. Mussel shells make natural containers for these tasty hors d'oeuvres.

◆

MAKES 40

2 lb (960 g) mussels
2 oz (60 g) spinach leaves, shredded
a few slices root ginger
1 tablespoon (15 ml) corn oil
1½ teaspoons (7.5 ml) crushed yellow bean paste
1 tablespoon (15 ml) tomato ketchup
½ teaspoon sugar
1 tablespoon (15 ml) Shaoshing wine
¼ teaspoon Worcestershire sauce
salt
4 thin slices of root ginger

◆

Cook the mussels with the ginger in a saucepan of boiling water for 1–2 minutes until all the mussels have opened. Strain in a colander and remove the mussel meat from each shell. Discard the larger half of each shell. Remove all traces of muscle and sinew from the smaller halves, using a sharp knife. Set aside.

Cut the thin slices of ginger into hairs-breadth strands, using a very sharp knife. Put the oil into a small pre-heated saucepan, then add the bean paste, tomato ketchup, sugar, wine, Worcestershire sauce, ginger and salt to taste. Heat gently until the mixture caramelizes. Add the mussels and turn them gently in the sauce so that they absorb the flavour.

Half-fill each prepared mussel shell with a little shredded spinach. Top each with mussel meat and a little of the sauce. Serve hot or cold.

◆◆◆

Left: Spinach-Bedded Coral Mussels,
right: Fragrant Fish *(p. 18).*

FRAGRANT FISH
illustrated on page 16–17

Although this is perfect for hors d'oeuvres it also makes an excellent main course, in larger quantities, perhaps served with plain boiled rice.

◆

SERVES 12

1½ lb (720 g) monkfish, cod or other firm white fish
1½ tablespoons (22.5 ml) chopped spring onion
1 tablespoon (15 ml) dark soy sauce
white pepper
2 tablespoons (30 ml) plain flour

for the coating sauce
1½ tablespoons (22.5 ml) dark soy sauce
1½ tablespoons (22.5 ml) malt vinegar
1½ tablespoons (22.5 ml) Shaoshing wine or dry sherry
2½ tablespoons (37.5 ml) sugar
¼–½ teaspoon 5-spice powder

for deep-frying
1 pint (600 ml) corn oil

Skin the fish and dry it thoroughly. Cut it into 3 × 2 × ½-in (7.5 × 5 × 1-cm) pieces. Put them into a bowl and add the spring onion, soy sauce and pepper to taste. Turn the fish to coat, then dust all over with flour, using a wire sieve or dredger.

Heat the oil to 400°F (200°C) in a wok or deep-fryer, add the fish and deep-fry for 7–8 minutes until firm, slightly crusty and brown at the edges. Remove with a slotted spoon and drain in a wire sieve. Leave to rest while making the sauce.

Heat all the sauce ingredients with 1½ tablespoons (22.5 ml) of water in a large, heavy saucepan, stirring occasionally, until the sauce is thickened and reduced by about one-third. Turn off the heat, add the fish to the pan and turn gently to coat with sauce. Leave until cold, then serve.

❖

SALMON ON DISPLAY
illustrated on page 8–9

To buy salmon specially for this recipe may not be necessary. If you already have a large piece for another dish, you would be able to remove the small amount needed from the tail end. Or you could use a salmon steak. It is not essential to use laver, available in packets from Asian grocers, or Japanese horseradish which may be difficult to come by; chives, lumpfish roe or mustard and cress make good alternative garnishes, and you could substitute English horseradish for the Japanese variety, or use English mustard. This dish may be prepared an hour or so in advance and wrapped in clingfilm until needed.

◆

MAKES 30

8 oz (240 g) fresh salmon, tail section, or fillet
8 oz (240 g) Chinese white radish
salt
½ teaspoon Japanese horseradish powder mixed with 1 teaspoon (5 ml) water, or 1 teaspoon (5 ml) creamed horseradish
1 sheet dry roasted laver, cut into thin strips

◆

Peel the radish and cut into round slices ⅛ in (3 mm) thick. Using a sharp knife, cut out different shapes, and set aside.

Skin the tail end of the salmon and halve it horizontally; using a very sharp knife, slice just above the bone, then turn the fish over and, holding it down firmly, repeat the operation, keeping as close to the bone as possible to avoid wastage.

Then slice it as you would smoked salmon. Holding the knife at an angle and starting at the wider end, cut wafer-thin slices towards the tail.

If you are using a salmon steak rather than the tail, first remove the skin, then, holding it firmly, cut it in thin slices across the grain of the flesh, working away from you and holding the knife at an angle.

Sprinkle the radish shapes with a little salt and spread them very thinly with horseradish cream. Top each with sliced salmon, trimming it neatly to fit, and decorate with laver.

❖

SPINACH SEAFOOD ROLLS
illustrated on page 31

Cheap, easily obtainable and subtle in flavour, spinach has a good colour, and its delicate strength makes it an ideal wrapping. Once cold, wrap the rolls in clingfilm until needed.

◆

MAKES 24

2 oz (60 g) fresh spinach leaves
4 oz (120 g) monkfish
$\frac{1}{2}$ egg white
$\frac{1}{2}$ teaspoon salt
$\frac{1}{2}$ teaspoon sugar
white pepper
$\frac{1}{2}$ teaspoon cornflour
3 ocean sticks (imitation crab sticks)

◆

Remove and discard the spinach stalks. Place the leaves in a sieve and pour half a kettleful of hot but not boiling water over them, so that they become flexible but are still firm. Remove, drain on kitchen paper and pat dry.

Remove and discard any grey parts from the monkfish. Cut the fish into small pieces and mince them, or process in a food processor.

Place the fish in a bowl with the egg white, salt, sugar, pepper and cornflour. Mix by turning a few times with chopsticks or a fork, to give the fish a firm texture.

Cut each ocean stick in half crossways, then cut each piece lengthways, to make 4 narrow strips.

Remove the thickest part of the central rib from the spinach leaves. You will need 12 pieces of leaf roughly 5 in (12.5 cm) square. It may be necessary to overlap two to obtain the necessary size or to cover cracks.

Take some of the minced fish mixture on the end of a knife and spread it centrally on the leaf at the end nearest to you. Place an ocean stick across it and top it with an equal amount of minced fish. Bring over the end of the spinach firmly, keeping it close to the filling. Fold in the two sides to secure the filling and roll to give a neat finish.

Steam the rolls over boiling water for about 4 minutes. Using a sharp knife, trim both ends of each roll neatly and cut the roll in two. Arrange attractively and serve.

TWIRLS OF TASTY SQUID
illustrated on page 20

Squid has an attractively firm texture and these spicy, deep-fried mouthfuls are simply irresistible.

◆

SERVES 12

$1\frac{1}{2}$ lb (720 g) baby squid
2 tablespoons (30 ml) dark soy sauce
2 tablespoons (30 ml) Hoi Sin sauce
1 tablespoon (15 ml) Shaoshing wine
2 tablespoons (30 ml) golden syrup
2 small cubes root ginger, crushed
1 teaspoon (5 ml) cornflour
$\frac{1}{4}$ teaspoon salt
white pepper
$\frac{1}{4}$ teaspoon 5-spice powder
$\frac{1}{2}$ fresh green chilli, very finely shredded
a little sesame oil
a little sugar

for deep-frying
1 pint (600 ml) corn oil

◆

Wash and dry the squid. Separate the heads from the bodies. Gently squeeze the glutinous membrane out of each body, keeping the top and the tentacles.

Make a cut the length of each squid and open it out flat. Gently score the surface in a criss-cross pattern, then cut crossways into 4 pieces.

In a bowl mix together the soy and Hoi Sin sauces, wine, golden syrup, the juice from the crushed ginger, cornflour, salt and pepper to taste. Add the squid, turn to coat and leave to marinate in the refrigerator for at least 2 hours.

Place the squid in a wire sieve and leave to drain, then sprinkle with the 5-spice powder.

Heat the oil in a wok or deep-fryer until almost smoking (about 325°F/160°C), add the squid and deep-fry for approximately 1 minute. Drain in a wire sieve.

Heat a second wok or frying pan to a very high temperature, add the squid and chilli and stir-fry without oil for about 2 minutes. Add a drop of sesame oil and sugar to taste, stir-fry quickly and serve.

19

Clockwise, from top: Chicken Squares, Bite-size Chicken Wings, Twirls of Tasty Squid *(p. 19)*.

CHICKEN SQUARES

Basically a variation on Sesame Prawn Toast (p. 12), these may be prepared and cooked several hours in advance, then reheated in a conventional oven (375°F/190°C/gas mark 5) for 10–15 minutes.

◆

MAKES 24

12 oz (360 g) boneless chicken breast, diced
2 oz (60 g) pork fat, diced
¾ teaspoon cornflour
1½ teaspoons (7.5 ml) salt
white pepper
1 teaspoon (5 ml) sugar
1 egg white
2 small cubes root ginger
½ oz (15 g) black sesame seeds
3 oz (90 g) white sesame seeds
6 slices brown bread, crusts removed

for deep-frying
1¾ pints (1 litre) corn oil

◆

Put the pork fat into a food processor and process briefly, then add the chicken, cornflour, salt, pepper to taste, sugar, egg white, the ginger, pressed through a garlic press, and 1 tablespoon (15 ml) water. Process to a coarse but evenly textured paste.

Spread the bread slices evenly with the mixture, using about 1 tablespoon (15 ml) for each slice, then cut into quarters. Trim the edges neatly.

Take a bread quarter and, holding it in the centre between fingers and thumb, lightly press down on to the white sesame seeds, to coat the surface evenly. Cover the centre where your thumb has been with black sesame seeds. Coat the remaining bread quarters in the same way.

Heat the oil to 275°F (140°C) in a wok or deep-fryer, add the bread squares, coated side down, and deep-fry for about 3 minutes, until light golden. Turn and fry for 1 further minute. Remove with a slotted spoon and drain on kitchen paper. Serve hot.

———— ❖ ————

BITE-SIZE CHICKEN WINGS

These luscious tidbits can be served either hot or cold. If you need larger quantities you can halve the frying time, which demands the cook's attention, then place the chicken pieces in a roasting tin in a pre-heated oven (375°F/190°C/gas mark 5) for 10 minutes, or cook them in a microwave oven.

◆

MAKES 12

12 chicken wings
½ teaspoon cornflour
salt and white pepper
1 tablespoon (15 ml) corn oil

for the marinade
1 tablespoon (15 ml) oyster sauce
1 tablespoon (15 ml) dark soy sauce
1 tablespoon (15 ml) Sweet and Chilli Sauce (p. 130)
2 tablespoons (30 ml) tomato ketchup
1 tablespoon (15 ml) Shaoshing wine
1-in (2.5-cm) cube root ginger
1 garlic clove, crushed
1 teaspoon (5 ml) sugar
1 tablespoon (15 ml) plum sauce

◆

Separate each chicken wing into 3 sections using a sharp, heavy knife to cut through the joints. Discard the bony end, reserve the middle for another recipe and take the meaty end for use here.

Take firm hold of the loose skin at the base (the thickest part), insert a small sharp knife under the skin and work the knife away from you, to separate the skin from the flesh. The skin can be removed without difficulty in one piece. Then push the flesh toward the far end before sprinkling the chicken with the cornflour, salt and pepper. Rub in well.

Mix all the marinade ingredients in a bowl, add the chicken, stir, then leave to marinate for an hour.

Heat the oil to a medium temperature in a frying pan and add the chicken. Turn the heat down slightly and fry for about 7–8 minutes, turning the pieces to brown.

Transfer to a heated serving dish and serve hot.

———— ❖ ————

21

SESAME CHICKEN BATONS

Spirals of chicken breast and French beans coated in roasted sesame seeds are delicious by themselves, or with one of the dipping sauces on pp. 130–133. They may be prepared and cooked several hours in advance and should be wrapped in clingfilm until needed.

◆

MAKES 12

3 oz (90 g) boneless chicken breast
2 oz (60 g) French beans
1 tablespoon (15 ml) white sesame seeds
1 tablespoon (15 ml) Hoi Sin sauce
1 tablespoon (15 ml) Sweet and Chilli Sauce (p. 130)

for deep-frying
1 pint (600 ml) corn oil

◆

To roast the sesame seeds, put them into a pre-heated wok or frying pan and stir-fry without oil over a moderate heat until they are golden and their nutty flavour becomes more pronounced. Remove from the heat and allow to cool; they may then be stored in an airtight container for future use.

Slice the chicken breast thinly lengthways and cut into long strips ¼ in (6 mm) wide. Top and tail the French beans and cut them into 2½-in (6-cm) lengths. Wrap the chicken round the length of the beans in a spiral fashion, leaving narrow gaps through which the green of the bean will show as a contrasting colour.

Mix the Hoi Sin and sweet and chilli sauces together in a bowl. Dab the chicken bâtons here and there with the mixture, so that the brown colour is delicately distributed rather than heavily applied, and sprinkle with roasted sesame seeds.

Heat the oil to 200°F (100°C) in a wok or deep-fryer and deep-fry the bâtons, a few at a time, for about 30 seconds or until the chicken turns white. Remove with a slotted spoon and drain on kitchen paper. Serve hot or cold.

CHICKEN MEDALLIONS
illustrated on pages 26–27

This recipe is not strictly speaking Chinese in origin, but it does come from South-East Asia and it is a particular favourite of mine, which is why I have included it here. If you are cooking for larger numbers, you may find it quicker to fry the medallions in batches, using a tablespoon (15 ml) oil for each batch, rather than grilling them. Roughly two minutes on each side should be long enough to cook them, at which point they will be firm to the touch and lightly tinged with brown.

◆

SERVES 12

1 lb (480 g) boneless chicken
¾ teaspoon salt
1 teaspoon (5 ml) cornflour

for the marinade
9 oz (270 g) Greek-strained natural yoghurt
2 tablespoons (30 ml) golden syrup
1 teaspoon (5 ml) ground cumin
½–1 teaspoon (2.5–5 ml) chilli powder
1-in (2.5-cm) cube root ginger
freshly ground black pepper
2 tablespoons (30 ml) corn oil

for the garnish
thin slices Chinese white radish
pomegranate seeds

◆

Cut the chicken into 2-in (5-cm) cubes. Mix the salt with the cornflour and use to dust the chicken pieces, rubbing the mixture in lightly.

In a bowl, thoroughly combine all the marinade ingredients. Add the chicken pieces and turn to coat. Leave to marinate for at least 30 minutes at room temperature, or for several hours in the refrigerator.

Remove the chicken pieces one by one, scraping off as much of the marinade as possible. Place them on a baking tray and grill under a pre-heated hot grill for approximately 3 minutes on each side, until cooked through and golden. Arrange on a serving dish and garnish with the white radish and pomegranate seeds, as shown in the photograph. Serve hot.

22

Clockwise, from top left: Mange-tout and Cucumber Rolls *(p. 33)*, Stuffed Cucumber, Okra and Mange-tout *(p. 33)*, Stuffed Brussels Sprouts *(p. 32)*, Sesame Chicken Batons.

DEEP-FRIED WUN-TUN

illustrated on pages 26–27

If you do not have time to make your own wun-tun skin you might be glad to know that it can be obtained fresh daily from any Chinese supermarket or grocery and, if bought in advance, can be stored in the freezer for future use.

These deep-fried dumplings could be served with a small helping of a simple spicy sauce such as sweet and chilli sauce, plum sauce or one of those to be found on pp. 130–133.

The dumplings may be prepared and cooked several hours in advance, then reheated just before they are needed in a microwave oven, or in a conventional oven (375°F/190°C/gas mark 5) for 10–15 minutes.

◆

MAKES 12

for the skin
6 oz (180 g) plain flour
$\frac{1}{4}$ teaspoon salt
2 eggs, beaten
a little cornflour
a little extra flour

for the filling
4 oz (120 g) pork tenderloin or fillet
2 small eggs, beaten
1 oz (30 g) canned bamboo shoots, drained and finely chopped
white pepper
$\frac{1}{4}$–$\frac{1}{2}$ teaspoon salt
$\frac{1}{4}$ teaspoon cornflour
1$\frac{1}{2}$ teaspoons (7.5 ml) finely chopped spring onion, white parts only
$\frac{1}{4}$ teaspoon sugar

for deep-frying
1$\frac{3}{4}$ pints (1 litre) corn oil

◆

To make the skin, sift the flour with the salt into a mixing bowl. Make a well in the centre and add the eggs and 1 tablespoon (15 ml) cold water. Using a fork, mix clockwise until the mixture forms a dough, then knead with the palms of your hands until pliable (it should be quite bouncy). If it seems rather sticky, dust it with a little flour.

Knead the dough for a further 5 minutes, then divide it into 3 equal portions. Place the pieces of dough in a bowl, with a little cornflour on the bottom to prevent them from sticking, and cover the bowl with a damp cloth to keep it from drying out.

Roll out one piece of dough at a time on a well-floured surface until paper-thin. Cut into 3-in (7.5-cm) squares and continue in the same way until all the dough is cut into squares. Dust the squares with flour, return to the floured bowl and cover again.

To make the filling, mince the pork, with a cleaver or in a food processor, and place it in a bowl. Mix in one of the eggs, then add all the remaining ingredients and stir well to blend thoroughly.

To make the wun-tun, take a dough square and place on a board or work surface. Using a teaspoon, place a small amount of the mixture in the corner nearest you and fold the point towards the centre to cover the meat. Then bring in the two adjacent corners so that the mixture is totally enclosed (see diagram). Dab with a little egg to seal. Continue in the same way until all the wun-tun are filled.

Heat the oil to 275°F (140°C) in a wok or deep-fryer, add the wun-tun and deep-fry until firm, crispy and light golden. Drain in a wire sieve, then on kitchen paper. Serve hot.

24

CURRY BEEF CUSHIONS

You may like to serve these tiny spicy pasties as I do, nestling in a knotted or twisted starched linen napkin. They may be prepared and cooked several hours in advance, then reheated in a microwave oven, or a conventional oven (325°F/160°C/gas mark 3) for 10–15 minutes.

◆

MAKES 30

7½-oz (225-g) packet shortcrust pastry
plain flour for dusting

for deep-frying
1¾ pints (1 litre) corn oil

for the filling
8 oz (240 g) finely minced beef
1 teaspoon (5 ml) cornflour
salt
white pepper
2 tablespoons (30 ml) corn oil
1 oz (30 g) green pepper, cored, seeded and very finely sliced
1 oz (30 g) leek, thinly sliced into rings
½ teaspoon sugar
½–1 tablespoon (7.5–15 ml) curry powder
1 teaspoon (5 ml) ground fennel
1 teaspoon (5 ml) cornflour mixed with 1 tablespoon (15 ml) water

◆

To make the filling, mix the beef with the cornflour, ½ teaspoon salt and pepper to taste. Set aside.

Heat 1 tablespoon (15 ml) oil in a pre-heated wok or frying pan, add the vegetables with a sprinkling of salt and stir-fry for 30 seconds, then transfer them to a side bowl.

In the same pan, heat the remaining oil, add the beef and stir-fry over a high heat for 1–1½ minutes. Return the vegetables to the pan, stirring well to mix. Add the sugar, curry powder, fennel, and the cornflour mixture and stir-fry briefly to blend well. Remove from the heat and allow to cool.

Roll out the pastry as thinly as possible on a floured surface. Using a fluted 2-in (5-cm) biscuit cutter, cut out as many shapes as possible. Put a small amount of the mixture in the centre of half the circles, leaving a narrow margin round the edges. Over each place a second circle to cover the filling. Brush the edges with water and press together gently to seal.

Heat the oil to a medium temperature, approximately 250°F (120°C) in a wok or deep-fryer, and deep-fry the 'cushions' a few at a time until light golden. Drain in a wire sieve, then on kitchen paper. Serve hot.

———————— ❖ ————————

LYCHEE SATELLITES
illustrated on pages 8–9

Here is an Oriental interpretation of English angels on horseback – prunes wrapped in bacon. Don't be disheartened if some breakages occur in the early stages when preparing the lychees; a very little practice makes perfect.

◆

MAKES 20

20 fresh lychees
2 oz (60 g) thin streaky bacon rashers, rinds removed
½ cucumber about 1½ in (3.5 cm) in diameter

◆

Grill the bacon until crisp but not dried out and cut it into pieces about 1 × ¼ in (2.5 cm × 6 mm).

Peel the lychees carefully, without piercing the flesh. Set the lychees stalk end down on a board. Make a criss-cross cut half-way down the fruit, and, with your fingers, ease the tops apart as if you were opening up a bud. Then, using a small, sharp pointed knife and working from the outside of the fruit, run the point of the knife round the edge where the flesh meets the stone, cutting in a small circle to release the stone (see diagram). Turn the stone very gently, and ease it out of the lychee.

Fill the cavity with 3–4 bacon pieces, leaving some showing at the top.

When all the lychees are similarly prepared, cut the unpeeled cucumber into slices ⅛ in (3 mm) thick. Neatly cut out the centres to leave a narrow green border and slip one ring over each lychee to encircle it. (Avoid making your rings too large at the outset as they could be too wide to fit snugly. You can always make them bigger if necessary).

———————— ❖ ————————

25

26

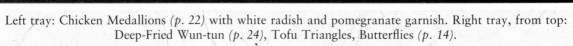

Left tray: Chicken Medallions *(p. 22)* with white radish and pomegranate garnish. Right tray, from top: Deep-Fried Wun-tun *(p. 24)*, Tofu Triangles, Butterflies *(p. 14)*.

TOFU TRIANGLES

The triangles may be prepared in advance, then reheated in a microwave oven, or in a conventional oven (325°F/160°C/gas mark 3) for 10–15 minutes.

◆

MAKES 20

9 oz (270 g) fresh tofu (beancurd)
1 egg white, lightly beaten
$\frac{1}{2}$ teaspoon salt
white pepper
1 oz (30 g) streaky bacon rashers, rinds removed
1 tablespoon (15 ml) finely chopped Chinese black mushrooms
1 tablespoon (15 ml) finely chopped coriander
1 egg, beaten
phyllo pastry sheets

for deep-frying
1$\frac{3}{4}$ pints (1 litre) corn oil

◆

To make the filling, drain the liquid from the tofu. Holding the tofu in a cloth, gently press between the hands to remove any excess moisture. Remove the surface skin with a knife.

Place the tofu in a food processor with the egg white, salt and pepper to taste and process briefly to make a coarse paste. Fry the bacon lightly, then chop finely. Add to the tofu paste with the mushroom and coriander. Stir well to mix. Set aside.

To make the triangles, take 2 phyllo pastry sheets together, making sure you handle them carefully as they tear easily. Return the remaining sheets to the bag to keep them from drying out.

Fold the double sheets in half lengthways and cut down the folds. Continue to fold and cut until you have 8 double strips, each about 10 × 2$\frac{1}{2}$ in (25 × 6 cm).

Fold one corner across to make a triangle. Put 1 teaspoon (5 ml) of the tofu mixture along the fold, keeping it away from the edges. Continue forming the triangles until you come to the end of the strip (see diagram). Lightly brush the edges with egg, to seal.

Heat the oil to 275°F (140°C) in a wok or deep-fryer. Add the triangles and deep-fry for 1 minute, turning once or twice, until a light golden-brown. Drain in a wire sieve, then on kitchen paper.

27

LAMB BALLS WITH MINT

Meat balls do not always conjure up an exciting image, but mint to give flavour and a little dressing with caramel does wonders for them. The balls may be prepared and cooked several hours in advance, then reheated in a microwave oven, or in a conventional oven (375°F/190°C/gas mark 5) for about 10 minutes.

◆

MAKES 24

12 oz (360 g) lean lamb leg steak
2–3 tablespoons (30–40 ml) chopped fresh mint
2 oz (60 g) pork fat
1 egg white
1 tablespoon (15 ml) light soy sauce
1½ teaspoons (7.5 ml) Shaoshing wine
¼–½ teaspoon salt
¼ teaspoon freshly ground black pepper
1 teaspoon (5 ml) sugar
1 teaspoon (5 ml) cornflour
1 oz (30 g) Spanish onion, chopped
1 tablespoon (15 ml) finely chopped spring onion
2 tablespoons (30 ml) finely chopped celery
2–3 oz (60–90 g) plain flour for coating

for deep-frying
1 pint (600 ml) corn oil

for the glazing sauce
1½ teaspoons (7.5 ml) light soy sauce
1½ teaspoons (7.5 ml) Shaoshing wine
1 tablespoon (15 ml) Sweet and Chilli Sauce (p. 130)
1 tablespoon (15 ml) Hoi Sin sauce
1 tablespoon (15 ml) corn oil

for the garnish
a little shredded coconut

◆

Mince the lamb and the pork fat finely with a cleaver or in a food processor. Put it into a bowl and mix well with the egg white, soy sauce, wine, salt, pepper, sugar and cornflour. Add the chopped vegetables and mint and mix again.

Heat the oil to 350°F (180°C) in a wok or deep-fryer. With floured hands, form the mixture into balls the size of large walnuts and coat each with flour. Deep-fry the balls, a few at a time, for about 2 minutes until browned and cooked through. Drain in a wire sieve, then on kitchen paper.

To make the sauce, mix all the ingredients, except the oil, together in a bowl. Heat the oil in a large heavy saucepan, then add the sauce mixture and bring gently to the boil, stirring. Turn off the heat. Put the lamb balls into the sauce and turn to coat evenly, then transfer to a heated serving dish and keep warm.

Fry the coconut gently in a frying pan without oil over a low to moderate heat, stirring until it becomes golden. Sprinkle over the lamb balls. Serve hot.

SPICED BANANA SLICES

The Orient merges with the Caribbean to produce this mouthwatering version of potato crisps.

◆

SERVES 12

2 large under-ripe bananas, weighing about 1 lb (480 g), peeled and cut diagonally into slices ⅛ in (3 mm) thick

for the coating
4 teaspoons (20 ml) paprika
2 teaspoons (10 ml) chilli powder
4 teaspoons (20 ml) ground turmeric
4 teaspoons (20 ml) ground cumin
a pinch of salt

for deep-frying
1¾ pints (1 litre) corn oil

◆

Blend together all the coating ingredients. Using a flour dredger, dust the banana slices all over with the mixture. Handle them gently so that they do not break.

Heat the oil to 250°F (120°C) in a wok or deep-fryer and deep-fry the banana slices in batches for about 1 minute. Drain in a wire sieve, then fry again briefly until crisp and golden, like potato crisps. Drain again in the sieve, then on kitchen paper. Serve hot or cold.

SWEET POTATO BALLS

The chicken and sweetcorn filling is the surprise element here. The balls may be made a day in advance and refrigerated before deep-frying.

◆

MAKES 20

1½ lb (600 g) sweet potato (smaller ones often have better flavour)
2 tablespoons (30 ml) plain flour
½ teaspoon salt
white pepper
2 oz (60 g) desiccated coconut

for the filling
1 pint (600 ml) corn oil
6 oz (180 g) minced chicken
½ teaspoon cornflour
½ teaspoon salt
white pepper
1 tablespoon (15 ml) corn oil
2 oz (60 g) Spanish onion, finely chopped
2 oz (60 g) sweetcorn kernels
1 teaspoon (5 ml) cornflour mixed with 1½ teaspoons cold water
2 tablespoons (30 ml) finely chopped parsley

for deep-frying
1¾ pints (1 litre) corn oil

◆

Peel the sweet potatoes, cut them into ⅛-in (3-mm) thick slices and lay them in a bamboo steamer or steaming rack. Steam over boiling water in a wok for about 10 minutes until the sweet potato is tender. Mash with salt and pepper and cool. Stir in the flour and set aside.

To make the filling, mix the chicken with the cornflour, salt and pepper to taste. Heat 1 tablespoon (15 ml) oil to a high temperature in a pre-heated wok or frying pan, add the onion and fry briefly, until just softened, then add the chicken mixture and stir-fry for about 1 minute.

Add the sweetcorn and cornflour mixture and stir-fry for 1 further minute. Stir in the parsley and transfer to a bowl. Allow to cool.

To make the balls, take a small teaspoonful of the mashed sweet potato in your hand and flatten it with your fingers. Put a very small amount – about ½ teaspoon – of the chicken mixture in the middle of the sweet potato and another small teaspoonful of sweet potato on top. (This could be a sticky operation, but don't be put off.) Mould into a walnut-sized ball.

Shape all the balls in the same way, then roll in coconut, to coat thinly, rounding them between the palms of your hands.

Heat the oil to 275°F (140°C) in a wok or deep-fryer and deep-fry the balls a few at a time for about 30 seconds to 1 minute at a steady temperature, until light golden. Drain in a wire sieve, then on kitchen paper. Serve hot.

❖

CARROT HEARTS
illustrated on pages 8–9

These may be reheated in a microwave, or in a conventional oven (325°F/160°C/gas mark 3) for 15 minutes.

◆

MAKES 30

3 medium carrots, sliced
salt
a pinch of sugar
2 spring onions, very finely chopped
freshly ground black pepper
a little plain flour
7½-oz (215-g) frozen puff pastry, thoroughly thawed

for deep-frying
1¾ pints (1 litre) corn oil

◆

Cook the carrots in a minimum of boiling salted water, with the sugar, until they are tender and the water has evaporated. Mash the carrots until smooth. Cool, then stir in the spring onions, season with pepper and set aside.

Roll out the pastry thinly on a floured surface, then cut out heart shapes with an aspic cutter. Lay out half the hearts and cover them with the carrot mixture, leaving a narrow margin around the edges. Cover each with a second heart and seal with a little water.

Heat the oil to 300°F (150°C) in a wok or deep-fryer and deep-fry the hearts for about 2 minutes, until puffed and light golden. Drain thoroughly. Serve hot.

❖

29

SPINACH WITH A DIFFERENCE

These may be prepared an hour or so in advance. Let them get cold before wrapping in clingfilm until needed: the bright colour of the spinach will not spoil.

◆

MAKES 12

6 large or 12 small spinach leaves
2 carrots
1 long stick celery
2 oz (60 g) bamboo shoots
2 leek leaves
1 tablespoon (15 ml) corn oil
$\frac{1}{4}$ teaspoon sugar
salt and white pepper
1 tablespoon (15 ml) oyster sauce

◆

Peel the carrot and cut it into matchstick strips. Cut the celery and bamboo shoots into similar sized strips.

Remove and discard the spinach stalks and place the leaves in a sieve or colander. Pour hot but not boiling water over them to make them flexible. Blanch the leek leaves for 20 seconds or until they are soft enough to use as ties. Drain well and cut into strips approximately $\frac{1}{8}$ in (3 mm) wide.

Heat the oil to a moderate to high temperature in a pre-heated wok or frying pan. Add the vegetables with the sugar, salt, pepper, and oyster sauce, and stir-fry for 10 seconds. Remove the vegetables from the pan while still crunchy and leave to cool.

If using large leaves, halve them lengthways, discarding the central rib, to make 4 × 2 in (10 × 5 cm) pieces. Take a few of the vegetable strips – roughly equal amounts of each kind and sufficient to make rolls of about $\frac{1}{2}$ in (1 cm) in diameter. Place the vegetables on a piece of spinach leaf and roll up neatly. Using a sharp knife, trim the ends to give a clean, neat finish.

Decorate each round the middle with a leek ribbon, the ends overlaid rather than tied.

QUAILS' EGGS WITH SPINACH

If you want to serve these hot, everything can be prepared well in advance and only the steaming done shortly before serving. If serving cold it is advisable to halve the eggs at the last minute, so that they remain fresh and bright.

◆

MAKES 24

12 quails' eggs
12 large fresh spinach leaves
4 Chinese black mushrooms, soaked and drained
1 lb (480 g) boneless chicken breast
1 egg white
$\frac{3}{4}$–1 teaspoon (4–5 ml) salt
$\frac{1}{4}$ teaspoon white pepper
1 teaspoon (5 ml) sugar
$\frac{1}{2}$ teaspoon cornflour

◆

Hard-boil the quails' eggs for 4 minutes, then remove the shell, keeping the white intact. Remove and discard the central ribs from the spinach leaves. Place the leaves in a sieve or colander. Pour a kettleful of hot but not boiling water over them, to make them flexible. Remove and drain on kitchen paper, then pat dry.

Chop the Chinese mushrooms as finely as possible. Finely mince the chicken with a cleaver or in a food processor. Mix it with the egg white, salt, pepper, sugar and cornflour and finally stir in the mushrooms.

Coat each egg with the mixture, moulding it on carefully and evenly to a thickness of approximately $\frac{1}{8}$ in (3 mm).

Wrap each egg in a spinach leaf, overlapping it where necessary so that there are no gaps. Trim away any surplus leaf as the wrapping should not be too thick.

Steam the spinach-wrapped eggs over boiling water for about 4 minutes. Remove and cut each in half crossways.

30

Clockwise, from top: Spinach with a Difference, Spinach Seafood Rolls *(p. 19)*, Quails' Eggs with Spinach.

31

DEEP-FRIED STUFFED MUSHROOMS

I suggest serving these on strands of uncooked wholewheat spaghetti with a couple of spring onion brushes (see pp. 134–135) placed at opposite corners to set off the dish.

◆

MAKES 20

20 mushrooms with stalks, the longer the better weighing about 6 oz (180 g)
salt
plain flour for dusting
1 egg, beaten
2 oz (60 g) dry white breadcrumbs

for the stuffing
6 oz (180 g) minced lamb
1 teaspoon (5 ml) cornflour
1 egg white
$\frac{1}{4}$ teaspoon salt
white pepper
sugar
1 tablespoon (15 ml) corn oil
1$\frac{1}{2}$ tablespoons (22.5 ml) oyster sauce
1 spring onion, finely chopped
3 thin slices root ginger, finely chopped
a small handful of coriander leaves

for deep-frying
1$\frac{3}{4}$ pints (1 litre) corn oil

◆

To make the stuffing, mix the lamb with the cornflour, egg white, salt and pepper and sugar to taste. Leave to stand for 20 minutes.

Heat 1 tablespoon (15 ml) oil to a high temperature in a pre-heated wok or frying pan, add the lamb mixture and stir-fry for 1 minute. Add the oyster sauce and cook for 1 further minute. Turn off the heat and blend in the spring onion, ginger and coriander. Allow to cool.

Wash and dry the mushrooms, then trim off the tip of each stalk. Now cut round the rim to a depth of about $\frac{1}{4}$ in (6 mm), creating a small circular groove. Lightly sprinkle the mushrooms inside and out with salt, then fill the grooves with the stuffing mixture, pressing down lightly.

Dust the stuffed mushrooms with flour and brush with beaten egg, then coat with the breadcrumbs. Heat the oil to 200°F (100°C) in a wok or deep-fryer, add the mushrooms stalk side down and deep-fry slowly for 1 minute so that the stuffing has a chance to cook right through. Towards the end of cooking, turn the mushrooms and continue frying until light golden all over. Drain in a wire sieve, then on kitchen paper. Serve hot.

❖

STUFFED BRUSSELS SPROUTS
illustrated on page 23

The humble Brussels sprout becomes something special when stuffed with prawns and coriander. These may be made several hours in advance.

◆

MAKES 12

12 fairly large Brussels sprouts
salt
2 oz (60 g) cooked peeled prawns
1 tablespoon (15 ml) corn oil
1 oz (30 g) Spanish onion, finely chopped
$\frac{1}{4}$ teaspoon sugar
white pepper
1 tablespoon (15 ml) finely chopped coriander

◆

Cut a thin slice from the bottom of each sprout so that it stands upright. Make 2 firm, fairly deep, criss-cross diagonal cuts in the top of each sprout. Hollow out the centre, leaving a neat casing to hold the filling.

Blanch the sprouts in well-salted boiling water for 2–3 minutes. Drain, refresh immediately under running water, then drain again on kitchen paper.

To make the filling, dry the prawns with kitchen paper, then chop them. Heat the oil to a high temperature in a small pan, add the onion and stir-fry until softened but not coloured. Add the prawns with the sugar, $\frac{1}{4}$ teaspoon salt and a sprinkling of pepper. Stir-fry for 1 minute, then turn off the heat and mix in the coriander. Cool, then use the filling to stuff the prepared Brussels sprouts.

❖

STUFFED CUCUMBER, OKRA AND MANGE-TOUT

illustrated on page 23

These vegetables, with their bright colours savoury filling and tapering shape, make ideal finger food.

◆

SERVES 12

12 okra
1 cucumber
2 oz (60 g) mange-tout

for the stuffing

8 oz (240 g) boneless chicken
2 Chinese black mushrooms, soaked and drained
2 oz (60 g) bamboo shoots, trimmed
1 tablespoon (15 ml) dark soy sauce
$\frac{1}{2}$ teaspoon cornflour
$1\frac{1}{2}$ tablespoons (22.5 ml) plum sauce
1 teaspoon (5 ml) sugar
2 tablespoons (30 ml) peanut or corn oil
salt and white pepper
1 tablespoon (15 ml) Shaoshing wine or medium sherry

◆

To make the stuffing, cut the Chinese mushrooms into tiny pieces, smaller than $\frac{1}{8}$ in (3 mm). Cut the bamboo shoots into tiny pieces and set both aside in a bowl.

Slice and then dice the chicken to the same size as the bamboo shoots. Put the chicken into a bowl with the soy sauce, cornflour, plum sauce and sugar. Stir to mix and leave to marinate for 30 minutes.

Heat half the oil to a high temperature in a pre-heated wok or frying pan, add the mushrooms and bamboo shoots with 2 pinches of salt and a little pepper and stir-fry for 30 seconds. Transfer the mixture to a bowl.

In the same wok heat the remaining oil, add the chicken and stir-fry for 1 minute, separating the tiny pieces as much as possible. Add the wine, continuing to stir-fry, then add the mushrooms and bamboo shoots. Stir-fry for 1 further minute, taste and adjust the seasoning if necessary, then set aside.

To prepare the vegetables, trim the top ends off the okra. Lay each okra flat on a work surface. Using a very sharp knife, cut lengthways and open gently. Remove the seeds. Blanch in boiling salted water for 10 seconds.

Drain and refresh under cold running water, then drain again. Dry inside and out with kitchen paper.

Remove any withered caps from the mange-tout. Using a very sharp knife, open the mange-tout lengthways along the edge where the peas are formed, leaving the pod intact. Ease the pocket apart slightly. Blanch the mange-tout in boiling salted water for 10 seconds. Drain and refresh as before. Drain again.

Split the cucumber in half lengthways. Cut each half diagonally crossways to make boat-shaped wedges, approximately 2 in (5 cm) long and $\frac{1}{2}$ in (1 cm) wide. Remove the pulp and seeds, leaving an $\frac{1}{8}$-in (3-mm) surround on all sides. Carefully fill all the prepared vegetables with the stuffing mixture.

❖

MANGE-TOUT AND CUCUMBER ROLLS

illustrated on page 23

These crisp rolls may be prepared several hours in advance and should be wrapped in clingfilm until needed.

◆

SERVES 12–16

Shar Shiu Pork (p. 40), cut into $\frac{1}{8}$-in (3-mm) thick slices
3 oz (90 g) fairly large mange-tout
1 teaspoon (5 ml) salt
$\frac{1}{2}$ cucumber

◆

Remove the caps from the mange-tout. Using a very sharp knife, cut the mange-tout open lengthways and separate each into two parts. Boil them in salted water for 30 seconds, then drain, refresh immediately under cold running water and drain again.

Cut the cucumber into lengths the same size as the mange-tout. Slice the cucumber into very thin strips approximately 1 in (2.5 cm) wide so that each has a narrow dark green edge formed by the skin.

Place a slice of pork on top of each piece of mange-tout and roll up neatly from one short end. Secure with a cocktail stick.

Roll the cucumber and pork in the same way, to give an attractive contrasting dark green edging.

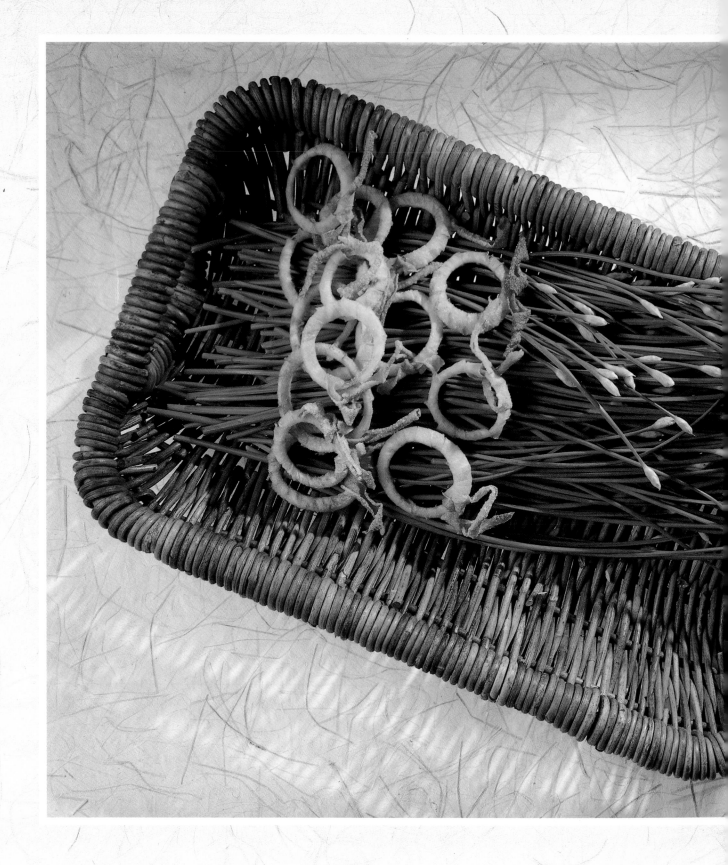

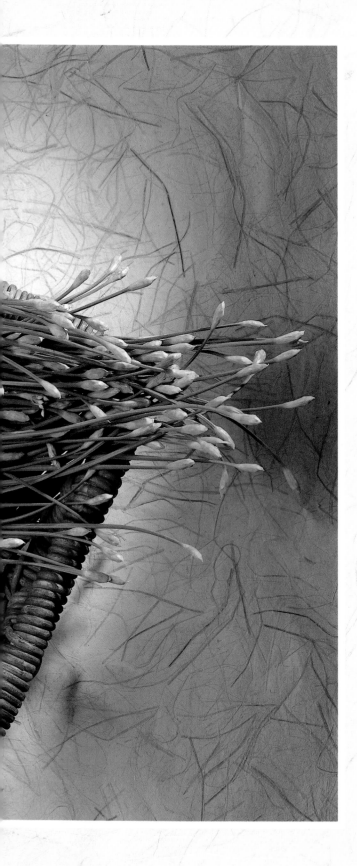

ONION CIRCLETS

Here is something delightfully simple – and cheap as well. The robust, commonplace onion is transformed into an aesthetically pleasing novelty. A 2-in (5-cm) diameter onion is the ideal size. When deep-frying, make sure the oil is not too hot – it is a good idea to test with one onion ring first. The circlets may be prepared several hours in advance, then deep-fried just before needed. Once cooked they can be kept hot in a conventional oven (325°F/ 160°C/gas mark 3) for 10–15 minutes.

◆

MAKES 40

1 large Spanish onion
spring roll paper
salt
1 egg, beaten

for deep-frying
1¾ pints (1 litre) corn oil

◆

Peel the onion and cut it into ¼-in (5-mm) rings. Cut a sheet of spring roll paper diagonally into ¼-in (6-mm) wide strips – as many as are needed to cover the onions. Keep the strips in a polythene bag until you are ready to use them, to prevent them from drying out and becoming too brittle to handle easily.

Sprinkle the onion rings with salt. Wrap each ring in a strip of spring roll paper. Start by leaving about 2 in (5 cm) hanging free, then bind the ring, overlapping the paper rather as one does with a bandage. Join a fresh strip of spring roll paper where necessary until the ring is covered. Finish off the wrapping with a simple knot.

Heat the oil to 300°F (150°C) in a wok or deep-fryer and gently deep-fry the onion rings a few at a time, until light golden. Remove with a slotted spoon and drain on kitchen paper. Serve hot.

Left: Onion Circlets.

SPICY PASTA

Although pasta is most familiar in Italian cooking, it actually originated in China, so I feel quite justified in making use of it. The type of pasta to be served is a matter of choice. As some kinds of pasta may take longer to cook than others, I advise separate cooking for each type and this I often do well in advance as I find the pasta then has plenty of time to drain and become firm. Of course it is perfectly possible to make the dish on the spur of the moment, but do be sure to drain the pasta thoroughly after cooking it. It is equally tasty served hot or cold.

◆

SERVES 12

1 oz (30 g) farfalle
1 oz (30 g) gnocchi
1 oz (30 g) fusilli
salt
1 tablespoon (15 ml) corn oil
1 large clove garlic, crushed
1 tablespoon (15 ml) tomato ketchup
$\frac{1}{2}$–1 teaspoon (2.5–5 ml) chilli bean sauce
1 teaspoon (5 ml) dark soy sauce

◆

Cook the pasta in boiling salted water for 5 minutes or until marginally undercooked (*al dente*).

Heat the oil in a non-stick frying pan and add the drained pasta, garlic, tomato ketchup, chilli bean and soy sauces.

Stir-fry for no more than 1 minute to blend all the ingredients. If you think more blending is needed, turn off the heat while continuing to stir. Arrange in an attractive pattern as finger food.

FROGS' LEGS WITH PLUM SAUCE

Frogs' legs, most often associated with French cuisine, are also familiar in China – where they are sometimes prescribed as a cure for rheumatism. They may be prepared and cooked several hours in advance, then reheated in a microwave oven, or in a conventional oven (325°F/160°C/gas mark 3) for 10–15 minutes. Mango chutney could be served as an alternative to plum sauce.

◆

SERVES 18

12 oz (360 g) frogs' legs, thawed if frozen
1 large tablespoon (15 ml) chopped parsley
$\frac{1}{2}$ teaspoon sugar
$\frac{1}{2}$ teaspoon salt
$\frac{1}{2}$-in (2.5-cm) cube root ginger, crushed
1–2 cloves garlic, crushed
2 tablespoons (30 ml) plain flour
1 egg, beaten
2 oz (60 g) dry white breadcrumbs

for deep-frying
1 pint (600 ml) corn oil

◆

Put the frogs' legs into a bowl with the parsley, sugar, salt, ginger and garlic. Leave to marinate in the refrigerator for at least 4 hours, or overnight.

Dust the frogs' legs lightly with the flour and coat with beaten egg, then with the breadcrumbs.

Heat the oil to 300°F (150°C) in a wok or deep-fryer, add the frogs' legs and deep-fry for about 1 minute, until golden. Drain in a wire sieve. Transfer to a heated serving dish and serve hot with plum sauce (p. 131).

Top: Spicy Pasta, centre: Frogs' Legs, below: Prawn Fingers *(p. 13)*.

BUFFET DISHES

This informal style of entertaining is less demanding of the hostess than a sit-down dinner. Most of the food can be laid out ready for the guests to help themselves, so the occasional sortie to the kitchen is likely to go unremarked. While at a small buffet it might be possible to have the dessert on display from the outset, it is generally more pleasing if the ravaged remains of the first courses are removed before the dessert is presented.

Food is conversation-inducing, so choose one or two unusual dishes, such as Banana and Fish Fritters, or Smoked Quails, to excite interest and provoke discussion. Some can be simple, with familiar ingredients presented in an exotic way, such as Szechuan Spicy Shredded Beef with colour-contrasting carrots (p. 56). The very simplest ingredients can be made to look pretty, as with Cucumber Flowers (p. 66). You might like to include at least one hot dish in your buffet spread, and you will find a selection of hot as well as cold food in this section. Several of the hors d'oeuvre dishes would, of course, be suitable for a buffet party too. Group the dishes on the serving table so that they are all easily accessible.

Although Chinese practice is to use bowls, I advise providing plates on which your guests can assemble the food of their choice, as it will look much more attractive served this way. It is a good idea to supply knives and forks as an alternative to chopsticks.

39

Clockwise, from left: Aubergine and Pork Muffins (*p. 65*), Sea Bass with Chinese Chives (*p. 86*), Crunchy Vegetable Stir-fry (*p. 60*), Mock Squid Decked with Seaweed (p. 47), Beribboned Spicy Beef (*p. 56*).

40

MIXED SEAFOOD WITH VEGETABLES

This colourful buffet centrepiece looks and tastes wonderful served with Shar-Shiu Pork.

◆

SERVES 16

8 oz (240 g) monkfish, skinned
8 oz (240 g) baby squid, cleaned
8 oz (240 g) French beans
8 oz (240 g) broccoli
salt and white pepper
½ teaspoon cornflour
2 slices root ginger
1 clove garlic, creamed
1 tablespoon (15 ml) Shaoshing wine
1 teaspoon (5 ml) sugar

for deep-frying
1 pint (600 ml) corn oil

◆

Cut the monkfish flesh into neat 1-in (2.5-cm) squares approximately ½ in (1 cm) thick. Place them in a dish and season with the cornflour, ¼ teaspoon salt and a sprinkling of pepper. Set aside to marinate.

Separate the squids' heads from the bodies. Gently squeeze the glutinous membrane out of the body and trim away the tentacles. Cut the squid open lengthways, lay them flat on a board and lightly score the surface in a criss-cross pattern. Cut into smallish pieces of roughly equal size and place in a bowl. Sprinkle with salt and pepper; leave to marinate.

Blanch the beans and the broccoli in boiling salted water for just 1 minute, then drain. Heat the oil to a high temperature in the same saucepan and very briefly fry the monkfish pieces, then the squid. Drain.

Put 2 tablespoons (30 ml) of the hot oil into a pre-heated wok or frying pan and add the ginger. Fry briefly to flavour the oil, then remove the ginger.

Quickly add the vegetables, monkfish and squid to the pan and add the garlic. Add the wine and sprinkle with the sugar and a little more salt to taste.

Stir-fry for just 30 seconds, then arrange in the centre of a heated serving dish, surrounded by thin slices of Shar-Shiu Pork.

SHAR-SHIU PORK

This red-coloured meat often hangs in rows alongside the roast duck in the windows of many Cantonese restaurants.

◆

SERVES 16

2 pork tenderloins, trimmed of any fat
salt and white pepper

for the marinade
1 tablespoon (15 ml) sesame paste
3 tablespoons (45 ml) dark soy sauce
2 tablespoons (30 ml) Sweet and Chilli Sauce (p. 130)
3 tablespoons (45 ml) golden syrup
1½ teaspoons (7.5 ml) sesame oil
2 tablespoons (30 ml) Shaoshing wine
1 spring onion, chopped into 1-in (2-cm) pieces
3 slices root ginger
½ teaspoon salt
white pepper
¼–½ teaspoon 5-spice powder
1 tablespoon (15 ml) Szechuan peppercorns and
3 cloves star anise (or equivalent quantity of
broken pieces) tied together in a muslin bag

◆

To make the marinade, heat the sesame paste with the soy and sweet and chilli sauces and syrup over a low heat. When blended, add the remaining marinade ingredients, with 10 fl oz (280 ml) water. Pour into a deep dish and allow to cool.

Pat the pork dry and score the surface lightly, making 4 or 5 long incisions. Sprinkle lightly with salt and pepper. Add the pork to the marinade and leave to marinate for at least 4 hours, turning once or twice.

Remove the pork from the marinade. Use your fingers to remove any excess marinade.

Ten minutes before you are ready to cook the pork, heat the oven to 475°F (240°C, gas mark 9).

Pass a skewer with a hook through one end of each tenderloin and hang them from the top shelf of the oven, placing them slightly apart. Use a roasting tin to catch the drips and roast for about 35 minutes.

Remove from the oven and remove the skewers. Allow to cool slightly, then cut the pork into thin, diagonal slices.

Above: Shar-Shiu Pork arranged around Mixed Seafood with Vegetables.

SALMON-RINGED ASPARAGUS

illustrated on pages 66–67

*This dish can be served equally well hot or cold –
even cold with a hot sauce. Very familiar starter
ingredients are given a completely novel treatment.*

◆

MAKES 20

1 ×2-lb (960 g) bundle asparagus, trimmed
12 oz (360 g) fresh salmon fillet
salt
1 slice dried roasted laver, cut into ¼-in (6-mm) strips

for the serving sauce
double quantity Fresh Herb Sauce (p. 132) or
White Radish Sauce (p. 131)

◆

Cut each asparagus spear in half diagonally, to give
lengths about 3 in (7.5 cm), and blanch them in boiling
water for 30 seconds. Drain, refresh under cold running
water, then drain again.

Cut the salmon along the grain into thin 4 × 1-in
(10 × 2.5-cm) strips. Trim the edges neatly.

Take 4 asparagus lengths – 2 spears and 2 stalks – and
place together in a bundle. Wrap a salmon strip round
each bundle. When all the asparagus and salmon
bundles are ready, place them in a greased ovenproof
dish, then on a steaming rack over boiling water in a
wok or saucepan, and steam for about 3 minutes.

Remove them from the steamer and when cool
enough to handle wrap a laver strip round the middle of
each salmon ring, overlapping the ends.

42

BANANA FISH FRITTERS

*The combination of fruit and fish is unusual in
Chinese cooking, but the flavour and texture of both
ingredients marry surprisingly well.*

◆

MAKES 10

12 oz (360 g) monkfish or cod fillet
2 slightly under-ripe bananas
½ teaspoon salt
¼ teaspoon white pepper
¼ teaspoon sugar
1–2 tablespoons (15–30 ml) chopped fennel
plain flour

for deep-frying
1¾ pints (1 litre) corn oil

for the batter
6 oz (180 g) plain flour
pinch of salt
salt and white pepper
1 tablespoon (15 ml) corn oil
2 medium egg whites

◆

To make the batter, sift the flour with the salt into a
mixing bowl. Make a well in the centre and gradually
stir in the oil and 7 fl oz (210 ml) iced water. Mix to a
smooth paste. Chill in the refrigerator for 30 minutes.

Skin and trim the fish and cut it into 2 × 3-in (5 × 7.5-
cm) slices about ¼ in (6 mm) thick. Put them into a bowl
and mix with the salt, pepper and sugar. Peel the
bananas and cut them into 3-in (7.5-cm) sections, then
crossways into slices.

Place a slice of banana on half the pieces of fish,
sprinkle the banana with the fennel and cover each with
a second piece of fish, to make a sandwich. Dust the
outside lightly with flour.

Whisk the egg whites until they stand in peaks, then
fold them gently into the batter, using a spatula.

Heat the oil to 350°F (180°C) in a wok or deep-fryer.

Dip the fish sandwiches into the batter, to coat, then
deep-fry in batches for 1–1½ minutes, until golden.
Remove with a slotted spoon and drain on kitchen
paper. Serve hot.

STEAMED SEA BASS
illustrated on pages 38–39

Normally the ingredients for this sauce are heated and added after, rather than before, the fish itself is cooked. I feel that flavouring should be part of the actual cooking process, and in this dish the flavours of the soy sauce and oil are mellowed and blend agreeably with the natural juices of the bass. If you have no means of steaming on top of the stove, the bass could be baked, with the flavourings, in a hot oven (425°F/220°C/gas mark 7), wrapped closely in greased kitchen foil in a roasting tin filled with boiling water. A large fish will cook in this way in about 40 minutes, and smaller fish in about 30 minutes.

◆

SERVES 16

1 large sea bass, weighing about 3 lb (1.5 kg), or 2 smaller fish making up the same weight, cleaned
4 slices root ginger
3 tablespoons (45 ml) dark soy sauce
3 tablespoons (45 ml) corn oil

for the garnish
12 thin slices root ginger, cut into hair's-breadth strands
3 oz (90 g) spring onions trimmed, cut in half lengthways, then diagonally into long strands, $\frac{1}{8}$ in (3 mm) wide

◆

Dry the bass well with kitchen paper. Score the back diagonally in a criss-cross pattern.

Lay the bass on its side in an ovenproof dish and season with salt and pepper. Put the slices of ginger inside the body cavity and spoon over the soy sauce and oil. Place in a fish kettle and pour in boiling water to come below the level of the dish. Steam the bass at a constant high temperature for about 13–14 minutes, topping up with more boiling water if necessary. (For 2 smaller fish, 7–8 minutes should be sufficient cooking time.)

Transfer the bass to a heated serving dish and garnish with the ginger and spring onion, mixed well together. Pour the cooking juices round the fish.

❖

FISH SURPRISE
illustrated on pages 66–67

Simplicity is the key note here. Very little in the way of actual cooking is required for this attractive dish. Cod fillet, cut across the grain, could be substituted for monkfish.

◆

SERVES 16

2 lb (960 g) monkfish, trimmed and cut into $\frac{1}{2}$ × 1 × 2-in (1 × 2.5 × 5-cm) pieces
1 oz (30 g) Chinese cellophane (transparent) noodles
salt and white pepper
3 tablespoons (45 ml) plain flour for coating

for deep-frying
1 pint (600 ml) corn oil

for the garnish
mustard and cress

for the serving sauce
double quantity Sweet and Chilli Sauce (p. 130)

◆

Heat the oil in a wok or deep-fryer to 250°F (120°C) and deep-fry the noodles in small batches. (They expand as soon as they make contact with the oil and are cooked almost immediately.) Remove with a slotted spoon and drain thoroughly on kitchen paper. They are now ready for use, or may be stored for a day in an airtight tin.

Slit each piece of fish open horizontally, cutting through 3 edges but keeping one long edge intact. Open the fish out like a book, season with salt and pepper, then dust with flour.

Reheat the oil in the wok or deep-fryer to 250°F (120°C), add the fish, deep-fry for about 30 seconds, then drain briefly in a wire sieve. Transfer the fish pieces to the centre of a pre-heated shallow serving dish. Arrange a border of the crispy noodles around the edge and scatter with mustard and cress.

Heat the sauce and spoon over half the quantity only, to dress the fish lightly. Serve the remaining sauce separately in a small bowl.

❖

CORAL AND PEARL BUTTERFLY PRAWNS

This is a dish of two quite distinctive and contrasting tastes – and colours, hence the title.

◆

SERVES 16

32 large peeled raw prawns, roughly 3–4 in
(7.5–10 cm), tails intact
1 teaspoon (5 ml) cornflour
salt and white pepper
1 carrot
1 courgette
3 tablespoons (45 ml) corn oil
3 slices root ginger
1 tablespoon (15 ml) dark soy sauce
1 tablespoon (15 ml) Sweet and Chilli Sauce (p. 130)
1 tablespoon (15 ml) tomato ketchup
1 teaspoon (5 ml) sugar
1 teaspoon (5 ml) sesame oil
1 large clove garlic, crushed
1 tablespoon (15 ml) Shaoshing wine

for the garnish
thinly sliced spring onions, green parts only

◆

Cut the prawns down the top of the spine, half-way down the body, making sure the other half remains joined. Devein the prawns and wash and dry them thoroughly.

Divide the prawns equally between 2 bowls. Add half the cornflour to each bowl and season with salt and pepper. Mix well.

Peel the carrot and cut it into strips twice the size of matchsticks. Peel the courgettes thickly (about $\frac{1}{8}$–$\frac{1}{4}$ in (3–6 m)). Discard the centres, or reserve for another use, and cut the green part into the same size strips as the carrot.

Remove the prawns from one bowl, and pierce a small hole through the centre of each body with a skewer. Insert one carrot and one courgette strip, drawing them evenly half-way through the prawn, but keeping the hole as small as possible.

Heat half the oil to a very high temperature in a pre-heated wok or frying pan, then add the ginger. Leave for

a few seconds to flavour the oil, then remove and add the prawns. Stir-fry for about 3 minutes, turning them gently to prevent the vegetable strips from falling out, until firm and opaque. Be careful not to overcook. Remove the prawns and keep warm in a hot oven with the heat turned off.

Wipe out the wok and heat the remaining oil to a very high temperature. Stir-fry the second batch of prawns for 1 minute, then add the soy sauce, sweet and chilli sauce, tomato ketchup, sugar, sesame oil and garlic. Finally add the wine, pouring it in at the side of the pan, not directly over the prawns, and stir-fry for 1 further minute.

The total cooking time should be about 4 minutes. If the prawns show signs of overbrowning, reduce the heat a little.

Place the prawns in the centre of a heated serving dish and surround them with the first batch of prawns with the vegetables inserted.

44

Top: Bang Bang Chicken *(p. 50)*, below: Coral and Pearl Butterfly Prawns.

45

46

Above: School of Whales.

SCHOOL OF WHALES

This amusing dish is usually confined to a Chinese banquet. Although exotic in appearance it is really quite easy to prepare.

◆

MAKES 10

1 fairly small white Chinese radish
sky-blue food colouring
20 raw peeled prawns, about 2–2½ in (5–6 cm), tails intact
1 small egg white
½ teaspoon cornflour
¼–½ teaspoon salt
white pepper
a few black sesame seeds

◆

To make the 'waves', peel the radish and leave it in a jar with enough blue food colouring to cover, for about 1 hour. Remove and stand on end to dry and allow the colour to set, then slice thinly. Cut the slices into quarters to form 'waves' with a delicate blue edging. Arrange the 'sea' on your chosen serving dish, ordering the waves as you like, ready for the whales to swim jauntily across.

Remove the tails from half the prawns. Cut them down the spine and devein them thoroughly. Mince the prawns, either with a cleaver or in a food processor, then add the egg white, cornflour, salt and pepper and stir well to mix. Set aside.

Cut the remaining prawns open lengthways. Open out flat to form a base and season with salt and pepper. Using a knife, put about 1 teaspoon (5 ml) of the minced prawn mixture on to each base and mould to look like a whale, as in the picture.

Arrange in a heatproof dish, place on a steaming rack over boiling water in a wok or saucepan and steam for about 4–5 minutes. Give each whale a pair of sesame seed eyes. The tails need no attention as they will automatically curl up. Serve hot.

MOCK SQUID DECKED WITH SEAWEED

illustrated on pages 38–39

Chicken, with its firm texture, is very like squid when cooked this way, but is bound to keep your guests guessing.

◆

MAKES 16

8 oz (240 g) boneless chicken breast
4 medium to large black Chinese mushrooms, soaked and drained
3 oz (90 g) bamboo shoots
4 oz (120 g) cooked ham, cut in 1 slice
salt and white pepper
½ teaspoon cornflour
¼ teaspoon ground Szechuan pepper
plain flour for dusting

for deep-frying
1 pint (600 ml) corn oil

◆

Slice the mushrooms thinly. Cut the bamboo shoots lengthways along the grain into 2½-in (6-cm) strips. Cut the ham into small strips of similar length. Group them all on a plate, season lightly and set aside.

Hold the chicken on a chopping board with your middle fingers and, using a sharp knife, cut it horizontally at a slight angle into thin slices, as for smoked salmon. There should be about 16 slices of approximately 2 × 3 in (5 × 7.5 cm). Put them into a bowl and sprinkle lightly with the cornflour, ¼ teaspoon salt and pepper to taste.

Take a chicken slice and across one end place 2 strips each of mushroom, bamboo shoot and ham, so that they come to the edge on one side, with half their length overhanging at the other. Roll up firmly and round off the end with your fingers. Dust lightly with flour.

Heat the oil to 275°F (140°C) in a wok or deep-fryer. Add the rolls, a few at a time, and deep-fry for about 1 minute, until light golden. Keep warm in the oven while frying the remainder.

For the 'seaweed' follow the recipe for Spare Ribs Served with Mock Seaweed and Prawn Balls (p. 58).

47

DEEP-FRIED STUFFED CHICKEN

It is unusual for the Chinese to stuff a simple dish like this. The result is a lovely colour contrast and light texture.
Stuffing and steaming the chicken may be done in advance.

◆

SERVES 16

4 chicken breasts, skin intact, weighing about 1½ lb (720 g)
salt and white pepper
plain flour for dusting
1 egg, beaten
2 oz (60 g) dry white breadcrumbs

for deep-frying
1 pint (600 ml) corn oil

for the stuffing
8 oz (240 g) taro
½ teaspoon salt
white pepper
2 oz (60 g) carrots

for the garnish
Chinese chives or cabbage leaves

◆

48

Steam the unpeeled taro for about 30 minutes or until soft. Using a potato masher, mash until creamy, and season with salt and pepper. Shred the carrots finely and mix them in.

Trim the chicken breasts neatly. Insert the blade of a small, sharp knife into the thicker end of each breast and work through the entire length of the breast, stretching it outwards slightly to make a cavity large enough to hold sufficient stuffing to be in proportion to the meat. Stuff the cavity with the taro mixture, using a knife to spread it out, and making sure you do not pierce the flesh. Tie each breast in three places with thread, so that it keeps a nice firm shape.

Lightly salt the breasts and place them on a rack over boiling water in a wok or saucepan and steam for 15 minutes, then take them out, remove the thread and leave to cool.

Dust the chicken breasts with seasoned flour, brush with egg and coat with the breadcrumbs. Heat the oil to 250°F (120°C) in a wok or deep-fryer, add the breasts and deep-fry slowly until golden on all sides. Remove and drain on kitchen paper, then cut crossways into ½-in (1-cm) slices. Arrange on a serving platter, with Chinese chives and serve with one of the sauces on pp. 130–133.

◆◆◆

PARTY VEGETABLES

Vegetables here take pride of place, appearing not in their time-honoured supporting role, but as stars in their own right. Graphic in form, strong in character, interesting in texture and offering natural colour contrast, they need no improvement or artifice to render them visually pleasing. The changing seasons bring new varieties, making possible the creating of seemingly endless refreshing alternatives to the predictable fish, meat and poultry theme for buffet fare.
On a purely practical level, too, they recommend themselves. They are readily available – even the more exotic ones can be found, reasonably priced, in any local supermarket. A little stir-frying here and there, the addition of some garlic and ginger, perhaps, and the preparation is minimal, the work load lightened, yet the results are gratifying.

My choice of vegetables on this occasion is: okra; mange-tout; broccoli; fresh lotus root which is imported, unusual in texture and form, sweet in flavour and can be eaten raw or cooked; Kenya beans tied with Chinese chive – a favourite among Chinese, but remember the flower is not for eating.

◆◆◆

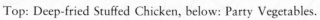
Top: Deep-fried Stuffed Chicken, below: Party Vegetables.

BANG BANG CHICKEN

illustrated on page 45

I was delighted to find this dish on the imaginative and highly selective menu of a trendy London restaurant, taking its place alongside French and Italian dishes. The chicken can be steamed a day in advance and you should be able to collect some chicken juice for use in a flavoursome sauce or to steam vegetables (p. 107). The sauce may also be prepared in advance and stored in a screwtop jar in the refrigerator.

◆

SERVES 16

3–3½lb (1.5–1.75 kg) ovenready chicken
salt and white pepper
4 slices root ginger
2 spring onions, cut into 4-in (10-cm) lengths
1 tablespoon (15 ml) corn oil

for the serving sauce

1 tablespoon (15 ml) roasted sesame seeds
1 teaspoon (5 ml) Szechuan peppercorns
1 teaspoon (5 ml) sesame paste
1½ teaspoons (7.5 ml) sesame oil
2 tablespoons (30 ml) Sweet and Chilli Sauce (p. 130)
2 tablespoons (30 ml) plum sauce
1½ teaspoons (7.5 ml) light soy sauce
1½ tablespoons (22.5 ml) Shaoshing wine
1–2 cloves garlic, crushed
a little salt and white pepper
1 tablespoon (15 ml) corn oil

for the garnish

1 tablespoon (15 ml) chopped spring onion
1½ teaspoons (7.5 ml) roasted sesame seeds

◆

Remove any fat from around the vent end of the chicken. Cut down the length of the breast-bone and open the chicken out. Season with salt and pepper.

Lay the opened-out chicken in a shallow heatproof dish with half the ginger and spring onion tucked underneath and the other half scattered on top. Pour the oil over the chicken.

Steam the chicken, still in the dish, on a rack over boiling water in a wok or saucepan for about 35–40 minutes, until cooked through. Allow to cool and reserve the chicken juices in the dish for another use.

To make the sauce, grind half the sesame seeds with the Szechuan peppercorns to a fairly fine texture, then add all the remaining sauce ingredients and blend well together. Set aside.

Remove all the skin from the chicken and cut the flesh into fairly small strips. Arrange the chicken neatly in a serving dish and pour some of the sauce over it. Serve the remaining sauce separately in a small bowl.

CHICKEN IN ASPIC

illustrated on page 61

These little moulds, which may be turned out in advance of serving and kept in the refrigerator, are my answer to œufs en gelée

◆

MAKES 10

2 oz (60 g) boneless, chicken breast
1 large Chinese black mushroom, soaked, drained and thinly sliced
a few coriander leaves

for the aspic

1 × ½-oz (15-g) sachet powdered gelatine
a few drops of sesame oil
1 teaspoon (5 ml) light soy sauce
1 teaspoon (5 ml) Shaoshing wine
½ teaspoon sugar
¼ teaspoon salt
¼ chicken stock cube

◆

Steam the chicken for 5–6 minutes as described in Bang Bang Chicken and cut it into small strips.

To make the aspic, dissolve the gelatine, in 10 fl oz (300 ml) hot water in a small saucepan, then add all the remaining aspic ingredients and simmer very gently for 5 minutes, without boiling.

Place a well-shaped coriander leaf, or part of one, with a piece of mushroom, in the base of each of 10 egg cups. Place 4 chicken strips on top, then pour in the aspic mixture to a depth of approximately 1 in (2.5 cm). Chill in the refrigerator until set, then turn out to serve.

CHICKEN WITH WALNUTS

Chicken thighs – both tender and inexpensive – are my choice for this dish as the colour of the meat is unimportant. The walnuts lose any bitterness when blanched, but retain their crunchiness. The dish can be reheated in a microwave oven, so may be prepared in advance.

◆

SERVES 8

1¼ lb (600 g) boneless chicken thighs, cut into 1-in (2.5 cm) cubes
4 oz (120 g) shelled walnuts
⅜ teaspoon salt
white pepper
1½ teaspoons (7.5 ml) dark soy sauce
1 teaspoon (5 ml) cornflour
8 fl oz (240 ml) chicken stock
2 teaspoons (1- ml) Hoi Sin sauce
1 teaspoon (5 ml) sugar

for deep-frying
1¾ pints (1 litre) corn oil

◆

Put the chicken into a bowl and add the salt, pepper, soy sauce and cornflour. Mix well and leave to marinate for 20 minutes.

Put the walnuts into a saucepan with the stock, bring to the boil, then simmer for 8 minutes. Strain in a wire sieve.

Heat the oil to 350°F (180°C) in a wok or deep-fryer, add the chicken and immediately turn off the heat. Leave for 20 seconds, then drain the chicken in a wire sieve.

Reheat 1 tablespoon (15 ml) of the hot oil to a very high temperature in a pre-heated wok or frying pan, add the walnuts and stir-fry for just 15 seconds. Return the chicken to the pan and stir-fry for 20 seconds. Add the Hoi Sin sauce and sugar and stir-fry for a further 15 seconds, then transfer to a heated serving dish.

SMOKED QUAILS
illustrated on page 57

This recipe combines 2 cooking methods – frying and roasting. The flavour of star anise, commonly identified with the aroma of Chinese cooking at its best, is particularly associated with braising and smoking.

◆

SERVES 8

16 quails, thoroughly thawed if frozen
salt and white pepper
4 tablespoons (60 ml) corn oil
carrot curls, to garnish

for the marinade
2½ tablespoons (37.5 ml) golden syrup or clear honey
4 tablespoons (60 ml) dark soy sauce
4 tablespoons (60 ml) Sweet and Chilli Sauce (p. 130) or tomato ketchup or half and half
4 cloves star anise (or the equivalent quantity of broken pieces)
½ teaspoon 5-spice powder
2 cloves garlic, crushed
4 tablespoons (60 ml) Shaoshing wine or dry sherry

for the smoking
2 tablespoons (30 ml) tea leaves, Chinese or Indian
1 tablespoon (15 ml) sugar

◆

Mix together all the marinade ingredients in a large bowl, add the quails and leave to marinate for several hours, then season lightly with salt and pepper.

Heat the oven to 400°F (200°C, gas mark 6). Heat the oil to 325°F (160°C) in a preheated wok with a rack, then reduce the heat and put in the quails. Fry until evenly browned all over, then transfer to a baking tray and roast in the oven for about 15 minutes until cooked through. Put the tea leaves and sugar into a clean wok. Place a wire rack on top and set over a high heat until the sugar starts to melt and the tea leaves are smoking, then place the quails on the rack and let them smoke for approximately 1 minute.

Transfer the quails to a heated serving platter, either whole, or cut into halves if you prefer, and garnish with the carrot curls.

51

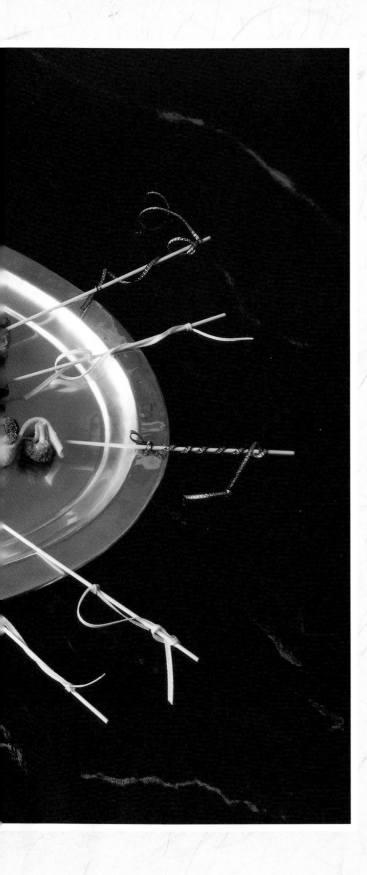

A SKEWER QUINTET

Traditionally the Chinese do not serve food on skewers, but these are such a convenient and versatile way of dispensing party food. This is my own original composition offering variations on a simple stir-fry theme, in which colour, texture and flavour combine harmoniously. The skewers can be served hot or cold as hors d'oeuvre, or as part of a buffet or dinner party.

CHICKEN

◆

MAKES 10

12 oz (360 g) boneless chicken
1-in (2.5-cm) cube root ginger, finely chopped
1 teaspoon (5 ml) dark soy sauce
1 teaspoon (5 ml) cornflour
¾ teaspoon sugar
½ teaspoon salt
white pepper
2 tablespoons (30 ml) corn oil
1 tablespoon (15 ml) Shaoshing wine
½ teaspoon sesame oil
1–2 teaspoons (5–10 ml) golden syrup

for the garnish
roasted sesame seeds

◆

Cut the chicken into 1-in (2.5-cm) cubes. Mix it with the ginger, soy sauce, cornflour, sugar, the salt, and pepper to taste.

Heat the oil in a pre-heated wok or frying pan, add the chicken and stir-fry for about 1 minute, then add the wine, sesame oil and golden syrup. Stir-fry for no more than 1 further minute.

Skewer the chicken – roughly 4 pieces to a skewer –

Left: A Skewer Quintet, including Vegetables *(p. 54)*, Prawn *(p. 55)*, Lamb *(p. 54)*, Chicken *(p. 53)* and Beef *(p. 55)*.

53

and dab with the small quantity of juice remaining in the pan. Place the skewers in a heated serving dish and scatter lightly with sesame seeds.

LAMB

◆

MAKES 10

1 lb (480 g) lean boneless leg of lamb
1 tablespoon (15 ml) corn oil
1 tablespoon (15 ml) dark soy sauce
2 teaspoons (10 ml) sugar

for the sauce

12 oz (360 g) roasted peanuts in the shell
6 oz (180 g) Spanish onion, chopped
1 large clove garlic, chopped
1½ tablespoons (22.5 ml) dark soy sauce
1½ tablespoons (22.5 ml) corn oil
½ teaspoon turmeric
1 tablespoon (15 ml) sugar
½ teaspoon salt
freshly ground black pepper
2 tablespoons (30 ml) Sweet and Chilli Sauce (p. 130)
1 teaspoon (5 ml) sesame oil

◆

Cut the lamb into 1-in (2.5-cm) cubes and flatten them with the side of a cleaver or a mallet, to tenderize. Place them in a bowl with the oil, soy sauce and sugar and leave to marinate for at least 1 hour. Thread 3 or 4 pieces of meat on to each skewer.

To make the sauce, shell the peanuts and remove the skins, to give a shelled weight of about 8 oz (240 g). Fry the nuts in a frying pan without oil until brown in places. (Although they are ready roasted, this will bring out the full richness of their flavour.) Allow the nuts to cool, then blend them in a food processor until reduced to a slightly sticky pulp. Transfer to a bowl.

Blend the onion in the food processor with the garlic and 1 tablespoon (15 ml) water until reduced to a watery paste.

Transfer the onion purée to a pre-heated saucepan and cook over a moderate heat, stirring constantly, for 5 minutes until most of the water has evaporated. Add the soy sauce, corn oil, turmeric, sugar, salt, pepper to taste and the ground peanuts. Gradually stir in 10 fl oz (300 ml) boiling water and when well combined add the sweet and chilli sauce and oil.

Cook over a very low heat for about 20 minutes, stirring occasionally, until thickened.

Place the skewers under a pre-heated grill and grill at the highest temperature for 4–6 minutes, turning from time to time, until the lamb is done to your liking.

To serve, place the skewers on individual dishes, accompanied by a little of the serving sauce. Any left over can be stored in a screwtop jar in the refrigerator.

VEGETABLE

◆

MAKES 10

8 oz (240 g) broccoli spears (choose ones with well-formed, easily separated florets)
2 long carrots
2 tablespoons (30 ml) corn oil
1 large clove garlic, thinly sliced
salt and white pepper

◆

Divide the broccoli into bite-sized florets, then peel the carrots and slice them thinly lengthways. (I find a cheese slicer does the job very well.)

Heat the oil to a medium to high temperature in a pre-heated wok or frying pan, add the garlic and stir-fry briefly, just long enough to draw out its flavour. Add the broccoli and carrots with a sprinkling of salt and pepper and 1 tablespoon (15 ml) water and stir-fry briefly for 1 minute or slightly longer, depending on how crunchy you like your vegetables. Make sure the heat does not increase so that scorching can occur.

Remove the vegetables from the pan and push them

on to skewers so that the carrot on each forms three spirals. Insert a piece of broccoli into each spiral. The structure of these skewers is such that they appear to advantage from any angle, so that they are not only edible, they can form part of your table decoration as well.

BEEF

MAKES 10

12 oz (360 g) fillet or rump steak
½ teaspoon cornflour
salt

for the sauce

1 tablespoon (15 ml) corn oil
2 tablespoons (30 ml) dark soy sauce
2 tablespoons (30 ml) golden syrup
2 tablespoons (30 ml) Sweet and Chilli Sauce (p. 130)
2 whole cloves star anise (or the equivalent quantity of broken pieces)
½ teaspoon sesame oil
2 teaspoons cornflour mixed with 2 tablespoons (30 ml) water

To make the sauce, heat the oil in a saucepan. Add all the remaining sauce ingredients except the cornflour mixture, one by one, and allow to simmer very gently for about 10 minutes, stirring from time to time. Add the cornflour mixture and stir until thickened. Remove from the heat and allow to cool. (The sauce coats the meat better when it is cold, and can be kept in a screwtop jar in the refrigerator for up to 1 week.)

Cut the steak in half lengthways and trim away any fat or gristle. Cut the steak crossways into rectangular slices ⅛ in (3 mm) thick. Rub the cornflour and a sprinkling of salt into the meat. Thread 2 pieces of meat on to each skewer, 'weaving' through each and taking care to secure both ends and the centre of each piece. Keep the meat as near the end of the skewer as possible, so that it can be easily removed.

Brush the pieces of meat with the sauce, then place the skewers under a pre-heated grill, at the highest temperature. Grill quickly, turning, so that the meat 'catches' slightly. It is usually possible to arrange the skewers so that the exposed part does not burn, but foil wrapped around the stick next to the meat will prevent this. If you use foil, remove it before serving the skewers.

PRAWNS

MAKES 10

20 raw peeled prawns about 2 in (5 cm) long (if unavailable, cooked prawns may be substituted)
½–1 teaspoon (2.5–5 ml) cornflour
salt and white pepper
1 tablespoon (15 ml) corn oil
1 clove garlic, crushed
1 tablespoon (15 ml) Sweet and Chilli Sauce (p. 130)
½–1 tablespoon (7.5–15 ml) tomato ketchup
1½ teaspoons (7.5 ml) dark soy sauce
1½ teaspoons (7.5 ml) Shaoshing wine
1 teaspoon (5 ml) sesame oil

Dry the prawns very thoroughly with kitchen paper, then mix them with the cornflour, salt and pepper.

Heat the oil to a high temperature in a pre-heated wok or frying pan and add the garlic. Fry for a few seconds, add the prawns and stir-fry for ½ minute, then add all the remaining ingredients. Stir-fry for 1 further minute and remove from the heat.

When the prawns are cool enough to handle, place 2 on each skewer. The skewer should go through the centre of the prawns set at angles to each other, balanced, rather like a piece of mobile sculpture.

55

BERIBBONED SPICY BEEF

illustrated on pages 38–39

Both the preparation of the Chinese radish for the ribbons and the marinating and deep-frying of the beef can be done well in advance, leaving only the final cooking to complete this dish.

◆

SERVES 16

2 lb (960 g) beef skirt, trimmed and thinly sliced across the grain
1 egg white
3–3½ tablespoons (45–52.5 ml) dark soy sauce
2 teaspoons (10 ml) cornflour
1–2 teaspoons (5–10 ml) chilli bean sauce
2 tablespoons (30 ml) Shaoshing wine
2 teaspoons (10 ml) sugar
white pepper

for deep-frying
1¾ pints (1 litre) corn oil

for the garnish
2 white Chinese radish

◆

56

To prepare the garnish, peel the radish, then pare it lengthways into strips ½ in (1 cm) thick, using a potato peeler. Place the strips between sheets of kitchen paper, to draw out as much moisture as possible, and chill them, still in the paper, in the refrigerator for a few hours until crisp.

Place the beef in a bowl with the egg white, 1½ tablespoons (22.5 ml) of the soy sauce and the cornflour. Stir well to mix, then leave to marinate for 30 minutes.

Heat the oil to 275°F (140°C) in a wok or deep-fryer and deep-fry the beef in 2 batches, each for about 30 seconds. Transfer to a wire sieve and leave to drain.

Heat a wok or frying pan to a high temperature, then add the beef, chilli bean sauce, wine, sugar, pepper to taste and the remaining soy sauce. Stir-fry for about 6 minutes until all the liquid has evaporated and the beef is beginning to 'catch' a little here and there.

Transfer the beef to a heated serving dish and surround with the radish ribbons.

SZECHUAN SPICY SHREDDED BEEF

The objective in this popular recipe is not to render a modest cut of meat soft and tender by means of long cooking, but to take advantage of its particular texture and, by brief cooking, turn it into something interesting.

◆

SERVES 16

2 lb (960 g) beef skirt
2 tablespoons (30 ml) dark soy sauce
1½ tablespoons (22.5 ml) plain flour
2 cloves garlic, creamed
1½ tablespoons (22.5 ml) Shaoshing wine
3 tablespoons (45 ml) red wine vinegar
1½ tablespoons (22.5 ml) crushed yellow bean paste
1½ teaspoons (7.5 ml) chilli bean paste
1½ tablespoons (22.5 ml) sugar
salt and white pepper
6 oz (180 g) carrots, finely shredded

for deep-frying
1¾ pints (1 litre) corn oil

◆

Cut the beef in half, then, holding it flat on a chopping board, cut it horizontally into slices about ¼ in (6 mm) thick. Cut across the grain – this is important – into thin narrow strips. Mix the beef strips with the soy sauce in a bowl and dust generously with flour so that the meat is lightly coated all over.

Heat the oil to 325°F (160°C) in a wok or deep-fryer, add the beef and deep-fry for about 3–4 minutes, separating the strips during cooking. Remove the beef and drain in a wire sieve.

Heat a clean wok or frying pan without oil to about 325°F (160°C). Add the beef and garlic and stir-fry for 2 minute, then add the wine, vinegar, yellow bean paste, chilli bean paste, sugar and salt and pepper to taste. Stir-fry for a further 3 minutes until the beef is firm and has absorbed both the moisture and the flavour.

Add the carrots, making sure they are evenly distributed through the beef. Stir-fry for 1 further minute, then transfer to a heated serving dish and serve immediately.

57

Top: Smoked Quails *(p. 51)*, below: Szechuan Spicy Shredded Beef.

SPARE RIBS SERVED WITH MOCK SEAWEED AND PRAWN BALLS

The prawn balls and seaweed give additional flavour, colour and texture to someimes hackneyed spare ribs. If spinach is unavailable use spring greens.

◆

SERVES 16

for the seaweed

1 lb (480 g) fresh spinach leaves or 2 lb (960 g) spring greens
salt and white pepper
caster sugar

for deep-frying

1¾ pints (1 litre) corn oil

for the spare ribs

4 lb (1.92 kg) pork spare ribs
2 tablespoons (30 ml) corn oil
2 slices root ginger
2 cloves garlic, crushed
2 oz (60 g) Spanish onion, thinly sliced

for the sauce

1 tablespoon (15 ml) corn oil
2 slices root ginger
2 cloves garlic, crushed
3 tablespoons (45 ml) light soy sauce
4 tablespoons (60 ml) tomato ketchup
2 tablespoons (30 ml) Shaoshing wine
2 tablespoons (30 ml) Hoi Sin sauce
2 tablespoons (30 ml) Sweet and Chilli Sauce (p. 130)
2 tablespoons (30 ml) golden syrup
2 teaspoons (10 ml) sesame oil
½ teaspoon 5-spice powder
2–3 whole cloves star anise (or equivalent quantity of broken pieces)
1 tablespoon (15 ml) Szechuan peppercorns
1 tablespoon (15 ml) whole black peppercorns

◆

To make the 'seaweed', wash the spinach and remove the central ribs. Dry thoroughly to remove all traces of moisture. Fold several leaves tightly together, rather like a cigar, and cut the roll lengthways into strips ⅛ in

58

(3 mm) thick. Separate the strands.

Heat the oil to 260°–275°F (130°–140°C) in a wok or deep-fryer. Deep-fry the spinach, a good handful at a time, for about 2–3 minutes, maintaining a constant temperature. Drain the spinach in a wire sieve, then on kitchen paper. The spinach will become crisp as it cools.

Transfer the spinach to a bowl and season with salt, pepper and a little sugar, then toss gently with the hands to allow the seasoning to penetrate. The spinach can be prepared well in advance and stored when completely cool in an airtight tin lined with greaseproof paper.

Heat half the oil in a pre-heated wok or large saucepan, add the ginger and garlic and fry for a few seconds, then add the onion and fry until just softened but not browned. Remove the ginger, garlic and onion from the pan with a slotted spoon. Add the spare ribs to the pan and fry briefly, turning them slowly until they are lightly browned and 'catch' lightly here and there.

Add all the sauce ingredients with 1 pint (600 ml) hot water to the pan and bring to the boil. Turn the heat down low and leave to simmer for about 45 minutes. Just before serving, strain off the sauce and spread out the spare ribs in a roasting tin. Roast in a pre-heated oven (350°F/180°C/gas mark 4) for 15–20 minutes.

◆

PRAWN-BALLS

These are delicious alone or with the Spare Ribs Served with Mock Seaweed recipe above.

◆

SERVES 16

8 oz (240 g) potatoes
¼ teaspoon salt
white pepper
½ teaspoon 5-spice powder
8 oz (240 g) peeled cooked prawns
1 egg, beaten

◆

Peel the potatoes and steam until tender. Mash well, seasoning with the salt, pepper to taste and the 5-spice powder. Shape the mixture into balls approximately 1½ in (3.5 cm) in diameter.

Dip the prawns in beaten egg. Place 6 to 7 prawns round each potato ball, pressing them on firmly.

Place the prawn balls on a well-greased baking tray and heat through in a pre-heated oven (400°F/200°C/gas mark 6) for 7–8 minutes.

LEMON-FLAVOURED SPARE RIBS

The addition of plenty of lemon zest and juice gives spare ribs a deliciously tangy, different flavour.

◆

SERVES 16

3 lb (1.5 kg) pork spare ribs
salt and white pepper
6 tablespoons (90 ml) Chinese red vinegar or malt vinegar
4 tablespoons (60 ml) sugar
1½ teaspoons (7.5 ml) dark soy sauce
finely grated zest and juice of 3 lemons
2 eggs, beaten
plain flour for dusting

for deep-frying
1¾ pints (1 litre) corn oil

◆

Chop the spare ribs into 3-in (7.5-cm) lengths. Season with salt and pepper and rub in well.

In a large bowl mix together the vinegar, sugar, ½ teaspoon salt, ¼ teaspoon pepper, soy sauce, lemon zest and juice. Add the spare ribs and leave to marinate for several hours.

Dip the spare ribs into the beaten egg, then dust with flour.

Heat the oil to 275°F (140°C) in a wok or deep-fryer and deep-fry the spare ribs in batches for 2 minutes until the pork is cooked through and a good rich colour. Drain in a wire sieve. Serve hot.

KOREAN PORK

This dish can be conveniently prepared in advance and left to stand for at least 1 hour before serving, so that the pork absorbs the flavours of the dressing. If left to stand for longer than 1 hour, cover the dish with clingfilm to prevent drying out.

◆

SERVES 16

3 lb (1.5 kg) boned shoulder or hand of pork
3 slices root ginger
½ teaspoon salt
white pepper

for the dressing
3 fl oz (90 ml) pork stock
4 spring onions, trimmed and chopped
2–3 large cloves garlic, crushed
1 teaspoon (5 ml) Shaoshing wine
½ teaspoon salt
¼ teaspoon sugar
white pepper

◆

Place the pork in a saucepan with 2 pints (1.2 litres) hot water, the ginger, salt and pepper to taste. Bring to the boil and boil for 2 minutes. Skim off any scum that may have risen to the surface, reduce the heat and simmer, covered, for 1½–2 hours, until the pork is tender when pierced with a fork. Remove the pork from the pan, reserving the stock, leave to cool, then wrap in clingfilm and chill in the refrigerator for 4–5 hours.

Carve the pork into thin slices and arrange in a shallow serving dish.

To make the dressing measure out 3 fl oz (90 ml) pork stock and combine with all the remaining ingredients, stirring well until thoroughly blended.

About 1 hour before serving, pour the dressing over the pork, mixing it in thoroughly.

59

COURGETTE CRADLES

These make ideal finger food – light, tasty and easy to handle.

◆

MAKES 16

3 courgettes
4 oz (120 g) crabmeat, fresh, frozen or canned
7 fresh spinach leaves
salt
1 tablespoon corn oil
1 teaspoon (5 ml) cornflour mixed with 1 tablespoon (15 ml) water
$\frac{1}{4}$–$\frac{1}{2}$ teaspoon sugar
white pepper
fresh chopped coriander

◆

Cut the courgettes into 2-in (5-cm) lengths. Using a vegetable corer, hollow out the insides, leaving an $\frac{1}{8}$-in (3-mm) shell. Blanch the courgettes in boiling salted water for 1–2 minutes, depending on how firm you like your vegetables. Drain and refresh immediately under cold running water, then drain again. Dry with kitchen paper.

Put the spinach leaves into a sieve and pour hot, but not boiling water over them. Squeeze out the excess water and cut into thin shreds.

If using frozen or canned crab, pat dry with kitchen paper. Heat the oil to a high temperature in a pre-heated wok or frying pan, add the crabmeat, the cornflour mixture, sugar, salt, and a generous sprinkling of pepper. Stir-fry quickly for about 1 minute.

Add the spinach and coriander and stir well to mix. Fill the centre of the courgettes with the mixture.

CRUNCHY VEGETABLE STIR-FRY

illustrated on pages 38–39

The vegetables should be cut into pieces of approximately the same size, to ensure quick, even cooking.

◆

SERVES 16

3 oz (90 g) green beans, topped, tailed and cut into 2-in (5-cm) pieces
4 oz (120 g) broccoli, sliced diagonally
4 oz (120 g) mange-tout, topped and tailed
2 sticks celery, sliced diagonally
2 oz (60 g) courgettes, cut into strips
salt
2 tablespoons (30 ml) corn oil
2 cloves garlic, sliced
4 thin slices root ginger

◆

Blanch the beans and broccoli in boiling salted water for just 30 seconds, then drain in a wire sieve.

Heat the oil in a pre-heated wok or large frying pan, add the garlic and ginger and stir-fry to release the flavours. Discard the garlic and ginger before they can start to burn.

Turn down the heat, put the mange-tout into the pan and stir-fry for 1 minute, then add the celery, courgettes, broccoli and beans and stir-fry for 1 further minute until the vegetables are cooked but still crisp and a bright green. Transfer to a serving dish.

Top: Chicken in Aspic *(p. 50)*, below: Courgette Cradles.

62

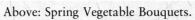
Above: Spring Vegetable Bouquets.

SPRING VEGETABLE BOUQUETS

Mundane vegetables can be transformed into a dish which would do credit to the florist's art.

◆

MAKES 16

1 long leek
8 large spring green leaves
8 large Chinese leaves
salt
1½ teaspoons (7.5 ml) corn oil
2 slices root ginger
2 oz (60 g) fresh bean sprouts
white pepper
2 oz (60 g) cooked ham, cut into fairly thick slices
4 Chinese black mushrooms, soaked and drained

to serve
double quantity Spring Onion and Ginger Sauce (p. 131)

◆

Discard the outer green leaves of the leek and cut the centre lengthways into strips like shoe laces, about ⅛ in (3 mm) wide. Run hot water over them to make them more flexible, then drain.

Remove and discard the central ribs from the spring green leaves. Divide each half leaf into two, making, as far as possible, a fan shape 6 in (15 cm) across at its widest point, with a depth of 3 in (7.5 cm). Blanch these in boiling salted water for 1 minute, drain and refresh under cold running water. Drain again and dry the leaves between sheets of kitchen paper.

Take the leafy parts of the Chinese leaves (reserve the lower parts for another use, such as stir-frying). Place them in a colander and hold them under hot running water for a short time until just flexible.

Heat the oil to a very high temperature in a pre-heated wok or frying pan. Add the ginger to flavour, then add the bean sprouts, season with salt and pepper and stir-fry for 10–15 seconds. Using a slotted spoon, transfer the bean sprouts to a bowl.

Cut the ham into strips ¼ in (6 mm) wide. Remove the stems from the mushrooms and slice the caps to the same size as the ham strips.

Place a piece of Chinese leaf on a piece of spring

63

green, both with the frilly edge at the top. Place a small bundle of bean sprouts, 4–5 strips of ham and two strips of mushroom down the centre.

Roll up from one corner, to make a cone shape with a scalloped edge at the top. Tie up the bouquet with a ribbon of leek and open up the top slightly, so that the heads of the flowers are well displayed. Serve with a very small amount of sauce – a coffee spoonful for each bouquet – and be sure to take some of the Spring Onion And Ginger Sauce (p. 131) with it.

ONION PASTIES
illustrated on pages 66–67

If not for immediate use the pasties may be placed on a wire rack and kept hot for up to 20 minutes in the oven (325°F/160°C/gas mark 3), or cooked as long as 3–4 hours in advance, left to cool, then reheated for 15 minutes in the oven (375°F/190°C/gas mark 5) immediately before serving.

◆

MAKES 4

for the pastry
8 oz (240 g) plain flour
$\frac{1}{8}$ teaspoon salt
1$\frac{1}{2}$ oz (45 g) lard
a little extra flour for dusting

for the filling
1$\frac{1}{2}$ tablespoons (22.5 ml) corn oil
1 lb (480 g) Spanish onions, finely sliced
$\frac{1}{2}$ teaspoon salt
white pepper
1 oz (30 g) spring onion, trimmed and finely chopped
1 oz (30 g) fresh coriander, finely chopped

for deep-frying
1$\frac{3}{4}$ pints (1 litre) corn oil

◆

To make the filling, heat 1$\frac{1}{2}$ tablespoons (22.5 ml) oil to a high temperature in a pre-heated wok or frying pan. Turn down the heat to moderate, add the Spanish onion, season with salt and pepper and stir-fry for about 1$\frac{1}{2}$ minutes until softened but not browned. Add

the spring onion and coriander and stir-fry briefly to mix. Transfer the filling to a bowl and allow to cool.

To make the pastry, sift the flour with the salt into a large mixing bowl. Make a well in the centre. Melt the lard and add to the bowl with 8 tablespoons (120 ml) hot water. Using a fork, briskly stir the mixture until it forms a dough.

In the mixing bowl, if this is large enough, or on a floured surface, knead the dough until smooth, soft and bouncy. Divide it into 4 equal pieces. Leave 3 of these in the bowl, covered with a damp cloth.

On a well-floured surface, using a floured rolling pin, roll out one piece of dough to a rectangle. Fold it into 3 so that it forms another rectangle and roll the three resulting thicknesses together, as for puff pastry (see diagram). Repeat this folding and rolling 3 times, the last time making the dough into a 6-in (15-cm) square instead of a rectangle. Trim the edges neatly.

Put a quarter of the onion filling in the centre of the pastry square. Bring all 4 corners into the centre, brush the edges with water or milk and seal the diagonal joins firmly, twisting them gently between finger and thumb to make attractive scalloped edges. (Any minor repairs can easily be made by smoothing the pastry together by hand, and sealing with a little liquid.) At each of the 4 corners give the pastry a little twist to finish off the joins, and a further twist in the centre will give the pasty a top-knot as a finishing touch. In the same way make the remaining dough into similarly filled pasties, 4 in all.

Heat the oil to 325°F (160°C) in a wok or deep-fryer. Add the pasties and deep-fry for about 5 minutes on each side, until an even golden-brown. If they seem to be browning too quickly, turn down the heat slightly. Remove with a slotted spoon and drain on kitchen paper and cut each into four before serving.

64

AUBERGINE AND PORK MUFFINS

illustrated on pages 38–39

Pork is not a 'must' in this dish. Lamb, beef or chicken could be substituted. The muffins can be kept warm in the oven (400°F/200°C/gas mark 6) for up to 20 minutes. If you find it more convenient to prepare them in advance, everything can be done 4–5 hours before serving. In this case the muffins only have to be reheated in the oven (400°F/200°C/ gas mark 6) for a good 20 minutes to make them ready to serve.

◆

MAKES 24

1½ lb (720 g) slender aubergines, about 2½ in (6 cm) in diameter,
cut into ⅛-in (3-mm) slices
1 teaspoon (5 ml) salt
plain flour for dusting

for the filling

1 lb (480 g) finely minced pork
3 tablespoons (45 ml) oyster sauce
2 tablespoons (30 ml) tomato purée
1 teaspoon (5 ml) cornflour
½ teaspoon salt
¼ teaspoon white pepper
1 teaspoon (5 ml) sugar
8 very thin slices root ginger, cut into hair's-breadth strands
1 egg white
1 tablespoon (15 ml) corn oil
3 spring onions, finely chopped

for deep-frying

1¾ pints (1 litre) corn oil

for the batter

12 oz (360 g) plain flour
⅛ teaspoon salt
3 tablespoons (45 ml) corn oil
3 egg whites

◆

Place the aubergines in a colander, sprinkle with the salt and leave to sweat for ½ hour.

Meanwhile make the batter. Sift the flour with the salt into a mixing bowl. Make a well in the centre and add the oil and ¾ pint (425 ml) water. Mix to a fairly thick, smooth consistency. Chill in the refrigerator for about 30 minutes.

Mix the pork with the oyster sauce, tomato purée, cornflour, salt, pepper, sugar, ginger and egg white. Stir until thoroughly combined.

Heat 1 tablespoon (15 ml) oil in a wok or frying pan until very hot, then add the pork mixture and stir-fry for 2 minutes. Add the spring onions and stir-fry for a further 30 seconds. Chill the stuffing mixture in the refrigerator for at least 30 minutes, until firm.

Rinse the aubergines under cold running water and pat them dry with kitchen paper. Sprinkle flour on one surface of the slices. Cover half the slices, on the floured side, with 1 teaspoon (5 ml) of the stuffing mixture to a depth of approximately ⅛ in (3 mm), keeping it level, and top each with a second slice of aubergine, floured side down. Press together lightly.

Whisk the 3 egg whites until they stand in peaks, then fold them gently into the batter, using a spatula. Heat the oil to 350°F (180°C) in a wok or deep-fryer. Dust the aubergine 'muffins' on both sides with flour and dip into the batter to coat thoroughly. Deep-fry the muffins in batches, keeping the temperature constant, for 1 minute on each side, until golden. Drain on a wire rack.

65

CUCUMBER FLOWERS

These are lovely as part of a buffet selection, and make most attractive garnishes, too. Part of their charm lies in the fact that no two are ever alike – and as their shape and flavour do not spoil, they may be prepared a few hours in advance.

◆

MAKES 30

2 cucumbers, very thinly sliced
4 oz (240 g) crabmeat, thoroughly thawed and drained if frozen
salt
2 teaspoons (10 ml) sugar
4 tablespoons (60 ml) rice or white wine vinegar
$\frac{1}{8}$ teaspoon chilli powder
white pepper

◆

Pat the cucumber slices dry between two sheets of kitchen paper. Put them into a colander and sprinkle them with salt to draw out any further moisture. Leave to drain for 30 minutes.

Press the cucumber gently with kitchen paper to remove as much water as possible. Place the cucumber slices in a bowl with a sprinkling of salt, the sugar and vinegar. Leave for 30 minutes, then drain in a wire sieve.

Using your fingers or chopsticks, pick up about 10 cucumber slices at a time and place them, well spaced, on a platter in raised sculpted heaps, reminiscent of full-blown roses, their 'petals' edged with green, and no two alike.

Carefully break up the crabmeat and sprinkle it with the chilli powder, and salt and pepper if you like. Top each cucumber flower with about $\frac{1}{2}$ teaspoon seasoned crabmeat.

66

Clockwise, from left: Fish Surprise *(p. 43)*, Salmon Ringed Asparagus *(p. 42)*, Cucumber Flowers, Onion Pasties *(p. 64)*.

DINNER DISHES

A Chinese dinner party, like any other, benefits from some advance planning and careful organization to prevent last-minute panics. Unless you are serving soup or a hot starter, aim to have the first course already laid out before the guests sit down.

Chinese food appears to best advantage on simple white dishes. If you are using individual serving bowls, these should be set on plates. An attractive option is to provide each guest with a set of 2 mussel shells containing soy sauce and chilli sauce.

Traditionally, fragrant tea is served throughout the meal, although some men like to drink whisky with food. Sometimes Japanese saké may be offered, heated like mulled wine. Personally, I prefer to serve a chilled white wine, such as a Touraine Sauvignon, Moselle or Gewürztraminer, or a light, fruity red, such as a Cabernet Sauvignon. All these wines go particularly well with Chinese food.

I always find 8 an ideal number for entertaining guests to dinner, so I have based all the recipes in the dinner section on this number. For 8, at least 2 main dishes will be needed. Choose a selection from the following: one braised or one roast dish, which can be prepared in advance; one or two stir-fried dishes, which can be kept warm in the oven for 10 minutes or so; one vegetable dish and one rice dish. Begin with a combination of two or three hors d'oeuvres, or a light Chinese soup could replace one of the starters.

Clockwise, from top: Peking Duck (*p. 92*), Rainbow Soup (*p. 71*), Mandarin Pancakes (*p. 109*), Seafood and Vegetable Fried Noodles (*p. 115*), Stir-fried Chicken, Prawns and Broad Beans (*p. 77*), Bean Sprouts with Fresh Herbs (*p. 102*).

BASIC STOCK

To make good home-made soup it is essential to have a tasty stock available. Chinese cooks like to start with a basic consommé made with fish, meat or poultry from which to create extravagant soups to grace a special occasion or a modest one made from odds and ends of everyday vegetables. This stock can also be used as the basis of a serving sauce. It can be frozen very successfully in small quantities in cartons for this purpose, so it is worth making larger quantities than needed for immediate use. The amounts given here are sufficient for 8 servings of soup.

◆

SERVES 8

about 3 lb (1.2 kg) meat, fish or poultry bones with a little of the flesh left on
3 slices root ginger
½ teaspoon salt
white pepper

◆

Bring 4 pints (2.4 litres) water to the boil in a saucepan and add all the ingredients. Boil briskly for 5 minutes, then skim off the scum which will have formed on the surface. Turn down the heat to a fairly low temperature and simmer uncovered, for about 2 hours, until the stock is reduced to about 2½ pints (1.5 litres), then strain through a fine wire sieve.

70

BEANCURD SOUP

illustrated on page 78

This highly versatile, nutritious vegetable can be cooked in all sorts of ways – stir-fried, steamed, braised and boiled. Here I have used it to make a light soup, with watercress for added piquancy.

◆

SERVES 8

6 oz (180 g) boneless chicken breast, shredded
12 oz (360 g) beancurd, cut into ½-in (1-cm) squares
2 bunches watercress, trimmed of stems
½ teaspoon cornflour
white pepper
1 tablespoon (15 ml) light soy sauce
2½ pints (1.5 litres) chicken or pork stock
1 spring onion, trimmed and finely chopped

◆

Mix the chicken with the cornflour, pepper to taste and soy sauce in a bowl and let it stand for 10 minutes. Bring the stock to the boil in a saucepan, then add the beancurd and simmer very gently for about 10 minutes.

Turn up the heat and add the watercress and chicken. Bring to the boil, then lower the heat and cook for 1 minute. Add the spring onion and serve in a heated tureen.

VELVET CHICKEN SOUP WITH LETTUCE

Using egg white in this way, to give a light, silky texture, is a technique almost exclusive to Chinese cooking.

◆

SERVES 8

2½ pints (1.5 litres) basic chicken stock, using 3 lb (1.2 kg) chicken carcass
3 oz (90 g) crisp lettuce (iceberg, Webb's Wonder or cos), cut into ⅛–¼ in (3–6 mm) shreds
5 egg whites

Before making the stock, remove any skin and visible fat from the chicken carcass. Follow the instructions for making basic stock (p. 70).

Just before serving, transfer the chicken stock to a clean pan and bring to the boil. Add the shredded lettuce and turn off the heat. Leave for 2–3 minutes to cool slightly, then gently stir in the egg whites, so that the soup becomes a soft velvety white but not cloudy. Serve immediately.

❖

RAINBOW SOUP

illustrated on page 69

This light, colourful soup is a perfect way to start a rich dinner; it won't spoil your appetite for the dishes that follow.

◆

SERVES 8

2½ pints (1.5 litres) seasoned pork stock
1 courgette
1 oz (30 g) carrots
1 oz (30 g) Chinese leaves (coarse white centre)
1 oz celery
1 oz red pepper, cored and seeded
salt
1 oz (30 g) radiccio
1 × 4-in (10-cm) square laver

◆

Peel the courgette fairly thickly (about ⅛ in/3 mm) and discard the centre. Cut the courgette skin and all the other vegetables and the laver into matchstick lengths. Bring the stock to the boil and add the carrots, followed by the courgette skin, Chinese leaves, celery and red pepper. Boil for 2 minutes, then taste and adjust the seasoning if necessary. Pour into a heated tureen.

Just before serving float the strips of radiccio and laver on the surface.

❖

DELICATE CHICKEN NOODLE SOUP

This light-hearted soup is delicious and made in an instant. You could, if you wish, prepare the ingredients well beforehand and have them ready, covered in clingfilm, but the actual cooking of the soup is amazingly quick, taking little more time than is needed to make a cup of tea. Serve the soup from a tureen.

◆

SERVES 8

6 oz (180 g) boneless chicken breast, finely shredded
1 oz (30 g) transparent noodles, soaked for 5 minutes in warm water, then drained and cut into 2-in (4-cm) lengths.
¼ teaspoon cornflour
¼ teaspoon salt
white pepper
2½ pints (1.5 litres) basic chicken stock
3–4 Chinese black mushrooms, soaked, drained and thinly sliced
2 oz (60 g) cooked ham, in one fairly thick slice, cut into fairly long, very thin shreds
4 oz (120 g) bean sprouts
5 oz (150 g) cucumber, seeds removed and cut into fairly long, very thin shreds

◆

Mix the chicken in a bowl with the cornflour, salt and pepper to taste. Bring the stock to the boil in a saucepan, then add the mushrooms, ham and chicken, in that order. As soon as the chicken becomes opaque – after about 5 seconds – turn off the heat.

Just before serving, reheat the soup and add the bean sprouts, cucumber and noodles, with a little extra salt if necessary.

❖

FISH SOUP
WITH CORIANDER

The fish should be cut into really thin strips, which are then blanched, rather than cooked, in the stock, just before serving.

◆

SERVES 8

2½ pints (1.5 litres) basic pork stock, also using 1 lb (480 g) pork shoulder steak finely chopped
8 oz (240 g) cod or haddock fillet, skinned and cut into very thin strips
¾ oz (22.5 g) coriander, finely chopped
1 teaspoon (5 ml) cornflour
⅛ teaspoon salt
white pepper
1 tablespoon (15 ml) Shaoshing wine

◆

Make the stock following the basic recipe given on p. 70 and including the extra meat. Reduce as per instructions.

Mix the fish in a bowl with the cornflour, salt and pepper to taste.

Bring the stock to the boil in a saucepan, add the wine and simmer gently for 5 minutes. Add the fish and coriander, and taste and adjust the seasoning if necessary. Serve in a heated tureen.

72

HOT AND SOUR SOUP

This is one of the most popular Chinese soups, with a unique combination of flavours that acts as an ideal appetizer.

◆

SERVES 8

6 oz (180 g) bamboo shoots
½ oz (15 g) (trimmed weight) wood ear, soaked and drained
2½ pints (1.5 litres) lightly seasoned basic chicken or pork stock
4 Chinese black mushrooms, soaked, drained and finely sliced
2 tablespoons (30 ml) dark soy sauce
5 tablespoons (75 ml) malt vinegar
½ teaspoon sesame oil
1 tablespoon (15 ml) cornflour mixed with 1 tablespoon (15 ml) water
white pepper
2 egg whites

◆

Cut the bamboo shoots lengthways into thin slices, then cut them along the grain into shreds thinner than matchsticks. Discard any hard pieces of wood ear and cut the remainder into ⅛-in (3-mm) shreds. Place the stock, bamboo shoots, wood ear and mushrooms in a saucepan and bring to the boil, then stir in the soy sauce, vinegar, sesame oil, cornflour mixture and pepper to taste.

Turn off the heat for a minute to allow the soup to cool slightly. Just before serving, add the egg whites, stirring them in gently with chopsticks or a spoon, so that the soup is streaked with delicate trails of white. Serve in a heated tureen.

SWEETCORN CHICKEN SOUP

This popular soup recommends itself by its warm, inviting colour. It is satisfying and substantial, but not so filling as to spoil one's appetite for any dishes that may follow.

◆

SERVES 8

8 oz (240 g) boneless chicken, finely minced
8 oz (240 g) thin streaky bacon rashers
2 × 14-oz (411-g) cans creamed sweetcorn
1 teaspoon (5 ml) cornflour
$\frac{1}{4}$ teaspoon salt
white pepper
$1\frac{1}{2}$ pints (900 ml) basic chicken stock
1 tablespoon (15 ml) cornflour mixed with 2 tablespoons (30 ml) water
pinch of salt
$\frac{1}{2}$ teaspoon sugar
2 eggs, beaten

for the garnish
1 oz (30 g) very finely chopped parsley

◆

Mix the chicken with the cornflour, salt and pepper in a bowl. Set aside. Fry the bacon until crisp, then chop very finely (this is best done in a food processor).

Heat the stock and the sweetcorn together in a saucepan. At about 140°F (70°C), well before it comes to the boil, add the chicken, stirring to separate the meat. Stir in the cornflour mixture and bring the soup to a gentle boil. Taste and adjust the seasoning, adding the sugar and salt and pepper as required.

Using a fork or chopstick, stir in the eggs with gentle wave-like movements, so the soup becomes lightly streaked. Serve the soup in a heated tureen with one-third of the bacon and parsley sprinkled on the centre of the surface to give it colour. Serve the remaining bacon and parsley in small bowls for guests to help themselves.

❖

SHARK FIN CHICKEN SOUP
illustrated on page 100

Any doubts about this soup, which may sound alien to Western ears, will be dispelled once it is tasted. It has a wonderful texture and is rich in calcium. It is definitely for a special occasion, as the shark fin is expensive, but there is a mystique attaching to it, and the Chinese experience is incomplete without it. It can easily be prepared in advance, and reheated and the chicken added just before serving.

◆

SERVES 8

$4\frac{1}{2}$ oz (135 g) prepared shark fin, soaked for 24 hours in lukewarm water
6 oz (120 g) boneless chicken breast, shredded finely
2–3 pints (1.5–2.8 litres) seasoned chicken stock
$\frac{1}{4}$ teaspoon cornflour
$\frac{1}{8}$ teaspoon salt
white pepper

for serving
2 oz (60 g) bean sprouts, topped and tailed
3 fl oz (90 ml) Chinese red vinegar

◆

Strain the shark fin and loosen the strands, drawing them apart to partially separate them. Strain the stock twice through a piece of muslin. Bring the stock to the boil in a saucepan, add the shark fin, then turn down the heat and simmer gently, covered, for about $1\frac{1}{2}$ hours.

Mix the chicken in a bowl with the cornflour, salt and pepper to taste. Add to the soup and cook for just 1 minute, then taste and adjust the seasoning if necessary. Pour into a heated tureen.

Place the bean sprouts and vinegar in separate bowls, for guests to add to their bowls of soup. (About 2 teaspoons (10 ml) vinegar and a few bean sprouts to each serving.)

❖

73

PRAWNS WITH SWEET PEPPER

A typical stir-fry dish. The ingredients are common in many Western recipes and therefore make an ideal introduction for the uninitiated.

◆

SERVES 8

1 lb (480 g) raw peeled medium prawns
1 tablespoon (15 ml) rock salt
2 small yellow peppers, cored, seeded and cut into thin rings
1 clove garlic, crushed
½ teaspoon salt
white pepper
½ teaspoon sugar
a few coriander leaves to garnish

for deep-frying
1 pint (600 ml) corn oil

◆

74

Cut the prawns down half their length of the spine, leaving the lower part uncut. Devein the prawns and rub them with the rock salt, leave them for 30 minutes, then rinse under a cold tap and pat dry with kitchen paper.

Heat the oil to 325°F (160°C) in a wok or deep-fryer, add the prawns and deep-fry for 30 seconds. Drain in a wire sieve.

Reheat 2 tablespoons (30 ml) of the hot oil in a second wok or frying pan, add the peppers with a pinch of salt and stir-fry for 30 seconds, then arrange on a heated serving platter.

In the same pan reheat a further 1 tablespoon (15 ml) of the hot oil, add the prawns and garlic, salt, pepper and sugar if using, and stir-fry for 1 minute. Spoon over the peppers and serve hot or cold.

Left: Salted Prawns with Chilli *(p. 7)*,
right: Prawns with Sweet Pepper.

SIZZLING PRAWNS WITH CRISPED RICE

illustrated on page 97

This is a most original, striking dish. Unlikely as it may seem, you start by collecting the caked rice that has stuck to the bottom of the saucepan during cooking. The rice should be at least a day old and can be up to three days old if it has been stored in a refrigerator. It is essential that it should have been correctly cooked in the first instance (see p. 112).

◆

SERVES 8

1 lb (480 g) cooked rice
1 lb (480 g) small peeled prawns
½ teaspoon cornflour
⅛ teaspoon salt
white pepper
4 oz (120 g) Spanish onion, diced fairly finely
2 oz (60 g) green pepper, cored, seeded and diced
2½ tablespoons (37.5 ml) tomato ketchup
1 tablespoon (15 ml) Sweet and Chilli Sauce (p. 130)
2 teaspoons (10 ml) light soy sauce
1 teaspoon (5 ml) sugar
⅛ teaspoon salt

for deep-frying
1 pint (600 ml) corn oil

◆

To make the crisped rice, scrape it from the bottom of the pan with a spatula. Clusters of grains are quite acceptable.

Heat the oil to 325°F (160°C) in a shallow frying pan, add the rice and deep-fry without stirring for 3–4 minutes at a constant temperature, until firm and lightly coloured. Turn the rice gently and cook for a further 2–3 minutes until light and firm to the touch. Remove with a slotted spoon and drain in a wire sieve.

Mix the prawns with the cornflour, salt and pepper. Reheat the oil to 325°F (160°C), add the prawns and deep-fry for just 30 seconds. Remove with a slotted spoon and drain in a wire sieve. Put an ovenproof serving dish to heat in a very hot oven.

Reheat 2 tablespoons (30 ml) of the hot oil to a high temperature in a pre-heated wok or frying pan, add the onions and green peppers with a sprinkling of salt and stir-fry for 20 seconds, then add the prawns and stir-fry for a further 30 seconds. Add the ketchup, sweet and chilli sauce, soy sauce, sugar and the cornflour mixture. Stir-fry for about 2 minutes to blend and thicken.

Transfer to a heated serving bowl. Transfer the crispy rice to the very hot dish heating in the oven. Pour the prawns over the rice at the table, making a point of pouring some over the bare surface of the dish which will cause the desired sizzling.

PRAWNS WITH CORIANDER

This simple dish speaks for itself, but by leaving half the shell in place the presentation is more interesting and the prawn meat is easily removed.

◆

SERVES 8

12 oz (360 g) medium-sized raw peeled prawns
1 tablespoon (15 ml) rock salt
1½ teaspoons (7.5 ml) finely shredded root ginger
salt and white pepper
a little Shaoshing wine or dry sherry
¼ teaspoon sugar

for deep-frying
1 pint (600 ml) corn oil

for the garnish
½ oz (15 g) fresh coriander leaves

◆

Cut the prawns down the spine and devein them. Rub the rock salt through the prawns and rinse them. Pat dry.

Heat the oil to 275°F (140°C) in a wok or deep-fryer, add the prawns and deep-fry very briefly, then drain.

Reheat 1 tablespoon (15 ml) of the hot oil to a high temperature in a pre-heated wok. Add the ginger and the prawns, salt and pepper, a few drops of wine and the sugar. Stir-fry for 1 minute, then scatter over the coriander leaves, separating any particularly large ones into smaller leaf shapes. Transfer to a heated serving dish and serve.

SALTED PRAWNS WITH CHILLI

illustrated on pages 74–75

In this recipe and the one for Prawns with Sweet Pepper (p. 75), using ingredients that are basically the same, I am presenting simple but decorative dishes, which require little in the way of attention and skill. They make a nice change from more robust food.

◆

SERVES 8

1 lb (480 g) raw prawns in the shell, about 2 in (5 cm) long
1 tablespoon (15 ml) rock salt
1 fresh green chilli, finely shredded
1 Spanish onion, cut into fine strands
¼ teaspoon salt
freshly ground black pepper

for deep-frying
1 pint (600 ml) corn oil

◆

Keeping the shells and tails intact, remove the legs from the prawns and devein them. Rub the prawns with rock salt and leave them for about 1 hour, then rinse under cold running water and pat dry with kitchen paper.

Heat the oil to about 325°F (160°C) in a wok or deep-fryer, add the prawns and deep-fry for about 30 seconds. Remove and drain in a wire sieve.

Heat a wok or frying pan until almost smoking, then add the prawns, chilli, onion, salt and pepper to taste. Stir-fry for 1½ minutes until the prawns are completely cooked and their outsides are glazed and crisp. They can be eaten with the fingers – shells included if you like to add roughage to your diet, or, if you find the prospect daunting, the shells are easily removed without losing the pleasant saltiness and good flavour.

STIR-FRIED CHICKEN, PRAWNS AND BROAD BEANS

It is well worth taking the trouble to skin the broad beans, in order to reveal their vibrant green which normally goes unappreciated.

◆

SERVES 8

8 oz (240 g) boneless chicken breast
8 oz (240 g) medium-size raw peeled prawns
1 lb (480 g) broad beans, thawed if frozen
1 teaspoon (5 ml) cornflour
salt and white pepper
1 teaspoon (5 ml) sugar

for deep-frying
1 pint (600 ml) corn oil

◆

Cut the chicken into pieces similar in size to a large broad bean. Remove any veins from the prawns and cut them into pieces roughly equal in size to the chicken. Put the chicken and prawns into a bowl and mix with the cornflour, ½ teaspoon salt and pepper to taste. Leave to stand while removing the skins from the broad beans.

Heat the oil to 250°F (120°C) in a wok or deep-fryer, add the chicken and prawns and deep-fry briefly until the pieces separate. While still slightly undercooked, remove them with a slotted spoon and put them in a wire sieve to drain.

Reheat 2 tablespoons (30 ml) of the hot oil in a pre-heated wok or frying pan. Add the broad beans with about ¼–½ teaspoon salt and stir-fry for about 1 minute.

Add the chicken and prawns and stir-fry for 1–2 minutes, then transfer to a heated serving dish.

77

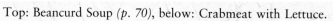

Top: Beancurd Soup *(p. 70)*, below: Crabmeat with Lettuce.

CRABMEAT WITH LETTUCE

In this light, informal dish, the lettuce is cooked briefly, which gives it a quite different flavour and texture. Crisp lettuce cooked in this way also makes an interesting and unusual vegetable accompaniment.

◆

SERVES 8

8 oz (240 g) fresh, frozen or canned crabmeat
1 iceberg or other crisp lettuce (slightly darker green lettuce gives better colour and flavour)
3 tablespoons (45 ml) corn oil
salt and white pepper
1 teaspoon (5 ml) sugar
2 teaspoons (10 ml) cornflour mixed with 4 tablespoons (60 ml) water
4 egg whites

◆

If using fresh crab, remove the meat, including the roe, from the shell. If using frozen or canned crab, press gently in a sieve to get rid of any excess moisture. Separate the lettuce leaves and tear them into pieces.

Heat half the oil to a high temperature in a pre-heated wok or frying pan, add the lettuce and a sprinkling of salt, and stir-fry quickly, turning the leaves, for 30 seconds to 1 minute, until the lettuce is slightly softened but still firm. Transfer to a heated serving dish.

In the same pan, heat the remaining oil, add the crabmeat with $\frac{1}{4}$ teaspoon salt, pepper to taste, the sugar and the cornflour mixture. Fry until the mixture becomes transparent, then blend in the egg whites. Turn off the heat under the pan and continue to stir gently until the egg white is set and the mixture is velvety in texture.

Spoon the crabmeat mixture over the lettuce. The dish will have a glistening, translucent quality and interesting colour variations.

SPICY MUSSELS
illustrated on page 88

Here is a dish that is not only delicious, but economical and simple to make. Clams could be substituted for the mussels.

◆

SERVES 8

3–3½ lb (1.2–1.5-kg) fresh mussels, scraped clean, then left in a bowl under gently running cold water for 1 hour, and strained in a colander just before using
2 tablespoons (30 ml) corn oil
1 tablespoon (15 ml) yellow bean sauce
1 tablespoon (15 ml) tomato purée
1 tablespoon (15 ml) Shaoshing wine
1 teaspoon (5 ml) sugar
1½ teaspoons (7.5 ml) dark soy sauce
2–3 fresh chillis, thinly sliced
2 × 2-in (5-cm) cubes root ginger, thinly sliced and cut into hair's-breadth strands
2 large cloves garlic, crushed
1 tablespoon (15 ml) cornflour mixed with 2 tablespoons (30 ml) water
3 spring onions, thinly sliced

◆

Heat the oil in a pre-heated wok or large saucepan until smoking. Add the mussels and stir-fry for about 3 minutes until they are all open and water comes out of them.

Ladle the mussels into a wire sieve and allow the surplus liquid to drain away, but keep back the liquid which is in the pan. The mussels can be kept hot in the oven pre-heated to 375°F (190°C, gas mark 5) in the sieve set over a heatproof bowl to catch any drips.

To the liquid in the pan, add the bean sauce, tomato purée, wine, sugar and soy sauce, then the chillis, ginger and garlic. Stir in the cornflour mixture.

Shake the excess water from the mussels and return them to the pan. Stir for about 1 minute in the sauce, until it clings here and there to the shells.

Transfer the mussels to a large heated serving platter and sprinkle with the spring onions. Turn them once or twice until everything is well blended.

79

LOBSTER WITH MONKFISH

This is a dish to appeal to the senses. If it sounds extravagant, console yourself with the thought that it is easy to prepare and dramatic in appearance despite its simplicity.

◆

SERVES 8

1 medium-size lobster, live or cooked
$1\frac{1}{4}$ lb (600 g) monkfish, boned and skinned
$\frac{1}{4}$–$\frac{1}{2}$ teaspoon salt
white pepper
1 teaspoon (5 ml) cornflour
1 teaspoon (5 ml) sugar
8 large raw peeled prawns
3 slices root ginger, finely shredded
2 tablespoons (30 ml) finely shredded spring onions, green parts only

for deep-frying
1 pint (600 ml) corn oil

◆

If you are using a live lobster, steam it for about 10 minutes over a high heat. Remove from the heat and separate the tail from the head. Turn the tail upside down and, using a pair of scissors, cut lengthways down the centre so that later the meat can be easily removed. Cut the lobster crossways into slices. Crack the claws and remove the meat. Cut the monkfish into $2 \times \frac{1}{2}$-in (5×1-cm) pieces. Put into a bowl with the salt, pepper to taste, cornflour and sugar.

Cut the prawns down the spine and devein them, then season lightly with salt and pepper.

Heat the oil to 200–300°F (100–150°C) in a wok or deep-fryer, add the monkfish and deep-fry, stirring gently to keep the pieces separate. Using a slotted spoon, transfer to a heated dish.

Deep-fry the prawns for about 30 seconds, until cooked and firm to the touch. Remove them from the oil.

Heat a wok over a high heat. Add 1 tablespoon (15 ml) of the hot oil, then add the monkfish, ginger,

Clockwise, from top left: Scallops Shanghai-style *(p. 82)*, Lobster with Monkfish, Steamed Monkfish *(p. 82)*

lobster slices and claw meat and stir-fry for 1 minute. Turn off the heat.

Remove the lobster slices and arrange them in the centre of a heated serving dish as shown in the picture. Place the monkfish and claw meat in more or less equal amounts on either side of the lobster, with a scattering of green spring onions to give a colour contrast with the whiteness of the fish. Arrange 4 prawns on either side to make an attractive edging and echo the colour of the lobster.

STEAMED MONKFISH
illustrated on pages 80–81

In this recipe the delicate natural flavour of the fish is displayed to advantage.

◆

SERVES 8

$1\frac{1}{4}$ lb (600 g) monkfish, cod or any other firm white fish
1 large Chinese black mushroom, soaked, drained and sliced
4 oz (120 g) canned bamboo shoots
$\frac{1}{2}$ teaspoon salt
white pepper
$\frac{1}{2}$ teaspoon cornflour
$\frac{1}{4}$ teaspoon sugar
$1\frac{1}{2}$ teaspoons (7.5 ml) Shaoshing wine
2 teaspoons (10 ml) corn oil

◆

Remove any skin, bones and unsightly tissue from the fish, leaving only the white flesh. Cut it into 2 × $1\frac{1}{2}$-in (5 × 3-cm) pieces approximately $\frac{1}{4}$–$\frac{1}{2}$ in (6 mm–1 cm) thick. Place the fish between kitchen paper and gently press out any moisture. Mix the fish in a bowl with the salt, pepper, cornflour and sugar.

Arrange the fish pieces in 2 rows in a heatproof dish. Cut the bamboo shoots into slices $\frac{1}{4}$ in (6 mm) thick. Tuck them between the pieces of fish. Arrange the sliced mushroom down the centre of each row.

Mix the wine with the oil and sprinkle over the fish. Place on a steaming rack over boiling water in a wok or saucepan and steam at a high temperature for about 5 minutes, until cooked.

82

SCALLOPS SHANGHAI-STYLE
illustrated on pages 80–81

Scallops are here given delicate treatment that complements their natural flavour, with celery and carrot chosen for their texture and colour.

◆

SERVES 8

16 scallops, thoroughly thawed if frozen
$\frac{1}{2}$ teaspoon cornflour
$\frac{1}{4}$–$\frac{1}{2}$ teaspoon salt
white pepper
$\frac{1}{2}$–1 teaspoon (2.5–5 ml) sugar
1 stick celery
1 carrot
1 tablespoon (15 ml) Shaoshing wine

for deep-frying
1 pint (600 ml) corn oil

Separate the roes from the white flesh of the scallops and reserve. (Make sure their delicate skins are not broken, or the white parts will be tainted.) Cut away any darkish veins from the white parts and dry. Put them into a bowl with the cornflour and season with salt, pepper and sugar.

Cut the celery and carrot into 2-in (5-cm) lengths, then into thin slices. (I find a cheese slicer or mandoline very helpful for this.) Finally cut the thinly sliced vegetables into fine strands, as shown in the picture.

Heat the oil to 250°F (120°C) in a wok or deep-fryer. Add the white parts of the scallops and deep-fry for just a few seconds to seal the surface and ensure that they retain their natural juices. Using a slotted spoon, transfer the scallops to a wire sieve.

Sprinkle the roes with a little salt and pepper. Deep-fry them for just under 30 seconds, until cooked. Transfer to a heated serving dish and keep warm.

Reheat 1 tablespoon (15 ml) of the hot oil in a pre-heated wok or frying pan, add the scallops and stir-fry for about 1 minute. Add the wine and stir-fry for 1 further minute. Add the celery and carrot, stir a few times, then spoon the mixture over the roes.

FANCY FISH CAKES WITH ASPARAGUS

illustrated on page 103

Don't be put off this recipe if it sounds like a lot of hard work! You will be surprised how quickly the ramekins can be assembled with just a little practice, and, best of all, they can be prepared a day in advance.

◆

MAKES 8

1 lb 4 oz (600 g) cod fillet or other firm white fish, skinned and finely minced
18 asparagus spears, cut diagonally
1 oz (30 g) bamboo shoots, cut into narrow strips just under 2½ in (6 cm) long
2 very large Chinese black mushrooms, soaked, drained and cut into narrow strips
2 oz (60 g) cooked ham in 1 slice, cut into narrow strips
1½ tablespoons (22.5 ml) corn oil
1 egg, beaten
1 teaspoon (5 ml) cornflour
2 egg whites
¾ teaspoon salt
¼ teaspoon white pepper
⅛ teaspoon sugar

for the serving sauce

1 teaspoon (5 ml) corn oil
½ pint (300 ml) seasoned chicken or pork stock
½ teaspoon light soy sauce
½ teaspoon Shaoshing wine
¼ teaspoon sesame oil
¼ teaspoon sugar
white pepper
2 teaspoons (10 ml) cornflour mixed with 2 tablespoons (30 ml) water

◆

To make the egg skin, heat the oil to a high temperature in a pre-heated small shallow frying pan. Pour in the egg and swirl round the pan as if making a pancake. When it is set and lightly browned, turn it and cook on the other side. Transfer to a plate and leave to cool completely, then cut into thin strips.

Put the fish into a bowl and mix with the cornflour, egg whites, salt, pepper and sugar. Stir well with chopsticks or a fork, until thoroughly blended.

To make the sauce, heat the oil in a saucepan, then add all the remaining sauce ingredients. Bring to the boil. Lower the heat and simmer for 5 minutes.

Lightly brush 8 × 2½-in (6-cm) ramekins with oil. Place 4 strips of bamboo shoot in the centre of each. Place a strip of mushroom, smooth side down, on either side, then a strip of ham on either side, then a strip of egg skin, to cover the base of each ramekin.

Spoon the fish mixture into the ramekins to within ½ in (1 cm) of the tops. Press down lightly and evenly, taking care not to dislodge the strips arranged on the bottom of each ramekin.

Steam the ramekins at a constant high temperature for about 4–5 minutes on a steaming rack over boiling water in a wok or saucepan. Allow to cool for 20 minutes, then unmould. If used later, cover with clingfilm and store in the refrigerator. To warm, or if the cakes are to be used immediately, place on a plate and warm gently or keep warm in a low oven.

Blanch the asparagus spears for 2–3 minutes in boiling salted water. Drain, refresh under cold running water, then drain again. Heat the remaining oil in a frying pan, add the asparagus and fry for 30 seconds, being careful not to break the tips. Arrange the asparagus in a formal criss-cross pattern across the centre of a heated shallow serving dish. Arrange the fish cakes in two rows at regular intervals in the diamond-shaped spaces created by the asparagus. Bring the sauce to the boil again and pour carefully around the arrangement.

83

SWEET AND SOUR FISH

For this dish, with its characteristically Chinese flavour, I have used yellow croaker which may be unfamiliar or difficult to obtain, although it can always be found frozen in Chinese supermarkets. However, you could use trout or grey mullet. You may prefer to serve portions of fish rather than a whole one, and I have found cod and haddock steaks highly suitable.

◆

SERVES 8

2 yellow croaker, each weighing 1 lb (480 g)
salt and white pepper
plain flour for dusting

for deep-frying
1¾ pints (1 litre) corn oil

for the batter
6 oz (180 g) plain flour
pinch of salt
1 tablespoon (15ml) corn oil
2 egg whites
white pepper

for the sauce
1 tablespoon (15 ml) tomato ketchup
3–4 teaspoons (15–20 ml) red wine vinegar
1 teaspoon (5 ml) light soy sauce
2 teaspoons (10 ml) sugar
4 oz (120 g) small peeled prawns
3 oz (90 g) mushrooms, sliced
1 fresh green chilli, finely shredded (optional)
2 slices root ginger, cut into fine strands
1 teaspoon (5 ml) cornflour mixed with 1 tablespoon (15 ml) water

◆

84

To make the batter, sift the flour with the salt into a mixing bowl. Gradually stir in the oil and 7 fl oz (210 ml) iced water. Mix in the egg and egg white, then add salt, pepper and the oil and stir to a smooth paste. Chill in the refrigerator for 30 minutes.

Clean and dry the fish, then season it liberally inside and out with salt and pepper. Dust lightly all over with flour. Whisk the egg whites until they stand in peaks, then fold them gently into the batter.

Heat the oil to 350°F (180°C) in a wok or deep-fryer.

Dip the fish into the batter to coat evenly and deep-fry, turning frequently, for about 5 minutes, until golden and cooked through. Either cook the fish one at a time or, if your pan allows, both together, allowing slightly longer in this case. Drain the fish on kitchen paper and keep on a heated serving dish while making the sauce.

Mix the ketchup, vinegar, soy sauce, sugar and 4 fl oz (120 ml) water together in a bowl. Reheat 1 tablespoon (15 ml) of the hot oil in a heated wok or frying pan, add the prawns and stir-fry for 30 seconds. Add the mushrooms, chilli and ginger, then stir in the cornflour mixture to thicken. Season to taste with salt and pepper. Pour the sauce over the fish just before serving.

❖

GRILLED MACKEREL WITH BLACK SOYA BEANS

Mackerel are now available virtually all year round, but grey mullet could also be used to good effect here.

◆

SERVES 8

2 fresh mackerel, filleted, total weight 2 lb (960 g)
2 tablespoons (30 ml) black soya beans
salt and white pepper
plain flour for dusting
1 tablespoon (15 ml) corn oil
1 tablespoon (15 ml) dark soy sauce
1 tablespoon (15 ml) finely chopped spring onion

◆

Wash the mackerel fillets and dry thoroughly. Score the skin in a criss-cross pattern, then season liberally with salt and pepper and dust with flour. Grill the mackerel fillets skin side uppermost, under a hot grill, about 5 in (12.5 cm) from the heat to prevent scorching, for 6–7 minutes, turning once, until firm and evenly browned.

Meanwhile heat the oil in a small saucepan, add the beans and stir-fry briefly, then add the soy sauce and 1 tablespoon (15 ml) water. Bring to the boil.

Transfer the mackerel to a heated serving dish. Sprinkle with the spring onion and spoon over the black bean sauce.

❖

85

Top: Grilled Mackerel with Black Soya Beans, below: Sea Bass with Chinese Chives *(p. 86).*

SEA BASS
WITH CHINESE CHIVES

illustrated on page 85

Chinese chives – quite unlike European chives, with a pronounced sweet flavour rather like Spanish onion – are an essential ingredient in this handsome dish.

◆

SERVES 8

2 sea bass, filleted, each weighing 1 lb (480 g), all scales removed

12 oz (360 g) Chinese chives, cut into 2-in (5-cm) lengths, flowers discarded

2 teaspoons (10 ml) cornflour

salt and white pepper

1 tablespoon (15 ml) Shaoshing wine

$\frac{1}{2}$ teaspoon sugar

for deep-frying

1 pint (600 ml) corn oil

◆

Wash and dry the bass fillets, then cut into $1\frac{1}{2} \times \frac{1}{2}$-in ($3 \times 1$-cm) pieces $\frac{1}{2}$ in (1 cm) thick. Dust them lightly all over with the cornflour and season with $\frac{1}{4}-\frac{1}{2}$ teaspoon salt and pepper to taste.

Heat the oil to 250°F (120°C) in a wok or deep-fryer, add the fish and fry quickly to seal and keep its shape. Remove from the oil and set aside.

Reheat 2 tablespoons of the hot oil in a pre-heated wok or frying pan, add the Chinese chives with a little salt and stir-fry for about 30 seconds. Add the bass to the pan, then add the wine, pouring it on to the side of the pan to heat and draw out its full flavour, gently turning the pieces of bass meanwhile. Add the sugar and stir very gently to avoid breaking up the fish. Transfer to a heated serving dish before serving.

STEAMED
TROUT IN LOTUS LEAF

Mackerel, grey mullet or yellow croaker could be substituted for the trout in this simple yet exotic dish.

◆

SERVES 8

2–3 trout, total weight 2 lb (960 g), cleaned with heads and tails intact

1 large dried lotus leaf, soaked in warm water for about 2 hours until flexible, then drained

a little corn oil for brushing

salt and white pepper

4–6 thin slices root ginger

for the serving sauce

1 tablespoon (15 ml) corn oil

1 tablespoon (15 ml) oyster sauce

2 tablespoons (30 ml) light soy sauce

3 fl oz (90 ml) chicken stock

4 Chinese black mushrooms, soaked, drained and thinly sliced

2 oz (60 g) bamboo shoots, cut into matchstick strips

1 spring onion, trimmed and finely shredded

1 teaspoon (5 ml) cornflour mixed with 1 tablespoon (15 ml) water

◆

Pat the lotus leaf dry, then brush the inside surface with a little oil. Take a piece large enough to wrap 1 trout, place the fish in the centre, sprinkle with a little salt and pepper and insert 2 of the ginger slices into the cavity. Turn in the edges and roll the trout in its leaf wrapper. Repeat with the remaining trout.

Steam the trout together on a rack over boiling water in a wok or saucepan for 6 minutes at a constant high temperature.

Meanwhile make the serving sauce. Place all the ingredients in a small saucepan, bring to the boil and cook for 30 seconds until well blended.

Check that the trout is cooked to your liking, then unwrap all the fish. Arrange the pieces of lotus leaf overlapping on a serving platter, then place the trout on top. Pour the sauce evenly over the fish.

STUFFED BABY SQUID
illustrated on page 94

This dish, with its distinctive rich yellow colour, looks every bit as good as it does in the photograph, and tastes every bit as good as it looks. What's more, as neither its colour nor texture deteriorates while waiting, it can conveniently be prepared well in advance.

◆

SERVES 8

10 baby squid, cleaned

for the stuffing

1½ tablespoons (22.5 ml) corn oil
1 oz (30 g) Spanish onion, chopped
1 oz (30 g) green pepper, cored, seeded and finely diced
1 clove garlic, crushed
salt and white pepper
2 oz (60 g) cooked rice
½ teaspoon curry powder
1 teaspoon (5 ml) light soy sauce
¼ teaspoon paprika
2 teaspoons (10 ml) cornflour mixed with 1 tablespoon (15 ml) chicken stock or water
½ teaspoon sugar
1 egg white

for the sauce

4 fl oz (120 ml) seasoned chicken stock
1 small clove garlic, crushed
⅛ teaspoon paprika
¼ teaspoon curry powder
¼ teaspoon sugar

◆

Remove the squids' heads, complete with tentacles, from the bodies. Then separate the heads and discard, keeping the tentacles. Gently squeeze the glutinous membrane from the body. Select two complete squid and chop into small pieces. Leave the remaining 8 whole.

To make the stuffing, heat 1½ teaspoons (7.5 ml) of the oil in a pre-heated wok or frying pan, add the onion, green pepper, garlic, salt and pepper, and stir-fry for about 30 seconds. Transfer the mixture to a mixing bowl with the chopped squid and rice. Mix well and add the remaining stuffing ingredients. Stir well to mix.

Use a teaspoon to half-fill each squid with the mixture. Insert a squid's head into the remaining space in the body cavity, pushing down well so that it does not become detached during cooking.

Heat the remaining oil in the pan, add the squid and fry for about 4 minutes over a moderate heat, turning frequently until lightly coloured. Do not worry if a set of tentacles should escape, as it can be replaced after frying. Check that the squid are neat and tidy, then transfer them to a dish and set aside while making the sauce.

To make the sauce, heat the remaining oil in the rinsed out pan and add all the remaining sauce ingredients. Simmer for about 5 minutes. Bring the sauce to the boil, then return the stuffed squid to the pan. Turn to coat in the sauce, then simmer gently for about 10 minutes, until the sauce is reduced by about half.

Top: Steamed Vegetables *(p. 107)*, centre: Spicy Mussels *(p. 79)*, below: Simple Baked Chicken.

SIMPLE BAKED CHICKEN

Minimal effort is required in the preparation of this dish: it is the combination of the flavourings that gives it its very special quality.

◆

SERVES 8

1 ×3½ lb (1.5 kg) ovenready chicken
salt and white pepper
1 tablespoon (15 ml) dark soy sauce
1 tablespoon (15 ml) corn oil
1 small Spanish onion, diced
1 ×2-in (5-cm) cube root ginger, finely chopped
3 cloves star anise, ground

for serving
double quantity Spicy Salt Dip (p. 133)

◆

Remove any fat from the chicken and sprinkle with salt and pepper. Brush the outside lightly with the soy sauce, then with the oil. Mix the onion, ginger and star anise together and place in the cavity, then wrap the chicken in lightly oiled greaseproof paper. Make several folds across the top, then turn in both edges, pleating the ends together so that they are well sealed and stay firmly in place. Leave to stand for 3–4 hours in a cool place, to allow the chicken to absorb the flavours.

Heat the oven 450°F (230°C, gas mark 8). Place the chicken in a roasting tin breast side down and roast for 30 minutes, then turn breast side up and roast for a further 30 minutes. Remove from the oven and unwrap the paper. When the chicken is cool enough to handle, chop it into bite-size pieces as described for Sweet Baby Chicken (right). Reassemble the pieces on a heated serving platter to give a spread-eagled appearance – a typical style of Chinese presentation. Serve with a Spicy Salt Dip in 8 individual mussel shells.

SWEET BABY CHICKEN

The tasty marinade gives the rather subtle flavour of poussin a special life.

◆

SERVES 8

2 ovenready poussins, each weighing 1 lb (480 g)
salt and white pepper

for the marinade
1 pint (600 ml) corn oil
4 tablespoons (60 ml) light soy sauce
4 tablespoons (60 ml) clear honey
2 tablespoons (30 ml) Shaoshing wine

for deep-frying
1¾ pints (1 litre) corn oil

for the garnish
1 pint (600 ml) corn oil
a bunch of watercress

◆

Rinse dry and season the poussins. In a large bowl, mix together all the marinade ingredients and put a spoonful of the mixture inside each poussin. Turn the poussins in the remaining marinade so that their surface is covered and marinate in the refrigerator for 4–5 hours.

Heat the oil to 250°F (120°C) in a wok or deep-fryer. Remove the poussins from the marinade and shake off any excess. Deep-fry the poussins for 8–10 minutes, first breast-side down, then on each side in turn and finally on their backs, until they are a rich brown all over. Adjust the temperature of the oil if necessary.

Remove the poussins from the pan and allow to cool slightly, then cut them in the traditional Chinese manner for poultry or game, using a meat cleaver or heavy knife. First remove the legs and the wings, separating them at the joints and again into portions of manageable size, but not overdoing it to a point where they look untidy. Cut down the length of the breast-bone so that the carcase is in two halves. Chop each half lengthways and the crossways into about 4 pieces (the number will vary according to the size of the poussin).

Arrange on serving plates as if the poussins were still whole, lying flat. Garnish with watercress sprigs.

89

90

CHICKEN WITH ALMONDS

Even those not very familiar with Chinese cuisine will immediately recognize this dish, a favourite on many Chinese restaurant- and takeaway-menus, but they will probably be surprised to discover how easy it is to cook at home.

◆

SERVES 8

1 lb (480 g) boneless chicken breast
3½ oz (100 g) blanched almonds
½ teaspoon cornflour
salt and white pepper
1 small egg white
1 clove garlic, thinly sliced
¾ tablespoon (12 ml) crushed yellow bean paste
1½ tablespoons (22.5 ml) tomato ketchup
1–1½ teaspoons (5–7.5 ml) sugar

for deep-frying
1 pint (600 ml) corn oil

◆

Place the almonds in a heavy frying pan without oil and stir over a gentle to moderate heat until golden-brown.

Cut the chicken into ½-in (1-cm) cubes. Put the chicken into a bowl and add the cornflour, salt, pepper and egg white. Stir well to mix.

Heat the oil to 275°F (140°C) in a wok or deep-fryer, add the chicken and deep-fry for 30 seconds (the pieces will separate naturally as they cook, although initially they may need to be kept apart). Drain in a wire sieve.

Reheat 2 tablespoons (30 ml) of the hot oil in a pre-heated wok. Add the partially cooked chicken with the garlic, yellow bean paste, tomato ketchup and sugar. Mix well together, making sure the chicken pieces are evenly coated with the mixture, then add the roasted almonds. Stir well and transfer to a heated serving dish.

DUCK WITH CHESTNUTS

If you are busy with other things in the kitchen, this dish is for you, as it requires little attention.

◆

SERVES 8

4½ lb (2.25 kg) ovenready duck
1 lb (480 g) cooked chestnuts, peeled
1 tablespoon (15 ml) corn oil
1 oz (30 g) Spanish onion, thinly sliced
3 thin slices root ginger
2 cloves garlic, crushed
salt and pepper
2 tablespoons (30 ml) oyster sauce
1 tablespoon (15 ml) dark soy sauce
2 tablespoons (30 ml) Shaoshing wine or dry sherry
1 tablespoon (15 ml) golden syrup
1 teaspoon (5 ml) cornflour mixed with 1 tablespoon (15 ml) water

◆

Dry the duck well with kitchen paper and remove the parson's nose and any loose skin and fat round the neck. Using a cleaver or poultry shears, split the duck open the length of the breast-bone and prick the outside skin here and there to release the fat during cooking.

Heat the oil to a high temperature in a wok or large flameproof casserole, add the duck, breast side down, and fry until evenly browned. Turn the duck and brown the underside as well. Drain off the excess fat.

Remove the duck and set aside. Drain off all but 1 tablespoon (15 ml) of the fat from the pan. Add the onion, ginger, garlic, salt and pepper and fry gently until lightly browned. Return the duck, breast side uppermost, to the pan and heat through over a moderate heat. Add the oyster sauce, soy sauce, wine, golden syrup and 1 pint (600 ml) hot water. Adjust the seasoning and bring the mixture to the boil.

Reduce the heat and braise the duck for about 1¼ hours, basting it from time to time. Add the chestnuts and cook for a further 30 minutes, or until the duck is tender, adding a little more water if necessary.

Transfer the duck and chestnuts to a heated, shallow serving dish and arrange them as shown in the photograph. Remove any ginger and garlic pieces and stir the cornflour mixture into the sauce, to thicken slightly. Bring to the boil and pour over the duck.

Top: Chicken with Almonds, below: Duck with Chestnuts.

PEKING DUCK

illustrated on pages 68–69

This is possibly the most celebrated Chinese dish of all, a pièce de résistance for any special occasion. I like to invite guests to help themselves to the duck, rather than carving it in advance; this way the meat is eaten at its most succulent and the party is given a nice informal touch.

◆

SERVES 8

2 ×4–4½-lb (2–2.5-kg) ovenready ducks
20 Mandarin Pancakes (p. 109)

for the coating sauce

3 tablespoons (45 ml) clear honey, or golden syrup, or maltose
1 tablespoon (15 ml) Shaoshing wine
1 tablespoon (15 ml) light soy sauce
1 teaspoon (5 ml) dark soy sauce
red food colouring
salt and white pepper

for the serving sauce

4 tablespoons (60 ml) Hoi Sin sauce
2 tablespoons (30 ml) plum sauce
¼ teaspoon sesame oil

for serving

8 spring onions, trimmed and cut into 4-in (10-cm) lengths
1 cucumber, cut into 4-in (10-cm) thin strips

◆

First make the coating sauce: dissolve the honey, syrup or maltose in 6 tablespoons (90 ml) hot water in a small saucepan. Add the wine, soy sauces, a little food colouring and salt and pepper to taste and set aside in a bowl.

Remove any excess fatty pieces from the ducks, plunge them into a saucepan of boiling water for 2 minutes, then remove and pat dry. Sprinkle the ducks lightly inside and out with salt and pepper. Insert a meat hook into the loose skin at each neck end, or tie a loop of string round the neck end if necessary, to secure the hook firmly. Brush all over with the coating sauce.

Hang the ducks in a cool, airy place for at least 7 hours, with a tray underneath to catch the drips. Brush them again with the coating sauce 3 or 4 times at roughly hourly intervals. After the final coating leave the ducks for at least 3 hours to allow them to dry thoroughly.

Prick the duck skin with a fork in about 12 places to release the fat.

Heat the oven to 375°F (190°C, gas mark 5). Hang the ducks from the meat hooks upside down in the oven, with a baking tray underneath to catch the drips, and roast for 1½ hours, or until cooked through. If the ducks show signs of overbrowning, cover them with kitchen foil. If it is not convenient to hang the ducks in the oven, roast them on a rack in a roasting tin, turning them over a couple of times during the cooking.

To make the serving sauce, mix all the ingredients with 2 tablespoons (30 ml) hot water and blend thoroughly.

When the ducks are cooked, transfer them to 2 heated serving dishes. Put the spring onions, cucumber and serving sauce in separate bowls. Supply 2 sharp knives so that guests may help themselves to the pieces of their choice, taking care to include some of the delicious skin.

To serve, put 2 bite-sized pieces of duck and some of the cucumber and spring onion on to a pancake. Spoon over a small amount of sauce, then roll up.

POMEGRANATE DUCK

illustrated on page 103

When an Italian friend introduced me to a braised dish with the interesting addition of pomegranates I was impressed and set about creating my own dish.

◆

SERVES 8

2 large or 3 smaller boneless duck breasts, total weight 1½ lb (720 g), unskinned
4 oz (120 g) pomegranate seeds (as red as possible)
1 tablespoon (15 ml) corn oil
3 slices root ginger
2 tablespoons (30 ml) light soy sauce
1 tablespoon (15 ml) Shaoshing wine
½ pint (280 ml) duck or chicken stock
1–2 teaspoons (5–10 ml) sugar
1½ teaspoons (7.5 ml) cornflour mixed with
2 tablespoons (30 ml) water

◆

Dry the duck well. Heat the oil to a high temperature in a pre-heated wok or frying pan. Add the ginger and stir-fry for 15–20 seconds, then add the duck, flesh side down, and fry for about 1 minute. Then turn skin side uppermost and fry for 2 minutes until light golden, pricking with a fork to release the fat.

Add the soy sauce, wine and stock to the pan and bring to the boil. Turn down the heat until the liquid is bubbling gently. Simmer uncovered for 30 minutes, turning the duck 3 times, until the meat is fractionally underdone and pinkish. (If the breasts are small they will cook in 20–25 minutes.) If you prefer well-cooked duck, cover the pan partially with a lid during cooking.

Add the cornflour mixture and sugar. Return the sauce to the boil until it thickens, then turn off the heat and remove the ginger. Add a little hot water to the sauce to make up to ¼ pint (150 ml). Remove from the heat.

Transfer the duck to a board and cut diagonally into slices 1½ in (6 mm) thick. Arrange the slices in 2 rows on a heated serving platter.

Return the sauce to the boil, then turn off the heat and add the pomegranate seeds, turning them gently in the sauce to retain their vibrant colour. Using a slotted spoon, arrange some of the pomegranate seeds along the slices of duck and pour the remaining sauce around.

PIQUANT DUCK WITH RED BEANCURD SAUCE

Duck is particularly popular with the Chinese. This dish is especially tasty and is found on many restaurant menus.

◆

SERVES 8

4 lb (1.8 kg) ovenready duck
2 oz (60 g) red (fermented) bean curd

for the marinade
2 tablespoons (30 ml) Sweet and Chilli Sauce (p. 130)
1½ tablespoons (22.5 ml) dark soy sauce
2 tablespoons (30 ml) golden syrup mixed with 2 tablespoons (30 ml) hot water
salt and white pepper
1 tablespoon (15 ml) sugar (optional)
1-in (2.5-cm) cube root ginger, crushed
1 large clove garlic, crushed

for deep-frying
1¾ pints (1 litre) corn oil

◆

Discard the tips of the duck wings, then halve the duck lengthways through the breast-bone, using a cleaver or poultry shears. Open out the duck, lay it in a bamboo steamer over boiling water in a wok or saucepan and steam for about 1½ hours.

Remove the duck and leave to cool slightly. Separate the legs at the joints and divide each leg into two. Remove both breasts from the body. Cut each breast crossways into 4 pieces. Remove the meat from the underside of the duck, and discard the carcass.

Place the beancurd and marinade ingredients in a large mixing bowl. Add the duck pieces and leave to marinate for several hours or overnight. Remove the duck pieces from the marinade and leave to drain in a wire sieve for 1–2 hours. Reserve the marinade.

Heat the oil to 350°F (180°C) in a wok or deep-fryer. Deep-fry the duck in three batches for 30 seconds. Drain, then transfer to a heated serving dish.

Add a little water and extra sugar, if liked, to the marinade and bring to the boil in a small saucepan. Pour into a small heated serving bowl to accompany the duck.

93

Top: Aromatic Duck with Lamb, below: Stuffed Baby Squid *(p. 87)*.

AROMATIC DUCK AND LAMB WITH LETTUCE LEAF WRAP

The whole of the first stage of this recipe can be carried out a day or two in advance, so that only the final roasting process remains to be done.

◆

SERVES 8

½ shoulder lamb weighing 2–2½ lb (960 g–1.2 kg)
4 lb (1.8 kg) ovenready duck
4 tablespoons (60 ml) corn oil
3 slices root ginger
1 large clove garlic
2 oz (60 g) Spanish onion, sliced
salt and white pepper

to serve
plum sauce
crisp lettuce (Webbs, cos or iceberg)

for the braising sauce
4 fl oz (120 ml) light soy sauce
5 tablespoons (75 ml) golden syrup
1 teaspoon (5 ml) 5-spice powder
1 tablespoon (15 ml) Shaoshing wine
1 carrot, halved
1 stick celery, halved
3 slices root ginger
1 large clove garlic
2 cloves star anise *and*
1 tablespoon (15 ml) Szechuan peppercorns *and*
1 tablespoon (15 ml) whole black peppercorns tied together in a muslin bag
1 teaspoon (5 ml) salt

◆

Heat half the oil in a large, heavy-based saucepan. Add the ginger and garlic, and fry briefly to flavour the oil. Add the lamb and brown over a moderate heat.

Halve the duck lengthways. Discard the bony ends of the wings and brown the duck lightly over a moderate heat in the ginger- and garlic-flavoured oil.

Heat the remaining oil in another very large saucepan. Sprinkle the onion with salt and fry it until just softened, but not coloured. Transfer the lamb and duck to this pan. Mix together all the braising ingredients with 4 pints (2.25 litres) water, then add to the pan.

Bring to the boil, then simmer the duck (breast uppermost) and the lamb for about 2 hours or until they are both tender, turning them occasionally. Remove from the heat and drain the lamb and duck thoroughly.

Heat the oven to moderate (325–350°F, 160–180°C, gas mark 3–4). Place the duck and the lamb on a rack in a roasting tin and roast for about 1 hour, until they are slightly crisp outside and tender and succulent inside. Drain very thoroughly on kitchen paper.

To serve, carve the lamb and duck into slices. Everyone then helps themselves, placing the meat on a lettuce leaf, and adding plum sauce before rolling to eat.

LUXURY CHOP SUEY

Unfortunately chop suey has too often earned a bad name – because of indifferent take-away standards. The addition of the duck lends a luxurious touch to what is basically a gutsy, very worthwhile dish.

◆

Serves 8

4 tablespoons (60 ml) oil
2 cloves garlic, bruised
12 oz (360 g) bean sprouts
¼–½ teaspoon salt and pepper to taste
8 oz (240 g) cooked Peking duck (p. 92), finely shredded
4 slices root ginger, cut into hair's-breadth shreds
1 tablespoon (15 ml) oyster sauce
1 egg skin (Fancy Fish Cake, p. 83), cut into fine shreds
4 spring onions, cut into fine strands

◆

Heat 2 tablespoons (30 ml) of the oil in a pre-heated wok or frying pan, add the garlic and fry for 30 seconds, pressing it to release the flavour. Discard the garlic.

Put the bean sprouts into the pan with salt and pepper to taste and stir-fry for about 40 seconds. Transfer to a heated dish, draining off any liquid. Heat the remaining oil in the pan. Add the duck, ginger and oyster sauce and stir-fry for about 2 minutes, then the bean sprouts, egg skin and spring onion. Stir-fry quickly, then serve.

95

BEEF
IN OYSTER SAUCE

Skirt of beef, beaten with a mallet or the back of a cleaver, to tenderize it, could almost replace the much more expensive fillet of beef. The round, full, entirely non-fishy flavour of oyster sauce combines brilliantly with soy sauce.

◆

SERVES 8

1 lb (480 g) fillet of beef, cut across the grain into 2 × 1 ×$\frac{1}{4}$ in
(5 ×2.5 cm ×6 mm) slices
1 egg white
1 teaspoon (5 ml) cornflour
white pepper
2 tablespoons (30 ml) dark soy sauce
12 oz (360 g) French beans, topped and tailed, then halved
crossways
3 tablespoons (45 ml) corn oil
salt
2 cloves garlic, crushed
2 slices root ginger
2 tablespoons (30 ml) oyster sauce
1 tablespoon (15 ml) Shaoshing wine
$\frac{1}{2}$–1 teaspoon sugar

◆

96

Mix the beef in a bowl with the egg white, cornflour, pepper to taste and the soy sauce. Leave to marinate for 20 minutes. Blanch the beans in boiling salted water for under 1 minute, then drain.

Heat the oil to a high temperature in a pre-heated wok or frying pan, add the beans with a pinch of salt and stir-fry the beans for about 1 minute. Transfer to a bowl. Heat the remaining oil to a high temperature.

Add the garlic and ginger to the pan and fry for 20–30 seconds, pressing to extract as much juice as possible. Discard the garlic and ginger and heat the oil until smoking, then add the beef. Leave for 10 seconds, then stir-fry for just under 1 minute. Add the oyster sauce, wine, 1 tablespoon (15 ml) water and the sugar, and stir-fry for 30 seconds until well blended. Mix in the beans, taste and adjust the seasoning if necessary, and transfer to a heated serving dish, as shown in the photograph.

❖

BRAISED SHIN OF BEEF

Here is something warming, comforting and substantial, that requires no last-minute attention.

◆

SERVES 16

4 lb (2 kg) whole rolled shin of beef
2 tablespoons (30 ml) corn oil
3 oz (90 g) Spanish onion, sliced
1 carrot, cut into large chunks
8 oz (240 g) okra, trimmed and blanched

for the braising sauce

3 tablespoons (45 ml) light soy sauce
3 tablespoons (45 ml) Shaoshing wine
1 tablespoon (15 ml) Hoi Sin sauce
1 tablespoon (15 ml) golden syrup
$\frac{1}{2}$ teaspoon 5-spice powder
1 whole fresh green chilli
$\frac{1}{4}$ teaspoon salt
white pepper
1 tablespoon (15 ml) cornflour mixed with
1 tablespoon (15 ml) water

◆

Heat 1 tablespoon (15 ml) of the oil in a pre-heated wok or large saucepan, add the beef and fry, turning, for about 5 minutes, until browned on all sides.

Remove the beef and set aside on a plate. Add the onion to the pan and stir-fry for 30 seconds. Return the beef to the pan, add the carrot with all the braising sauce ingredients except the cornflour mixture, together with 3 pints (1.75 litres) water, and bring to the boil. Reduce the heat and simmer, uncovered, for 3$\frac{1}{2}$ hours, or until the beef is tender, and the water reduced by three-quarters.

Remove the beef from the pan and allow to cool slightly. Reserve the stock. Carve the beef into slices and arrange in a shallow heated serving dish.

Heat the remaining oil in the pan to a moderate temperature, add the okra and chilli and stir-fry for 2 minutes, then transfer to the dish with the beef.

Discard the chilli from it and stir in the cornflour mixture and the reserved stock. Bring to the boil and pour over the meat and vegetables.

❖

Clockwise, from left: Beef in Oyster Sauce, Tofu with Vegetables *(p. 108)*,
Sizzling Prawns with Crisped Rice *(p. 76)*.

MINCED
BEEF WITH MUSHROOMS

*If you wish to prepare this dish in advance, the meat
can be cooked beforehand so that all that remains to
be done is to stir-fry the mushrooms and put them
on a platter, heat the meat in a microwave oven, or
by stir-frying at a high temperature for 1 minute,
then adding the coriander.*

◆

SERVES 8

1 lb (480 g) minced beef
2 lb (960 g) medium button mushrooms, thinly sliced
1 teaspoon (5 ml) cornflour
salt and white pepper
5 tablespoons (75 ml) corn oil
3 oz (90 g) bamboo shoots, finely chopped
1 oz (30 g) Chinese preserved cabbage, rinsed, diced and finely
chopped
1 tablespoon (15 ml) light soy sauce
$\frac{1}{4}$ teaspoon chilli oil
1 tablespoon (15 ml) Shaoshing wine
1 teaspoon (5 ml) sugar
3 tablespoons (45 ml) chopped coriander or parsley

◆

Put the minced beef into a bowl with the cornflour, a
pinch of salt and pepper to taste, and leave to marinate
for 20 minutes.

Heat 1 tablespoon (15 ml) of the oil in a pre-heated
wok or frying pan, add the bamboo shoots and Chinese
cabbage, stir-fry for 1 minute, then transfer to a bowl.

Add the mushrooms to the pan in 2 batches, each
accompanied by $\frac{1}{4}$ teaspoon salt and 1$\frac{1}{2}$ tablespoons
(22.5 ml) corn oil heated to a high temperature. Stir-fry
for just under 1 minute, until still firm. Transfer the
mushrooms to a heated shallow serving dish.

Heat the remaining corn oil to a high temperature in
the pan, add the beef and stir-fry for 1$\frac{1}{2}$ minutes.

Add the reserved bamboo shoots and Chinese cabbage to the pan with the chilli oil, wine and sugar and
stir-fry for a further 30 seconds. Now add the coriander, mixing it in evenly, and spoon the mixture over the
centre of the mushrooms, leaving some exposed to view
as a border.

98

CALVES' LIVER
WITH LEEKS

*This is altogether lighter, more appetizing and
delicately flavoured than the commonplace fried
liver, bacon and onions. You will find strips of liver
more tempting than the customary large slices. You
can cook this dish a couple of hours before it is
needed and reheat in a microwave oven, in which
case the liver is better slightly underdone in the first
instance.*

◆

SERVES 8

1 lb (480 g) calves' liver, cut diagonally into 2 ×1-in (5 ×2-cm)
strips
12 oz (360 g) leeks, halved lengthways and cut diagonally into
pieces $\frac{1}{4}$ in (6 mm) wide
1$\frac{1}{2}$ tablespoons (22.5 ml) dark soy sauce
white pepper
2$\frac{1}{2}$ tablespoons (37.5 ml) corn oil
3 oz (90 g) thin rashers smoked streaky bacon, cut into
matchstick strips
1$\frac{1}{2}$ tablespoons (22.5 ml) Shaoshing wine
$\frac{1}{2}$–1 teaspoon (2.5–5 ml) sugar
white pepper

◆

Put the liver into a bowl with 1 tablespoon (15 ml) of the
soy sauce and a sprinkling of pepper. Leave to marinate
for about 20 minutes.

Heat 1 tablespoon (15 ml) of the oil to a high
temperature in a pre-heated wok or frying pan. Add the
leeks with a couple of pinches of salt and stir-fry for 1$\frac{1}{2}$
minutes, then transfer to a bowl.

Heat the remaining oil in the pan to a high temperature, add the bacon and stir-fry for 1$\frac{1}{2}$ minutes. Add the
liver and stir-fry for 1 minute. Add the wine and the
remaining soy sauce and stir-fry for 1 further minute.
Add the leeks and stir-fry for a further 30 seconds. The
liver will now be just done. If you want it pink, reduce
the time slightly – by 15 seconds or thereabouts.
Transfer to a heated serving dish and serve immediately.

CHICKEN LIVERS WITH HONEY SAUCE

This can be re-heated in a microwave oven so you may prefer to make it a day in advance. The livers could be served with lightly cooked lettuce leaves (see p. 81) rather than spinach, as a Chinese version of the nouvelle cuisine salade tiède.

◆

SERVES 8

1 lb (480 g) chicken livers, trimmed and any large pieces halved
1 tablespoon (15 ml) clear honey
6 thin slices root ginger, cut into hair's-breadth shreds
white pepper
3 tablespoons (45 ml) dark soy sauce
6 oz (180 g) Spanish onions, cut in half, then cut diagonally into small segments
salt
1 tablespoon (15 ml) Shaoshing wine
1½ lb (720 g) fresh spinach, washed and trimmed, fine stalks left on

◆

Put the chicken livers into a bowl with 1 tablespoon (15 ml) of the soy sauce, the ginger and a sprinkling of pepper and leave to marinate for 20 minutes.

Heat 1 tablespoon (15 ml) of the oil in a pre-heated wok or frying pan, add the onions with ⅛ teaspoon salt and stir-fry for just under 1 minute, until still firm and crunchy. Transfer to a bowl.

Heat 1 further tablespoon (15 ml) of the oil to a high temperature in the wiped-out pan. Add the chicken livers and stir-fry for 1 minute, then add the remaining soy sauce and the honey. Stir-fry for 1 minute, then return the onions to the pan and stir-fry for a further 30 seconds, until the sauce thickens and coats the livers. Turn off the heat.

Heat the remaining oil to a high temperature in a second pre-heated wok or frying pan. Add the spinach with a sprinkling of salt and stir-fry for just 1 minute until softened but still firm, and emerald green.

Transfer the chicken livers to one end of a heated serving dish. Using a slotted spoon, transfer the spinach to the other end of the dish. Serve immediately.

STIR-FRIED LAMB WITH GREEN PEPPERS

This is a very simple stir-fry, using only two main ingredients, so ideal to prepare when you are acquiring the skill of this fundamental Chinese cooking technique.

◆

SERVES 8

1 lb (480 g) boneless leg or lean shoulder of lamb
4 oz (120 g) green pepper, cored, seeded and cut into chunks
1 teaspoon (5 ml) cornflour
1 small egg white
1½ teaspoons (7.5 ml) dark soy sauce
white pepper
3 tablespoons (45 ml) corn oil
3 oz (90 g) Spanish onion, cut into chunks
1 tablespoon (15 ml) black soya beans
2 cloves garlic, crushed
1 tablespoon (15 ml) oyster sauce
1 tablespoon (15 ml) Shaoshing wine
sugar

◆

Cut the lamb into thin slices across the grain and beat with the flat of a meat cleaver or mallet to tenderize. Mix the lamb with the cornflour, egg white, soy sauce and a little pepper. Set aside to allow the flavours to absorb.

Heat 1 tablespoon (15 ml) of the oil in a pre-heated wok or frying pan, add the onion and stir-fry briefly until glazed but still firm. Add the green pepper and stir-fry for a further 30 seconds. Heat the rest of the oil to a very high temperature, and stir-fry the beans for 30 seconds. Add the garlic and stir-fry briefly again. Add the lamb, oyster sauce and wine and a little sugar to taste. Stir-fry for 1 minute, then return the vegetables to the pan and stir-fry for a further 30 seconds. Transfer to a heated serving dish and serve immediately.

99

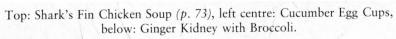

Top: Shark's Fin Chicken Soup *(p. 73)*, left centre: Cucumber Egg Cups,
below: Ginger Kidney with Broccoli.

GINGER KIDNEY WITH BROCCOLI

The Chinese use pigs' kidneys for their robust flavour, rather than lamb's or veal kidneys. Pre-soaking them removes some of their pungency.

◆

SERVES 8

6 pigs' kidneys
8 oz (240 g) green broccoli
salt
9 fl oz (270 ml) corn oil
3–4 tablespoons (45–60 ml) root ginger, very finely shredded
1 tablespoon (15 ml) dark soy sauce
1 tablespoon (15 ml) Shaoshing wine
$\frac{1}{2}$ teaspoon sugar
white pepper

◆

Halve the kidneys horizontally and leave them to soak in cold water for 4–5 hours, changing the water from time to time. Remove the kidneys, dry with kitchen paper and score a criss-cross pattern on the skin of each. Cut the kidneys into bite-sized chunks, discarding the cores, and mix them with $\frac{1}{4}$–$\frac{1}{2}$ teaspoon salt.

Trim the ends of the broccoli. Remove the stringy outside of the stalks and slice the spears diagonally, so that they are tapered and delicate-looking, and most of them have a share of both stalk and flower – a typically Chinese way of presenting this type of vegetable.

Blanch the prepared broccoli in boiling, salted water for 30 seconds, then drain in a wire sieve and set aside.

Heat the oil in a saucepan to a moderate temperature and quickly run the kidneys through it to seal them and remove any excess liquid. Reheat a tablespoon (15 ml) of the hot oil in a pre-heated wok or frying pan, add the broccoli and stir-fry for 30 seconds. Remove with a slotted spoon and set aside.

Reheat a further 2 tablespoons (30 ml) of the hot oil in the pan, add the kidney and ginger and stir-fry for about 30 seconds. Add the soy sauce, wine, sugar and pepper to taste and stir-fry for a further 30 seconds.

In a heated serving dish, arrange the broccoli in two small clusters, with a band of kidney alongside. Pour the cooking juices over or serve in a sauceboat.

CUCUMBER EGG CUPS

These would be ideal for a summer dinner party.

◆

SERVES 8

1 long cucumber, ideally $1\frac{1}{2}$ in (3.5 cm) in diameter
8 quails' eggs
salt
2 teaspoons (10 ml) corn oil
2 slices root ginger, bruised
2 cloves garlic, bruised
3 oz (90 g) fresh bean sprouts

for the serving sauce
1 teaspoon (5 ml) corn oil
6 fl oz (180 ml) chicken stock
$\frac{1}{2}$ teaspoon light soy sauce
$\frac{1}{4}$ teaspoon sugar
white pepper
$1\frac{1}{2}$ teaspoons (7.5 ml) Shaoshing wine
2 slices root ginger
1 tablespoon (15 ml) cornflour mixed with 1 tablespoon water

for the garnish
1 tablespoon (15 ml) shredded egg skin (see Fancy Fish Cakes with Asparagus p. 83).
$\frac{1}{2}$ oz (15 g) fresh bean sprouts

◆

Cut the cucumber into $1\frac{1}{2}$-in (3.5-cm) lengths. Make criss-cross cuts in the top of each piece to a depth of $\frac{1}{2}$ in (1 cm). Hollow out the centres, to leave an $\frac{1}{8}$-in (3-mm) shell. Sprinkle the cucumber pieces liberally with salt. Steam for 3 minutes on a rack over boiling water in a saucepan, transfer to a heatproof dish and set aside.

Heat the oil in a pre-heated wok or frying pan, add the garlic and ginger and stir-fry for 20 seconds, pressing to extract the full flavour. Discard the spices.

Add the bean sprouts with $\frac{1}{4}$ teaspoon salt to the pan. Stir-fry for about 40 seconds until softened but still crunchy. Transfer to a plate to drain and cool.

Fill the cucumber cases three-quarters full with the bean sprouts, to form little nests. Break an egg into each case and salt them. Steam on high for 3 minutes.

To make the sauce, heat the oil in a small saucepan and add all the remaining sauce ingredients. Boil for 5 minutes, then turn off the heat and add the garnishes.

STUFFED TOFU PUFFS

Deep-fried tofu puffs with a prawn and vegetable filling are served with a deliciously simple savoury sauce.

◆

SERVES 8

1 lb (480 g) fresh tofu (beancurd) (3 squares)

for deep-frying
1 pint (600 ml) corn oil

for the stuffing
4 oz (120 g) fresh peeled raw prawns or 6 oz (180 g) frozen prawns, well drained
2 oz (60 g) bamboo shoots, cut into matchstick strips, then into tiny cubes
2 Chinese black mushrooms, soaked, drained and cut into matchstick strips, then into tiny cubes
1½ teaspoons (7.5 ml) cornflour
1 egg white
¼ teaspoon salt
¼ teaspoon sugar
white pepper

for the sauce
7 fl oz (210 ml) chicken stock
1 tablespoon (15 ml) oyster sauce
¼ teaspoon sesame oil
salt and white pepper
¼ teaspoon sugar
2 teaspoons (10 ml) cornflour mixed with 2 tablespoons (30 ml) water

for the garnish
2 long Spring Onion Brushes (pp. 134–135)

◆

Drain the tofu on kitchen paper for at least 1 hour, then cut each square in half horizontally, then diagonally crossways, to give 12 triangles.

Heat the oil to 325°F (160°C) in a wok or deep-fryer, add the tofu and deep-fry for about 5–6 minutes, turning so that it colours evenly, until firm to the touch. Drain in a wire sieve.

To make the stuffing, mix the prawns in a bowl with the cornflour, egg white, salt, sugar and pepper. Add the bamboo shoots and mushrooms and stir well to mix. Next cut an opening in the longest side of each triangle, working towards the centre but keeping the other 2 sides intact. Using a small pointed knife, put in a small teaspoonful of the mixture so each triangle is sufficiently filled, but not over-full. Smooth the edges, leaving a little of the filling showing.

Reheat 2 tablespoons (30 ml) of the hot oil to a moderate to high temperature in a pre-heated wok or frying pan, add the triangles, one by one, to brown the filled edges, then turn and fry, turning again, until light golden on all sides. This will take 7–8 minutes altogether.

Add all the sauce ingredients and bring gently to the boil. Turn down the heat and simmer the triangles for 10 minutes, turning once.

Arrange the tofu triangles on a pre-heated serving dish. Either pour the sauce decoratively over the puffs or serve separately in a sauceboat.

BEAN SPROUTS WITH FRESH HERBS
illustrated on pages 68–69

If the bean sprouts have a somewhat rusty appearance, rinse in cold water to refresh them.

◆

SERVES 8

1 lb (480 g) fresh bean sprouts
1 oz (30 g) coriander leaves
1 bunch radishes
1 tablespoon (15 ml) corn oil
1 large clove garlic, sliced
3–4 thin slices root ginger
¾ teaspoon salt
white pepper

◆

Chop the coriander and slice the radishes thinly.

Heat the oil to a high temperature in a pre-heated wok or frying pan with the garlic and ginger. Let them flavour in the oil, then remove and add the bean sprouts, pepper and salt. Stir-fry for no more than 1 minute, then quickly mix in the coriander and the radishes. Transfer to a heated serving dish.

Top: Fancy Fish Cakes With Asparagus *(p. 83)*, left: Pomegranate Duck *(p. 93)*, right: Stuffed Tofu Puffs.

STEAMED TOFU HEARTS

You may immediately protest that this cannot possibly be Szechuan in origin since dishes of the region are normally both rich and spicy, yet this is indeed the case. On first being introduced to it in a restaurant in Hong Kong I, too, was surprised and then delighted by its delicacy and subtlety.

◆

SERVES 8

$1\frac{1}{4}$lb (600 g) fresh tofu (beancurd)
2 oz (60 g) raw peeled prawns
3 egg whites
$\frac{1}{2}$ teaspoon sugar
salt and white pepper
$\frac{1}{2}$-in (1-cm) cube root ginger
$1\frac{1}{2}$ tablespoons (22.5 ml) finely chopped parsley
a little corn oil

for the sauce

1 tablespoon (15 ml) corn oil
$\frac{1}{2}$ pint (280 ml) lightly seasoned chicken stock
1 tablespoon (15 ml) Shaoshing wine
$\frac{1}{4}$–$\frac{1}{2}$ teaspoon sugar
2 teaspoons (10 ml) cornflour mixed with 1 tablespoon (15 ml) water

for the garnish

green vegetables
1 cooked prawn, cut horizontally into 2 halves

◆

Drain the liquid from the tofu. Trim off the skin and place the tofu in the food processor. Add 2 of the egg whites, the sugar, $\frac{1}{4}$ teaspoon salt and pepper to taste. Process to a paste and transfer the mixture to a bowl.

To make the filling, place the prawns in the food processor and, using a garlic press, crush the ginger over them. Add three pinches of salt, a generous sprinkling of white pepper, the remaining egg white and approximately one-fifth of the tofu paste. Process to a paste and mix in the parsley with a fork.

To make the hearts, dampen a 12 × 18-in (30 × 46-cm) piece of muslin and brush corn oil over a 12 × 10-in (30 × 22.5-cm) area in the centre. Using a knife, spread the plain tofu paste evenly over an 8 × 10-in (20 × 25-cm) area to a thickness of $\frac{1}{4}$ in (6 mm), rather like making a swiss roll. Keep the sides neat, but bevelled like the edge of a mirror. This tapering will ensure a neat and delicate shape.

Borrow a second pair of hands to help you raise the muslin spread with tofu paste and place it in a steamer. Make good any breaks in the curd. The edges of the muslin may rest lightly on the surface.

With the lid on, steam the tofu for approximately 3 minutes, or until it is firm. Take the steamer off the water but leave the muslin in the steamer.

Starting from the centre, spread the prawn filling evenly across the width of the tofu in a band approximately 2 in (5 cm) wide.

Keeping the filling nearest to you, take hold of the unfilled muslin at the far corners and bring them over towards you, to form a roll. Pat gently to secure the edges firmly, making sure they are well sealed. Steam the roll for about 10 minutes.

Meanwhile, to make the sauce, put all the sauce ingredients into a saucepan and bring to the boil. Turn off the heat. Lift the tofu roll out of the steamer and remove the muslin. Cut the roll into sixteen $\frac{1}{4}$-in (6-cm) slices and arrange them in pairs on a heated serving dish, so that each pair form a heart. Arrange the hearts in a cluster to form a flower. Decorate the centre with the prawn slices. Finally, bring the sauce to the boil again and pour over the entire dish.

◆

Top: Steamed Stripy Tofu (*p. 108*), below: Steamed Tofu Hearts.

Above: Tofu and Spinach Island.

TOFU AND SPINACH ISLAND

Tofu gives exactly the light, firm texture required for this terrine-type dish.

◆

SERVES 8

1 lb (480 g) fresh tofu (beancurd) (approximately 4 squares)
4 oz (120 g) fresh spinach leaves (sufficient to line and cover a
6-in (15-cm) cake tin)
4 oz (120 g) peeled prawns
salt
white pepper
2 egg whites
½ teaspoon sugar
1 carrot, peeled, blanched and finely diced
2 oz (60 g) cooked ham, finely diced
4 Chinese black mushrooms, soaked, drained and finely chopped
1 oz (30 g) green pepper, cored, seeded and finely diced
2 tablespoons (30 ml) corn oil
½ teaspoon cornflour
1 carrot, cut into matchstick strips
1 teaspoon (5 ml) tomato purée
1½ teaspoons (7.5 ml) Shaoshing wine
4 tablespoons (60 ml) seasoned chicken stock or water
1 tablespoon (15 ml) cornflour mixed with 1 tablespoon (15 ml)
water
1–2 thin slices root ginger, cut into slivers

◆

Remove the stalks from the spinach and blanch the leaves in boiling salted water for approximately 30 seconds, then drain thoroughly and dry on kitchen paper.

Drain the liquid from the tofu, then, holding it in a cloth, gently press between the hands to remove any excess moisture. Remove the surface skin with a knife. Cut up the tofu and place in a food processor with the egg whites, ¾ teaspoon salt, ¼ teaspoon pepper and the sugar. Work to a smooth paste (or use a potato masher). Add the diced carrot, ham, mushrooms and green pepper and stir well to mix.

Grease the cake tin with half the oil and line it with spinach leaves. Fill the tin with the tofu mixture, then level the top and cover with the remaining spinach leaves. Use more pieces of spinach leaf to cover any gaps and tidy around the edges, which will just overlap.

Place the tin in a wok half-filled with boiling water and steam for about 25 minutes. Remove the tin from the wok and unmould on to the centre of a heated serving dish. Use kitchen paper to absorb any excess moisture which may appear. Keep warm.

Mix the prawns with the cornflour and season with ½ teaspoon salt and pepper to taste. Heat the remaining oil to a high temperature in a pre-heated wok or frying pan, add the prawns and stir-fry for 30 seconds, then add the carrot, tomato purée, wine, chicken stock, cornflour mixture and ginger. Stir-fry for just 2 minutes.

Spoon the sauce round the spinach and tofu mould, making sure the prawns and carrots are evenly distributed, for the best effect.

STEAMED VEGETABLES

The chicken juice is obtained by steaming either a whole chicken or pieces with ginger and spring onion (see Bang Bang Chicken, p. 50), and can be kept in reserve for future use. It would be a shame to throw away something as good as this! Use it to add delicious flavour to your steamed vegetables.

◆

SERVES 8

1½ lb (720 g) firm slender leeks
8 firm Brussels sprouts
1 tablespoon (15 ml) corn oil
2 thin slices root ginger
½ teaspoon salt
1½ fl oz (45 ml) seasoned chicken juice

◆

Wash and drain the leeks and cut them into 2-in (5-cm) pieces. Arrange them diagonally across the centre of a heatproof platter. Trim the sprouts and make 2 cross cuts in their tops so that they cook quickly. Place them on the platter with the oil and ginger. Sprinkle with salt.

Place the dish on a rack in a wok half-filled with boiling water, cover and steam for 7–8 minutes, until cooked to your liking. Warm the chicken juice and pour the hot juice over the vegetables before serving.

107

STEAMED STRIPY TOFU

illustrated on page 105

This is not unlike a vegetable mousse. Vegetarians could replace the chicken stock with a well-flavoured vegetable stock.

◆

SERVES 8

8 oz (240 g) fresh spinach leaves
1¼ lb (600 g) fresh tofu (beancurd)
1 lb (480 g) Chinese leaves
½–1-in (1–2.5-cm) cube root ginger
½ teaspoon salt
¼ teaspoon white pepper
2 egg whites
¼ teaspoon caster sugar

for the serving sauce

6 fl oz (180 ml) chicken stock, preferably home-made
2 teaspoons (10 ml) oyster sauce
2 slices root ginger
1 teaspoon (5 ml) cornflour mixed with 2 tablespoons (30 ml) water

for the garnish
Ribbons Of Leek (p. 134–135)

◆

Plunge the washed spinach into boiling water and immediately remove and strain under cold running water. Squeeze out all the moisture, then cut the leaves into small pieces and reserve.

Drain the liquid from the tofu. Remove the surface skin with a knife. Cut the tofu into small pieces and place in a food processor with the salt, pepper, 1 egg white and the sugar. Using a garlic press, crush the ginger over the tofu. Process to a paste and transfer three-quarters of the mixture to a bowl. Add the spinach to the remaining tofu paste, together with the second egg white and process again, stopping before the small pieces of spinach become unrecognizable.

Grease 8 ramekins 2½ in (6 cm) in diameter and spoon in the tofu mixture to a depth of ½ in (1 cm), leaving a ½-in (1-cm) central canal. Fill this with the spinach mixture. Level the surface and do not worry if the spinach merges somewhat with the tofu as these moulds will be turned out to serve.

Place the ramekins in a steamer over briskly boiling

water and steam for approximately 3–4 minutes. Take out the ramekins, run a knife around the edge of each and turn out on to a plate. Arrange the moulds carefully on a pre-heated serving dish or in separate bowls.

To make the serving sauce, place all the sauce ingredients in a small saucepan and bring to the boil. Pour the sauce evenly over the moulds, and garnish with ribbons of leek.

❖

TOFU WITH VEGETABLES

Deep-frying gives tofu a wonderful puffy lightness, quite unlike the texture of steamed tofu.

◆

SERVES 8

12 oz (360 g) fresh tofu (beancurd)
2 slices root ginger
1 oz (30 g) streaky bacon, rinds removed and shredded
3–4 Chinese black mushrooms, soaked, drained and shredded
1 oz (30 g) bamboo shoots, shredded
2 tablespoons (30 ml) oyster sauce
1 tablespoon (15 ml) dark soy sauce
1 tablespoon (15 ml) Shaoshing wine or dry sherry
½ pint (300 ml) chicken stock, preferably home-made
2 teaspoons (10 ml) cornflour mixed with 1 tablespoon (15 ml) water
salt and white pepper

for deep-frying
1¾ pints (1 litre) corn oil

for the garnish
1 tablespoon (15 ml) spring onion, shredded

◆

Drain the liquid from the tofu. Holding the tofu in a cloth, gently press between the hands to remove any excess moisture. Cut the tofu into 2½ × 1½-in (6 × 3-cm) pieces, ½ in (1 cm) thick. Lay the pieces on a cloth and dry again.

Heat the oil to 350°F (180°C) in a wok or deep-fryer. Add the tofu pieces and deep-fry for 7–8 minutes, maintaining a constant temperature and turning from time to time, until golden and firm to the touch. Drain in a wire sieve.

Reheat 2 tablespoons (30 ml) of the hot oil in a pre-heated wok or frying pan. Add the ginger, bacon, mushrooms and bamboo shoots and stir-fry for about 30 seconds. Add the oyster sauce, soy sauce, wine and stock.

Bring to the boil, then stir in the cornflour mixture until the sauce thickens. Season with salt and pepper. Add the tofu pieces to the pan, turn down the heat and simmer for about 15 minutes. Transfer to a heated serving dish and garnish with the spring onions just before serving.

STEAMED BA-CHOY WITH BACON

This inexpensive yet very tasty dish is perfect if you are entertaining on a budget.

◆

SERVES 8

1½ lb (720 g) young ba-choy
2 oz (60 g) streaky bacon rashers, rinds removed and cut into fine strips
2 tablespoons (30 ml) ginger-flavoured chicken stock, preferably home-made
salt

◆

Arrange some of the ba-choy around a plate, white stalks towards the rim, leaves towards the centre. Trim the stalks a little if necessary. Over these place a second layer of bay-choy, reversing the direction of the leaves. In this layer the white stalks should be fractionally shorter. Any leftover green parts can be added to give depth at the centre.

Pour the chicken stock over the bay-choy and season lightly with salt. To complete the flower-like arrangement place the bacon in a circle, like a garland, so that it comes between the white stalks and the outer band of green. Then place the plate on a rack over boiling water in a wok or saucepan, cover and steam for 7–8 minutes until the ba-choy is cooked. Serve hot.

MANDARIN PANCAKES

illustrated on pages 68–69

These pancakes, the traditional accompaniment to Peking duck, may be bought ready-made, but will give none of the satisfaction of making one's own. They can be made well in advance. To reheat just before serving, steam them for about 4–5 minutes at a high temperature. Wrap a teacloth over the lid of the pan to prevent the condensation from spoiling the pancakes.

◆

MAKES 20

10 oz (300 g) plain flour
2 pinches salt
1 tablespoon (15 ml) corn oil
extra flour for dusting
4 teaspoons (20 ml) sesame oil

◆

Sift the flour with the salt into a mixing bowl and make a well in the centre. Add 4 fl oz (120 ml) boiling water, then the corn oil, and stir with a fork for 2–3 minutes until the mixture forms a dough. Transfer to a floured surface and knead lightly for about 5 minutes, until soft and bouncy. If the dough seems too sticky, dust with a little flour. Divide the dough into 4 equal pieces and form each one into a roll about 1 in (2.5 cm) in diameter. Divide each roll into 5 equal pieces.

Flatten each piece of dough between the palms of your hands, to make a circle about 2 in (5 cm) in diameter. Brush 10 of the circles lightly on one side only with sesame oil. Cover with the remaining circles, making sure the edges are exactly aligned. Roll them out on a well-floured surface until each pair combines to make a very thin circular pancake 5 in (12.5 cm) in diameter, making 10 in all.

Fry each pancake in a pre-heated small shallow frying pan without oil, for 1½–2 minutes, turning once, until light, firm to the touch and browned in places.

Allow to cool slightly, then carefully peel apart the 2 layers, to give 20 very thin pancakes. Shake off any excess flour.

RICE AND NOODLES

Rice is a staple food for the Chinese. It gives bulk to their diet and is eaten to clear the palate after foods of very distinct or pronounced flavours. For this reason it is traditionally served plain-boiled throughout the dinner. In Chinese cooking, rice is by definition always the long-grain variety and must be cooked correctly, according to the method given on p. 112.

There is a general preference in the West for fried rather than boiled rice. A very simple version of fried rice can be made by frying a finely diced Spanish onion until softened and lightly coloured, stirring in cooked rice until thoroughly coated, then adding a beaten egg and stir-frying until the egg is set. Extra ingredients may be added to this basic mixture, to make a dish in its own right, like Savoury Rice with Lamb (p. 116). If it is more convenient to cook rice in advance, it can be reheated in the oven to 350°F (180°C, gas mark 4) for 30 minutes, in an ovenproof dish tightly covered with foil perforated twice to allow the steam to escape.

Chinese egg noodles are lighter than Italian, and are satisfying without being unduly filling. Cooked with vegetables or meat in a light-textured sauce, the Chinese eat them for breakfast, lunch and dinner, and as a snack at any time – even late at night, as they are very easy to digest. If noodles are to be fried, they must be rinsed under cold running water after boiling and allowed to dry thoroughly before frying.

Clockwise, from left: Fried Rice with Celery (p. 112), Noodles with a Spicy Meat Sauce (p. 119), Crab and Golden Lily Mushroom Fried Rice (p. 114), Steamed Rice with Chicken and Chinese Sausage (p. 118), Rice Wrapped in Lotus Leaf (p. 114).

111

CHINESE BOILED RICE

This is a simple, failsafe method of preparing plain rice.

◆

SERVES 8

1 lb (480 g) long-grain rice

◆

Place the rice in a saucepan and fill it with cold water. Stir well, then drain. Repeat 3–4 times.

Pour in cold water to ½ in (1 cm) above the level of the rice. Cover and bring to the boil.

Reduce the heat, and cook, half-covered, until the water above the rice has disappeared. Cover fully and cook over a very low heat for a further 20 minutes, until the rice is light and fluffy.

❖

112

FRIED RICE WITH CELERY

illustrated on pages 110–111

This dish has most attractive, pale colours, and – perhaps surprisingly – a strong, very good flavour.

◆

SERVES 8

1 lb (480 g) cooked long-grain rice
6 oz (180 g) pork tenderloin
½ teaspoon cornflour
salt and white pepper
1 teaspoon (5 ml) light soy sauce
1 tablespoon oyster sauce
½ teaspoon sugar
4 tablespoons (60 ml) corn oil
4 sticks celery, cut into strips twice the size of matchsticks

◆

Cut the pork into thin strips and mix with the cornflour, soy sauce, oyster sauce, sugar and salt and pepper to taste. Set aside for the flavours to absorb.

Heat half the oil to a high temperature in a pre-heated wok or frying pan, add the rice and stir-fry with ⅛ teaspoon salt for just over 3 minutes. Transfer the rice to a bowl.

In the same pan, cleaned if necessary, heat a further tablespoon (15 ml) oil, add a little salt and stir-fry the celery for just another 30 seconds, then transfer it to a separate bowl.

Heat the remaining oil in the pan, add the pork and stir-fry for about 1 minute, until opaque. Add the celery, then the rice, and quickly stir to mix well, so that the celery will remain crisp. Transfer to a heated serving dish and serve.

❖

FRIED RICE WITH MUSHROOMS

illustrated on pages 116–117

This is fried rice with a difference! If the mushroom and wood ear look uninviting to European eyes before cooking, when they are combined with the right sauce to complement their texture, you will be delightfully surprised by the result.

◆

SERVES 8

1 lb (480 g) cooked long-grain rice
1 oz (30 g) wood ear, soaked until soft, then rinsed, drained and shredded
4–5 Chinese black mushrooms, soaked, drained and shredded
4 oz (120 g) boneless chicken breast
½ teaspoon cornflour
salt and white pepper
1 teaspoon (5 ml) sugar
4 tablespoons (60 ml) corn oil
2 oz (60 g) Spanish onion, thinly sliced
1 tablespoon (15 ml) oyster sauce

◆

Cut the chicken into matchstick pieces and mix in a bowl with the cornflour, ¼ teaspoon salt, a sprinkling of pepper and half the sugar.

Heat 1 tablespoon (15 ml) of the oil in a pre-heated wok or frying pan, add the onion and stir-fry for 1 minute, then add the wood ear and Chinese mushrooms. Stir-fry for 1 further minute over a medium to high heat, then transfer to a heated serving dish.

Heat 1 further tablespoon (15 ml) oil in the pan and when it is very hot add the chicken and stir-fry for just over 1 minute. Transfer the chicken to the dish.

Heat the remaining oil in the pan, add the chicken and the mushrooms together with the rice, oyster sauce and the remaining sugar. Stir-fry for 1 minute, then serve.

'EIGHT JEWELS' RICE
illustrated on pages 110–111

This is a traditional name for a classical stir-fry rice dish with more ingredients than usual, guaranteeing no two mouthfuls will offer exactly the same flavours.

◆

SERVES 8

1 lb (480 g) cooked long-grain rice
8 oz (240 g) boneless chicken, steamed or poached, then diced
4 oz (120 g) small cooked prawns, well drained
2 oz (60 g) cooked ham, cut into $\frac{1}{4}$-in (6-mm) dice
4 oz (120 g) fresh or frozen crabmeat, well drained
4 oz (120 g) canned water chestnuts, drained and diced
4 Chinese black mushrooms, soaked, drained and diced
4 oz (120 g) frozen peas, defrosted
6 oz (180 g) Spanish onion, diced
3 tablespoons (45 ml) corn oil
$\frac{1}{2}$ teaspoon salt
2 tablespoons (30 ml) oyster sauce
white pepper
$\frac{1}{4}$ teaspoon sugar

◆

Heat half the oil in a pre-heated wok or frying pan, add the rice and half the salt and stir-fry for 3 minutes. Transfer to a dish and set aside.

Heat the remaining oil to a high temperature in the wiped out pan, add the onion with the remaining salt and stir-fry until just softened but not browned. Add the water chestnuts and stir well again.

Add the chicken, prawns, ham, mushrooms, peas and crabmeat one at a time, stir-frying between each addition. Add the oyster sauce, pepper to taste and the sugar and blend well with all the remaining ingredients. Return the rice to the pan and stir-fry for 2 minutes, then transfer to a heated dish to serve.

SPRING ONION BEEF FRIED RICE
illustrated on pages 116–117

This would be delicious as a supper dish, rather like a risotto, as well as part of a dinner menu.

◆

SERVES 8

8 oz (240 g) sirloin or rump steak
1 lb (480 g) cooked long-grain rice
2 oz (60 g) spring onions
2 cloves garlic
2 tablespoons (30 ml) corn oil
$\frac{1}{2}$ teaspoon salt
white pepper
$1\frac{1}{2}$ teaspoons (7.5 ml) dark soy sauce

◆

Heat half the oil in a pre-heated wok or non-stick frying pan. Add the steak and fry on both sides, until it is brown outside but remains pink in the centre. Remove from the heat.

Holding the spring onions together in a bunch, cut them across into tiny pieces. Take the beef from the wok and cut it into strips and then into tiny cubes.

Heat the remaining oil in the pan. Fry the rice for about 3 minutes before adding the beef with the salt, a sprinkling of pepper and the soy sauce and stir well to mix. Stir-fry for 1 minute, then transfer to a heated serving dish before serving.

113

114

CRAB AND GOLDEN LILY MUSHROOM FRIED RICE

illustrated on pages 110–111

This dish can be prepared fully in advance, then covered in kitchen foil with a slit in the top to allow steam to escape, and reheated in the oven (370°F/ 190°C/gas mark 5) for about 15 minutes, before garnishing with the coriander as a finishing touch. It would be delicious served with a simple vegetable, as a lunch dish.

◆

SERVES 8

3 tablespoons (45 ml) corn oil
1 lb (480 g) cooked long-grain rice
¼ teaspoon salt
6 oz (180 g) fresh crabmeat or 8 oz (240 g) frozen crabmeat, well drained
8 oz (240 g) fresh golden lily mushrooms (or a 7 oz/210 g vacuum pack) rinsed under cold running water, then drained on kitchen paper
1 tablespoon light soy sauce
1½ tablespoons (22.5 ml) oyster sauce
pepper to taste
⅛–¼ teaspoon salt

◆

Heat half the oil to a high temperature in a pre-heated wok or frying-pan, add the rice with the salt and stir-fry for 2–3 minutes. Transfer to a bowl, scraping up any grains which may stick to the pan.

Heat the remaining oil to a very high temperature in the pan, add the crabmeat and stir-fry for 30 seconds, then add the mushrooms and stir-fry for a further 30 seconds.

Add the soy sauce, oyster sauce and pepper to taste and stir-fry for 1 further minute, until thoroughly blended. Return the rice to the pan and stir-fry for 1 further minute, then add the coriander. Stir well and transfer to a heated serving dish.

RICE WRAPPED IN LOTUS LEAF

illustrated on pages 110–111

I serve these on side plates to be eaten as an accompaniment throughout the meal, like bread. The filling does not have to be pork. You can also make bigger bundles – steaming them for 5–10 minutes longer – which can be shared between two or more people.

◆

MAKES 8

1 lb (480 g) (uncooked weight) glutinous rice, boiled or steamed
4 lotus leaves
1 lb (480 g) fresh pork belly rashers, cut into 1½-in (3-cm) lengths
1 tablespoon (15 ml) corn oil
2 oz (60 g) Spanish onion, sliced
2 Chinese wind-dried pork sausages, cut diagonally into fairly thin slices
3 slices root ginger
2 tablespoons (30 ml) dark soy sauce
⅛ teaspoon 5-spice powder
white pepper
1 teaspoon (5 ml) sugar
8 fresh chestnuts, peeled
4 oz (120 g) bamboo shoots, cut into bite-sized chunks
4 fairly large Chinese black mushrooms, soaked, drained and halved

◆

Heat the oil to a high temperature in a saucepan, add the onion and fry for 30 seconds. Add the sausage, pork and ginger and stir-fry for 2–3 minutes, until the outside 'catches' slightly.

Add the soy sauce, 5-spice powder, pepper, sugar and 6 fl oz (180 ml) water. Turn down the heat and leave to simmer for 30 minutes, then add the chestnuts and cook for a further 30 minutes until the sausage, pork and chestnuts are tender.

Divide the cooked rice into 8 portions. Halve one portion and pat it into a cup shape in the palm of your hand. Add 2 pieces each of sausage, pork and bamboo shoot, a piece of chestnut and a piece of mushroom. Use the rest of the portion of rice to cover the filling and mould into a square shape. Repeat until all the ingredients are used up.

Lightly grease the lotus leaves on one side and divide each of them into 4. The number depends on the size of the leaves, but the area should be approximately 9 in (18 cm) square. Put a rice mould in the centre of each leaf wrapping. Fold in one end, followed by the two sides, and working away from you turn the near edge over so it meets up with the far corner, to make a parcel. The leaves resemble damp kitchen paper which clings and remains in place.

Steam the parcels in 2 batches if necessary on a rack over boiling water in a wok or saucepan for 20–25 minutes until cooked through. Serve with the leaf turned back – remember that it is inedible – leaving the contents revealed.

SEAFOOD AND VEGETABLE FRIED NOODLES

The noodles can be cooked up to a day in advance and kept covered in clingfilm in the refrigerator, which leaves only the final stages of cooking to be done at the last moment. Alternatively you can prepare the whole dish ahead of time and reheat it in a microwave oven.

◆

SERVES 8

8 oz (240 g) thread egg noodles
8 oz (240 g) peeled, raw, medium prawns
4 scallops
8 oz (240 g) cucumber
4 oz (120 g) celery
1 teaspoon (5 ml) cornflour
salt and white pepper
1 tablespoon (15 ml) oyster sauce
1½ teaspoons (7.5 ml) cornflour mixed with 3 fl oz (90 ml) stock or water
½ teaspoon sugar

for deep-frying
1 pint (600 ml) corn oil

◆

Clean and thoroughly devein the prawns. Separate the roes from the scallops. Remove any traces of veins and cut the white flesh into slices.

Cut the cucumber in half lengthways and scoop out the seeds. Cut crossways diagonally into fairly thin slices. Set aside. Cut the celery in similar slices.

Put the prawns and sliced scallops into a bowl and mix with the cornflour, ¼ teaspoon salt, and pepper to taste. Set aside. Cook the noodles in boiling salted water for 1½ minutes, until cooked but still firm. Drain, rinse under cold running water and set aside.

Heat the oil to 350°F (180°C) in a wok or deep-fryer. Turn off the heat under the pan and place the prawns and sliced scallops in the oil for 20 seconds. Transfer to a sieve. Add the roes to the oil very briefly, removing them as soon as their colour changes. Transfer to the sieve with the other seafood and leave to drain.

Heat 1½ tablespoons (22.5 ml) of the hot oil in a pre-heated wok or frying pan, add half the noodles and leave them undisturbed for 1½ minutes while they firm up, then fry for a further 1½–2 minutes, turning occasionally. Keep warm on a hot serving platter in a low oven while you fry the remaining noodles in the same way. Add them to the platter.

Wipe the pan clean, heat 2 tablespoons (30 ml) of the oil before adding the cucumber and celery with ⅛ teaspoon salt and stir-fry for about 1 minute, then return the prawns, scallops and their roes to the pan with the oyster sauce, soy sauce and cornflour mixture. Bring to the boil, add the sugar and check the seasoning, then spoon the mixture on to the centre of the noodles on the serving platter, leaving some of the noodles showing round the edge.

115

SAVOURY RICE WITH LAMB

This is an ideal dish for using up the remains of a Sunday roast with a minimum of trouble. Beef or pork may be used instead of lamb.

◆

SERVES 8

8 oz (240 g) (or whatever amount is available) sliced roast lamb
8 oz (240 g) crisp lettuce leaves (cos, iceberg, Webbs)
1 lb (480 g) cooked long-grain rice
4 tablespoons (60 ml) corn oil
salt and white pepper
2 oz (60 g) Spanish onion, sliced
3 tablespoons (45 ml) oyster sauce
$\frac{1}{2}$ teaspoon sugar
1 fresh green chilli, sliced
several stalks of fresh coriander, finely chopped

◆

116

Cut the slices of lamb into narrow 2-in (5-cm) strips. Cut the lettuce into 1-in (2.5-cm) strips.

Heat 2 tablespoons (30 ml) of the oil to a high temperature in a pre-heated wok or frying pan, add the rice with $\frac{1}{2}$ teaspoon salt and stir-fry for 3 minutes. Transfer to a bowl.

In the same pan heat the remaining oil, add the onion and the chilli with a little salt and pepper and stir-fry for 30 seconds. Add the lamb and stir-fry for about 2 minutes, then return the rice to the pan. Add the oyster sauce and the sugar and stir-fry briefly, making sure the rice and meat are well mixed. Add the lettuce and the coriander, then immediately remove the pan from the heat to prevent the lettuce from becoming too limp, stirring gently. Transfer to a heated serving dish and serve.

Top right: Fried Rice with Mushrooms *(p. 112)*, top left: Savoury Rice with Lamb, below: Spring Onion Beef Fried Rice *(p. 113)*.

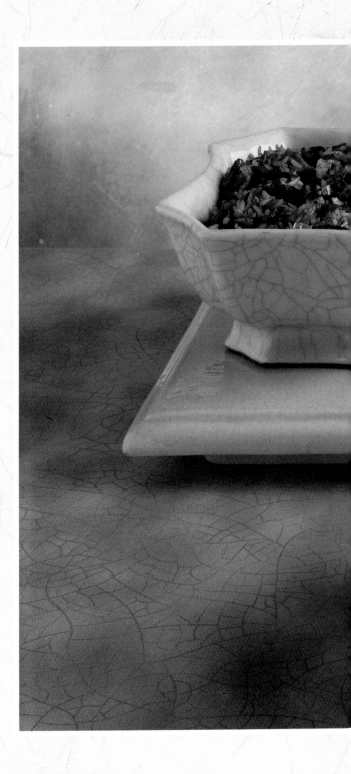

STEAMED RICE WITH CHICKEN AND CHINESE SAUSAGE

illustrated on pages 110–111

More subtle-tasting than fried rice, this classical Chinese dish is a meal in itself.

◆

SERVES 8

12 oz (360 g) long-grain rice
8 oz (240 g) boneless chicken breast
2 Chinese wind-dried sausages, thinly sliced diagonally
1 tablespoon (15 ml) light soy sauce
$\frac{1}{2}$ teaspoon cornflour
pinch of salt
white pepper
sugar
2 oz (60 g) bamboo shoots, thickly sliced
3 large Chinese black mushrooms, soaked, drained and sliced
2 tablespoons (30 ml) oyster sauce
2 very thin slices root ginger, very finely shredded

for the garnish
1 tablespoon (15 ml) finely chopped spring onion

◆

Cut the chicken into smallish chunks and mix them in a bowl with the soy sauce, cornflour, salt, and a little pepper and sugar. Set aside for the flavours to absorb.

Wash the rice thoroughly, changing the water several times to remove starchiness (see p. 112), then place it in a shallow ovenproof dish. Steam on a rack over boiling water in a wok at a high temperature for 15 minutes.

Turn off the heat and arrange the chicken on the centre of the rice, and the bamboo shoots in 2 rows at the edges with the mushroom and sausage inside them, making a formal arrangement. Spoon over the oyster sauce and sprinkle with the ginger.

Top up the pan with boiling water if necessary, then steam 10 minutes more at a high temperature.

Reduce the heat to simmering point and continue to steam for a further 10 minutes, then test the rice and cook a little longer if necessary. Present the dish at the table with the arrangement undisturbed, then, just before serving, mix all the ingredients gently together.

BEEF NOODLES WITH BEAN SPROUTS

It is possible to prepare the noodles a day or two in advance and store in a bowl covered with clingfilm in the refrigerator. The rice stick lends bulk to this popular restaurant dish.

◆

SERVES 8

1 lb (480 g) dry rice stick, $\frac{1}{2}$ in (1 cm) wide
1 lb (480 g) fillet or sirloin steak
1 lb (480 g) fresh bean sprouts
salt and white pepper
1 teaspoon (5 ml) sugar
$\frac{1}{2}$ teaspoon cornflour
1 egg white
1 tablespoon (15 ml) light soy sauce
7 tablespoons (105 ml) corn oil
3 slices root ginger
2 spring onions, finely shredded

◆

A few hours in advance, soak the rice stick in a large bowl of cold water to cover. It is ready for use when almost double its original size. Drain thoroughly in a wire sieve.

Cut the beef across the grain into thin slices. Put them into a bowl with $\frac{1}{4}$ teaspoon of salt, pepper to taste, the sugar, cornflour, egg white and light soy sauce. Mix well and leave to marinate.

Heat $1\frac{1}{2}$ tablespoons (22.5 ml) of the oil in a pre-heated wok or large frying pan. When the oil is very hot add half the noodles with 2 pinches of salt and stir-fry for about 2 minutes. Transfer to a bowl. Fry the remaining noodles in the same way and put them with the rest.

Heat 2 tablespoons (30 ml) of the oil in the pan and add the ginger, bean sprouts and $\frac{1}{4}$ teaspoon salt and stir-fry for 30 seconds. Transfer to a bowl.

Heat the remaining oil to a high temperature. Add the beef and fry, stirring constantly, for just 1 minute.

Return the noodles to the pan and stir well to mix for no longer than 2 minutes.

Finally add the spring onion and stir-fry for a further 30 seconds before serving.

118

NOODLES WITH A SPICY MEAT SAUCE

Just a little cabbage pickled in Szechuan style with salt and chilli gives this dish its character.

◆

SERVES 8

6 oz (180 g) pork tenderloin or boned pork chop
1 oz (30 g) Szechuan preserved cabbage
3 oz (90 g) bamboo shoots
6 oz (180 g) fine egg noodles
½ teaspoon cornflour
salt and white pepper
2 tablespoons (30 ml) corn oil
1½ teaspoons (7.5 ml) dark soy sauce
1½ teaspoons (7.5 ml) crushed yellow bean paste
1 teaspoon (5 ml) chilli bean sauce
1 tablespoon (15 ml) Shaoshing wine
1 teaspoon (5 ml) sugar

for the garnish
1 spring onion, finely chopped

◆

Mince the pork, using a cleaver or food processor, and mix it with the cornflour, and salt and pepper to taste in a bowl. Set aside.

Rinse the cabbage and mince it finely with the bamboo shoots. Bring a saucepan of salted water to the boil for the noodles.

Heat half the oil in a pre-heated wok or frying pan, add the vegetable mixture and stir-fry for 1 minute, then remove from the pan and set aside.

In the same pan heat the remaining oil to a high temperature, then add the minced pork and stir-fry for about 1 minute. Add the soy sauce, the yellow bean paste, chilli bean sauce, wine, sugar and 1 tablespoon (15 ml) water. Stir-fry for up to 1 minute, then turn off the heat. Return the vegetables to the pan and stir well.

Boil the noodles for 1–1½ minutes, until cooked, testing with a single strand. Strain quickly and transfer to a heated serving dish, then spoon the pork mixture on top. Toss and mix it with the noodles, sprinkle with the spring onion and serve.

SHELL PASTA WITH CHICKEN

illustrated on page 121

I happened to have these ingredients available in the kitchen one day and combined them in what turned out to be a very pleasing dish.

◆

SERVES 8

6 oz (180 g) medium pasta shells
6 oz (180 g) boneless chicken breast
1 teaspoon (5 ml) cornflour
salt and white pepper
12 oz (360 g) fresh bean sprouts
1 bunch radishes
4 tablespoons (60 ml) corn oil
2 slices root ginger
1 tablespoon (15 ml) tomato ketchup
1 tablespoon (15 ml) Sweet and Chilli Sauce (p. 130)
1 clove garlic, crushed

◆

Cook the pasta in boiling salted water for about 5 minutes, until marginally underdone (*al dente*). Drain and refresh the pasta under cold running water, then drain again and leave to rest in a wire sieve.

Cut the chicken into small thin strips and mix it with the cornflour, salt and pepper to taste. Rinse the bean sprouts in a colander under cold running water, then drain thoroughly. Slice the radishes thinly.

Heat 1 tablespoon (15 ml) of the oil in a pre-heated wok or frying pan. Add the bean sprouts, the ginger and some salt and stir-fry on high for 30 seconds. Then remove from the pan with a slotted spoon and set aside.

In the same pan, cleaned if necessary, heat another tablespoon (15 ml) of the oil over a high heat, add the chicken and stir-fry for about 1 minute until the pieces are white and have separated, then transfer to a bowl.

Quickly rinse the pan under hot water, then heat the remaining oil with the tomato ketchup, sweet and chilli sauce and garlic. Return the pasta shells to the pan and stir-fry briefly, mixing well. Return the chicken and the drained bean sprouts to the pan, turn off the heat. Add the radishes just before serving, so that they retain their fresh crispness and pink edging.

120

LOBSTER NOODLES

*Fresh live lobsters undoubtedly give the best results
here. Cooked ones will do, but the texture of the
flesh will not be as good, since the preparation of
this dish involves stir-frying, which means further
cooking. In the case of the noodles, and at the risk
of sounding contradictory, it must be said that the
fresh variety should be avoided as they easily
become soggy during cooking. Packaged noodles are
the ones to use.*

◆

SERVES 8

2 small live lobsters, each about 1 lb (480 g)
5 oz (150 g) egg noodles
salt
5 oz (150 g) spinach noodles about $\frac{1}{8}$ in (3 mm) wide
4 tablespoons (60 ml) corn oil
4 thin rings Spanish onion
3 or 4 slices root ginger, very finely shredded
2 spring onions, finely shredded
white pepper

◆

Cook the egg and spinach noodles in boiling salted
water for just a few minutes, keeping the strands
separate and testing frequently. Remove from the heat
while still just underdone (*al dente*), drain and rinse
under cold running water. Drain again and leave in a
sieve for 1–2 hours to dry out.

Cut each lobster into about 6 even-sized pieces.
Separate the claws into two parts and crack them with a
hammer, then extract the meat.

Heat half the oil in a pre-heated wok or frying pan,
add the Spanish onion with a little salt, and stir-fry until
softened, then transfer to a plate.

Add the noodles to the same pan and stir-fry for 3–4
minutes, then set aside with the onions.

Wipe out the pan, heat the remaining oil, and add the
lobster claw meat. Stir-fry for about 3 minutes. Add the
remaining lobster and pepper to taste with the ginger
and stir-fry for a further 3 minutes, until the lobster is
firm and opaque. Return the noodles and Spanish onion
to the pan, add the spring onions and stir-fry for about 1
minute. Transfer to a heated serving dish with the
cooking juices and serve immediately.

FRIED NOODLES
SINGAPORE STYLE

*It may seem surprising to include a dish which uses
curry powder, not a classic Chinese spice. However,
all the other ingredients and the method are truly
Chinese and it is very popular throughout the
Chinese community. The Chinese fish cake has to be
bought fresh from a Chinese grocery.*

◆

SERVES 8

6 oz (180 g) thin rice sticks (meifun)
4 tablespoons (60 ml) corn oil
$\frac{1}{2}$ teaspoon salt
3 oz (90 g) cooked peeled prawns
6 oz (180 g) Shar-Shiu Pork (p. 40), cut into matchstick shreds
3 oz (90 g) Chinese fish cake, cut into matchstick shreds
1 small green sweet pepper, cored, seeded and cut into thin
rings
$\frac{1}{2}$ teaspoon sugar
1$\frac{1}{2}$ teaspoons (7.5 ml) curry powder
2 teaspoons (10 ml) dark soy sauce
pepper

◆

Plung the rice sticks into boiling salted water to
separate the fine strands, then drain immediately. Run
under cold running water and leave in a sieve for 1 hour
to dry out.

Heat half the oil in a pre-heated wok or frying pan,
add the rice sticks and half the salt and fry over a high
heat for 2 minutes, then transfer to a heated serving
dish.

Heat the remaining oil in the same pan, add the
prawns with the remaining salt and stir-fry for 30
seconds. Add the pork, fish cake and green pepper.
Sprinkle with the sugar, curry powder, soy sauce and
pepper and stir-fry for a further 30 seconds. Spoon over
the rice sticks and serve.

Top: Fried Noodles Singapore-style, centre: Lobster Noodles, below: Shell Pasta with Chicken *(p. 119)*.

121

SWEETS AND DESSERTS

Even devotees of Chinese cuisine will probably agree that it offers little in the way of desserts. The best-known of these must without doubt be toffee apples, beloved of Chinese restaurants. Fresh fruit is a particular favourite with the Chinese, but too often little thought is given to ways of presenting it.

In this section, along with a few classic desserts I have included others entirely of my own creation, most of which are based on fruit. One of the simplest yet most stunning ways of presenting fruit for the dessert course, indulging your guests with a touch of sheer luxury, is to make a selection from the following: strawberries, raspberries, blackberries, blueberries, black, red and white currants, green and black grapes, cherries, paw paw, mangoes, star fruit, kiwi, lychees, pomegranates, water melon and clementines. Hull, peel and slice the fruit as necessary, then arrange them symmetrically on a large glass serving platter. Each fruit will contribute its own particular beauty of form, texture and colour to a visually impressive and memorable dish with which to conclude a meal.

Clockwise, from left: Gift-wrapped Mango and Strawberry *(p. 125)*, Melon and Ginger Sorbet Plus *(p. 128)*, Nectarines with Poached Meringue *(p. 129)*, Tofu with Sweet Bean Filling *(p. 126)*, Sweet Walnut Stars *(p. 124)*, Caramelized Fruit, Lattice Layers with Fruit *(p. 129)*.

SWEET WALNUT STARS
illustrated on pages 122–123

A departure from the traditional way of serving pancakes with beanpaste – folded, deep-fried and cut into strips – these stars lend unremarkable ingredients elegance and a touch of romance. They may be briefly reheated in the oven without impairing their colour, texture or flavour.

◆

SERVES 8

2 oz (60 g) shelled walnuts
2 oz (60 g) sweet black bean paste
a little icing sugar, sifted
a little extra flour mixed with water

for the batter
6 oz (180 g) plain flour
a pinch of salt
2 eggs, beaten
½ pint (300 ml) milk

for deep-frying
1 pint (600 ml) corn oil

◆

124

To make the batter, sift the flour with the salt into a mixing bowl. Make a well in the centre, add the eggs and gradually stir in the flour. Gradually add the milk, beating well after each addition until the mixture is smooth. Chill in the refrigerator for 30 minutes.

Make the pancakes in the usual way (p. 109) until all the batter is used up. Using a small star cutter, cut out as many star shapes from the pancakes as possible and pair them off.

Crush the walnuts into small pieces in a bowl and mix them with the sweet black bean paste. Put a small blob of the walnut mixture in the centre of each of a pair of stars and cover it with the other, sealing the edges with the flour and water mixture. Heat the oil to 275°F (140°C) in a wok or deep-fryer, add the stars and deep-fry until light golden on both sides. Drain in a wire sieve, then on kitchen paper. Dust lightly with icing sugar to serve.

ALMOND JELLY AND REDCURRANT SAUCE
illustrated on page 127

This nursery pudding is usually served cut into cubes, but here it is elegantly moulded and served with a redcurrant sauce.

◆

SERVES 8

for the jelly
½ oz (15 g) agar agar squares, soaked in cold water for 30 minutes
1 teaspoon (5 ml) almond essence
3 tablespoons (45 ml) evaporated milk
2 tablespoons (30 ml) milk
3 oz (90 g) caster sugar

for the serving sauce
1½ lb (720 g) redcurrants
¼ pint (150 ml) water
4–5 oz (120–150 g) caster sugar

for the decoration
1 lb (480 g) blackcurrants or blackberries preferably in clusters on stalks, frosted with caster sugar

◆

To make the serving sauce, put the redcurrants, sugar and water into a saucepan, bring to the boil, then simmer for 10 minutes. Press through a nylon sieve and leave to cool.

Remove the agar agar from the soaking water, and shake it gently so the excess water runs out.

Put the agar agar into the saucepan with 1¾ pints (1 litre) hot water, the almond essence, evaporated milk, milk and sugar and bring to the boil, skimming off any scum which may appear on the surface. Turn the heat to very low and simmer for about 20 minutes, or until the agar agar is completely dissolved. Pour the mixture through a wire sieve lined with muslin into a wetted 2-pint (1.2-litre) jelly mould. Chill until set.

To unmould, run a knife round the edge of the jelly, then stand the mould in a bowl of hot water for a few minutes. Turn out the jelly on to a serving dish. Just before serving decorate with the frosted fruit. Accompany with the redcurrant sauce in a sauce-boat.

GIFT-WRAPPED MANGO AND STRAWBERRY

illustrated on page 125

Since fruit is the usual end to a Chinese meal, I have devised a recipe which uses fruit in a more exciting way.

◆

SERVES 8

for the pancakes
7 oz (210 g) plain flour
2 pinches of salt
2 eggs, beaten
12 fl oz (360 ml) milk
2 tablespoons (30 ml) corn oil, for frying
a little beaten egg for sealing

for the serving sauce
8 oz (240 g) fresh or frozen, thawed raspberries
juice of $\frac{1}{2}$ lemon
1 tablespoon (15 ml) water
1–2 tablespoons (15–30 ml) caster sugar

for the filling
6 oz (180 g) strawberries, hulled and cut into fairly small pieces
2 ripe, firm mangoes, stoned and cut into fairly small pieces
2 tablespoons (30 ml) caster sugar

for a finishing touch
1–2 teaspoons (5–10 ml) ground ginger
2 tablespoons (30 ml) caster sugar
1 tablespoon (15 ml) icing sugar

for the decoration
2 lb (960 g) strawberries, halved

◆

To make the pancake batter, sift the flour with the salt into a mixing bowl. Make a well in the centre, add the eggs and a little milk and stir well. Gradually stir in the remaining milk, to make a smooth batter. Set aside.

To make the serving sauce, press the raspberries through a fine nylon sieve, then blend the purée with the remaining sauce ingredients. Pour into a jug and chill.

Brush a pre-heated crêpe pan with a little of the oil, heat again and use the batter to make 10 pancakes, adding more oil to the pan as necessary.

Mix the fruit for the filling with the sugar in a bowl.

To make the parcels, place a tablespoonful of the fruit towards one side of the pancake, turn the edge over so that the fruit is just covered, then turn in the sides to hold it in place and fold over, keeping the fruit well together as you do so. Slightly undercut the bottom edge of the pancake so that it is no longer visible.

Continue in this way until you have 8 parcels each measuring about $2\frac{1}{2} \times 2 \times 1\frac{1}{4}$ in (6.5 × 5 × 3 cm). Cut $\frac{1}{4}$-in (6 mm) strips across the centre of the remaining pancakes. Make a light, loose knot in the centre of 8 of the longest strips. Now lay 8 of the shorter strips across the longer sides of the parcels. Lay the knotted strips across the shorter sides, tucking the ends neatly underneath and sealing in position with a dab of egg.

Sprinkle the tops of the parcels lightly with ginger and caster sugar, and place under a pre-heated grill until the sugar melts and the fruit inside warms through (about 2–3 minutes). Put the parcels on a serving platter and dust with icing sugar. Decorate with strawberries and accompany with the raspberry serving sauce.

ICE-CAPPED PUDDINGS

This dish brings back memories of a Chinese childhood and arouses feelings of nostalgia. We ate it cold in cafés on the way home from school in summer and had it served hot as a comforting, filling bed-time snack during winter.

◆

SERVES 8

12 oz (360 g) red beans
6 oz (180 g) Chinese slab sugar or natural sugar
1 pint (600 ml) lemon or orange sorbet

◆

Rinse the beans and put them into a saucepan with the sugar and 7 pints (4 litres) water. Bring to the boil and boil for 5 minutes, then simmer, covered, over a very low heat for $3\frac{1}{2}$ hours until the beans are creamy and most of the water is absorbed.

Allow the beans to cool, then chill in the refrigerator. Serve in individual dishes with a topping of sorbet.

BLACK AND WHITE MARBLE PUDDING
illustrated on page 127

This is a combination of two traditional Chinese creamed rice desserts. Blanched bitter almonds are available only from Oriental food shops.

◆

SERVES 8

for dessert 1
8 oz (240 g) roasted black sesame seeds
4–5 oz (120–150 g) caster sugar
2 oz (60 g) long-grain rice, washed
2 pints (1.2 litres) hot water
1 tablespoon (15 ml) cornflour mixed with 1 tablespoon (15 ml) water

for dessert 2
4 oz (120 g) blanched almonds *and*
4 oz (120 g) blanched bitter almonds, soaked together in a little boiling water for 1 hour
2 pints (1.2 litres) hot water
2 oz (60 g) long-grain rice, washed
4–5 oz (120–150 g) caster sugar
1 tablespoon (15 ml) cornflour mixed with 1 tablespoon (15 ml) water

◆

126

To make dessert 1, put the sesame seeds, sugar, rice and water into a heavy saucepan and cook gently, half-covered, for 1 hour, until the liquid is reduced by half and the rice is mushy. Pour it, a little at a time, through a wire sieve into a bowl, stirring quite vigorously so that only the coarse particles remain in the sieve. Scrape the underside of the sieve and add this to the mixture. Process in a blender or food processor until creamy, bring to the boil in the rinsed out pan, then stir in the cornflour mixture and, when thickened, pour into a jug. Allow to cool, then chill thoroughly.

To make dessert 2, drain the almonds and process them, a quarter at a time, with a quarter of the hot water, in a blender or food processor, then press through a fairly small sieve lined with a layer of muslin into a second heavy saucepan. Make sure all the liquid is squeezed through. Add the rice and sugar, bring to the boil, then simmer, half-covered, for 1 hour until the liquid is reduced by half and the rice is mushy. Process in a blender or food processor until creamy. Bring to the boil in the rinsed-out pan, stir in the cornflour mixture and when it has thickened, allow to cool, then chill.

Place a 6-in (15-cm) loose-based cake tin, with the base removed, on a serving dish. Pour the black cream into the centre of the tin and the white cream around it.

Just before presenting the dish, lift away the cake tin carefully, leaving behind two clearly defined rings of colour. On serving swirl the serving spoon to create a marbled effect.

TOFU WITH SWEET BEAN FILLING AND PINE NUTS
illustrated on pages 122–123

This is a traditional teatime delicacy sold in Chinese bakeries.

◆

MAKES 16

1 lb (480 g) fresh tofu (beancurd)
5–6 tablespoons (75–90 ml) sweet black bean paste
32 pine nuts

for deep-frying
1 pint (600 ml) corn oil

◆

Drain the liquid from the tofu and remove any excess moisture. Remove the surface skin with a knife. Cut each piece of tofu into 4 squares, making 16 in all.

Heat the oil to 275°F (140°C) in a wok or deep-fryer. Add the tofu and deep-fry for at least 7–8 minutes until light golden. Drain in a wire sieve and leave to cool.

Cut a square in each tofu top and hollow out the interiors, leaving a casing sufficient to hold the filling. Fill with sweet black bean paste and top each with 2 pine nuts. Place on a baking tray and heat in a pre-heated (400°F/200°C/gas mark 6) for 6–7 minutes. Serve hot.

Top: Almond Jelly with Redcurrant Sauce *(p. 124)*, below: Black and White Marble Pudding.

MELON AND GINGER SORBET PLUS

illustrated on pages 122–123

Ginger, traditionally teamed with melon, lends zest to this refreshing, beautifully tinted sorbet, served accompanied by crisp rolled wafers and toasted coconut.

◆

SERVES 8

for the galettes
3 egg whites
2 oz (60 g) caster sugar
2 oz (60 g) plain flour, sifted
2 oz (60 g) butter, melted

for the sorbet
1 ripe honeydew melon, peeled and seeds removed
4 oz (120 g) caster sugar
2 × 2-in (5-cm) cubes root ginger
1 egg white

for the decoration
½ oz (15 g) roasted shredded coconut (p. 136–7)

◆

To make the sorbet, bring ¼ pint (300 ml) of water to the boil with the ginger and sugar in a saucepan, then simmer, covered, for 10 minutes. Remove from the heat and allow to cool, then strain.

Process the melon flesh to a smooth purée, then mix with the ginger syrup. Then whip the egg white until it holds soft peaks and fold gently into the purée. Pour into a metal mould and freeze until slushy, then beat well and freeze again until firm.

Heat the oven to 350°F (180°C, gas mark 4).

To make the galettes, whisk the egg whites lightly with the sugar, until just mixed, then add the flour and melted butter. Stir well until thickened and set aside for a few minutes.

Spoon very small quantities of the mixture – about 1½ teaspoons (7.5 ml) – in batches of 6 on to a non-stick baking sheet spacing them out well. Using the back of the spoon, spread out very thinly in a circular movement to make circles 4 in (10 cm) in diameter.

Bake in the oven for 5–6 minutes, until the edges are tinged with brown and the surface a somewhat patchy light gold. Remove the baking sheet from the oven and quickly curl up each circle to form a tube, overlapping the edges. Arrange the galettes join sides down on a platter as shown in the picture, with the roasted coconut scattered in between.

If the sorbet was frozen in a mould, quickly dip it into hot water and turn out. Place the sorbet on a glass dish. Serve with the coconut and galettes.

POACHED PEARS WITH LOTUS SEEDS

illustrated on pages 122–123

The crunchy texture of lotus seeds, particularly associated with Chinese cuisine, contrasts excitingly with the smoothness of the pears.

◆

SERVES 8

8 small comice pears, peeled and cored, tops reserved and bases levelled
2 oz (60 g) dry lotus seeds, soaked in water for 1 hour
3 tablespoons (45 ml) clear honey
3–4 slices root ginger

◆

Put the lotus seeds, honey and ¾ pint (450 ml) of water into a saucepan. Bring to the boil, then simmer for 30 minutes until the seeds are still intact, but softened.

Remove half the seeds, using a slotted spoon, and process to a paste with 1 tablespoon of the honeyed water in a food processor, or use a potato masher. Use to fill the cavity of each pear.

Replace the tops on the pears and place in a saucepan with the remaining honeyed water and lotus seeds. Add the ginger and a further ¼ pint (150 ml) water, bring to the boil and simmer for about 15 minutes.

Remove the ginger slices, then arrange the pears on a serving dish with the lotus seeds scattered around them. Serve hot or chilled.

LATTICE
LAYERS WITH FRUIT
illustrated on pages 122–123

The wun-tun pastry is available fresh daily from Chinese food shops, or you can make your own (p. 24). The latticed squares may be assembled and fried in advance, then allowed to cool completely and stored in an airtight tin, in layers separated by greaseproof paper, a day before.

◆

SERVES 8

6 oz (180 g) wun-tun pastry in 3-in (7.5-cm) squares (allow 3 squares per person)
1 egg, beaten
a little plain flour for dusting
2½–3 lb (1.2–1.4 kg) raspberries
4 oz (120 g) almonds, roasted and ground
2 oz (60 g) demerara or icing sugar

for deep-frying
1 pint (600 ml) corn oil

◆

Cut each wun-tun pastry square into 4 equal strips. On a floured surface, lay 4 pastry strips horizontally, parallel to each other, ¼ in (6 mm) apart. Brush a further 4 pastry strips lightly with egg and arrange them vertically in the same way, weaving them in and out of the horizontal strips or lay on top, if easier, so that they adhere and form a latticed square, with all the edges overhanging. As each square is woven, carefully transfer it to a light floured board or work surface. Continue until you have 24 latticed squares.

Heat the oil to 300°F (150°C) in a large shallow frying pan, add the latticed squares one at a time and fry very briefly, removing as soon as the pastry is puffed and golden, and transfer to kitchen paper to drain. Arrange 8 latticed squares on a large serving dish as a base, then spoon over half the raspberries in a layer. Arrange a further 8 latticed squares on top, followed by the remaining raspberries. Finish with a final layer of latticed squares and sprinkle the top with the almonds mixed with the sugar.

NECTARINES
WITH POACHED MERINGUE
illustrated on pages 122–123

Firm, smooth-skinned nectarines make an especially good base for the meringue, but skinned fresh peaches could be used if nectarines are unavailable.

◆

SERVES 8

8 large firm, ripe nectarines
2 tablespoons (30 ml) clear honey
3 egg whites
a pinch of salt
1 pint (600 ml) milk

for the serving sauce
8 oz (240 g) blackberries
3 tablespoons (45 ml) caster sugar

for the decoration
1 lb (480 g) ripe blackberries and a few blackberry leaves if possible

◆

Halve the nectarines, remove the stones and hollow out the centres slightly. Put the honey in a saucepan with 1 pint (600 ml) water and bring to the boil. Add the nectarines and return to the boil, then simmer for 5–6 minutes until tender but still firm. Remove from the pan and leave to cool.

Whisk the egg whites with the salt until they stand in peaks.

Heat the milk in a saucepan to a very gentle simmer. Take a heaped dessertspoonful of the beaten egg and round the surface with another spoon. Slip into the milk, a few at a time, and poach very gently for 1 minute. Turn very carefully with a slotted spoon and poach for a further 1 minute. Drain on kitchen paper, then put a meringue into each nectarine half, arranged on a serving platter, trimming a little where necessary.

To make the sauce, bring the blackberries, 3 fl oz (90 ml) water and the sugar to the boil, then simmer for 5 minutes. Press through a sieve.

Decorate the nectarine meringues with 6 blackberries, and accompany with the sauce in a jug.

129

SAUCES AND DIPS

Most Chinese like to serve something spicy with their food to stimulate the appetite and a traditional dinner service will always include a dish for sauce. Chilli and soy sauce – both straight from the bottle – will generally be offered at home and in restaurants too; the equivalent of the Western bottle of ketchup and just as imaginative!

Surely the carefully prepared dishes deserve something better and, although each one is carefully seasoned to bring out its own particular taste and character, a well-chosen sauce can certainly be complementary. I like to add the freshness of radish, ginger, coriander or Spanish onion, all of which combine well with basic ingredients to add to the interest.

Most commonly seen are probably spring onion and ginger in soy sauce, which can be served with steamed chicken or fish, and the classical spicy salt dip which may accompany both steamed and deep-fried chicken. You may well find Aromatic Duck and Lamb with Lettuce Leaf Wrap more exciting with Szechuan sauce. Try Prawn Fingers in their delicate, crispy pastry with savoury plum or sweet and chilli sauce, or Banana Fish Fritters with white radish sauce. The subtle flavour of deep-fried Stuffed Chicken or succulent Braised Shin of Beef may be highlighted with mustard sauce. Monkfish in its turn will enjoy the company of a sauce of fresh herbs.

Of course, these accompaniments need not be relegated to Chinese dishes alone; they could well be served with any food – whatever its country of origin.

SWEET AND CHILLI SAUCE

This is a sauce basic to Chinese cuisine, as you can see from the recipes in the body of the book. It can be used as a dipping sauce with such dishes as Pacific Prawns with French Bean Bales, Sesame Prawn Toast, or Deep-Fried Wun-Tun.

2 teaspoons (10 ml) corn oil
½ fresh chilli, thinly sliced
2 tablespoons (30 ml) tomato ketchup
2 teaspoons (10 ml) light soy sauce
2 teaspoons (10 ml) red wine vinegar
1 teaspoon (5 ml) sugar
1 clove garlic, crushed

Heat the oil in a small frying pan, add the garlic and chilli and fry gently for about 1 minute. Add all the remaining ingredients and stir well to blend. A commercially bottled version is also available.

SZECHUAN SAUCE

This nutty, garlicky accent would complent dishes like Sesame Chicken Bâtons, Mixed Seafood with Vegetables, and Stuffed Tofu Puffs.

1½ teaspoons (7.5 ml) corn oil
1 tablespoon (15 ml) light soy sauce
1 tablespoon (15 ml) white wine vinegar
¼ teaspoon sesame oil
1 teaspoon (5 ml) sesame paste
1 teaspoon (5 ml) chilli bean sauce
1½ teaspoons (7.5 ml) water
1 clove garlic, crushed
1 spring onion, finely chopped

Heat the oil in a small saucepan, then add all the remaining ingredients in the listed order and bring gently to the boil.

MUSTARD SAUCE

*This warm, green-flecked sauce is very versatile,
going well with such diverse tastes as Deep-Fried
Stuffed Chicken, Braised Shin of Beef or Tofu with
Vegetables.*

◆

MAKES ABOUT 3 TABLESPOONS (45 ML)8

1 tablespoon (15 ml) corn oil
2 tablespoons (30 ml) light soy sauce
1 tablespoon (15 ml) white wine vinegar
1½ teaspoons (7.5 ml) made mustard
½ teaspoon sugar
1 tablespoon (15 ml) mustard and cress

◆

Heat the oil in a small saucepan over a moderate heat,
add all the ingredients and blend well. Heat through for
1 minute, then stir in the mustard and cress.

SPRING ONION
AND GINGER SAUCE

*Try this sauce with vegetables – for example:
Stuffed Brussels Sprouts, Spinach and Seafood Rolls,
or Party Vegetables.*

◆

1 tablespoon (15 ml) corn oil
2 spring onions, finely shredded
2 slices root ginger, finely shredded
1½ tablespoons (22.5 ml) dark soy sauce
sugar

◆

Heat the oil in a frying pan, add the onion and ginger
and fry gently for 1 minute. Add the soy sauce and a
little sugar to taste and fry for a further 1–2 minutes.

WHITE RADISH SAUCE

*Sharp and cleansing, this is especially flavourful with
Banana Fish Fritters, Grilled Mackerel with Black
Soya Beans, and Lobster with Monkfish.*

◆

1 tablespoon (15 ml) dark soy sauce
2 tablepoons (30 ml) takara mirin (Japanese seasoning)
1 teaspoon (5 ml) grated root ginger
1 tablespoon (15 ml) grated white radish

◆

Put the soy sauce and takara mirin into a small
saucepan with 2 tablespoons (30 ml) water. Bring to the
boil, then add the ginger and allow to infuse. Turn off
the heat, add the radish, and blend well.

SAVOURY PLUM SAUCE

*This traditional sauce is used classically with Peking
Duck, but also goes well with dishes like Half
Moons and Butterflies, and Tofu Triangles.*

◆

1 tablespoon (15 ml) corn oil
1½ teaspoons (7.5 ml) finely shredded ginger
2 tablespoons (30 ml) plum sauce
1 tablespoon (15 ml) oyster sauce
1 tablespoon (15 ml) Shaoshing wine
white pepper

◆

Heat the oil in a small saucepan over a moderate heat,
add the ginger and fry for 30 seconds, then add all the
remaining ingredients and heat through for 1 minute.

SWEET BEAN SAUCE

This is a classic accompaniment to poultry dishes such as Chicken and Asparagus Rolls, Aromatic Duck and Lamb with Lettuce Leaf Wrap, and Chicken Squares.

◆

1 tablespoon (15 ml) corn oil
2 cloves garlic, crushed
2 × 2-in (5-cm) cubes root ginger, crushed
1 tablespoon (15 ml) crushed yellow bean paste
1 tablespoon (15 ml) light soy sauce
2 teaspoons (10 ml) sugar

◆

Heat the oil in a small saucepan over a moderate heat, then add remaining ingredients in the listed order.

FISH SAUCE

This somewhat salty, fishy condiment perks up vegetables and fish dishes, including Onion Pasties, Steamed Stripy Tofu, and Scallops Shanghai-style.

◆

1 teaspoon (5 ml) corn oil
½ teaspoon fish sauce delicacy
1 tablespoon (15 ml) white wine vinegar
2 teaspoons (10 ml) light soy sauce
1 teaspoon (5 ml) sugar

Heat the oil in a small saucepan over a moderate heat. Stir in all the remaining ingredients and let them blend well together for a minute or so.

GINGER AND VINEGAR SAUCE

A very piquant accompaniment to dishes like Shark Fin Soup, Chicken Squares, or Salmon Ring With Asparagus.

◆

1 tablespoon (15 ml) root ginger, finely shredded
3 tablespoons (45 ml) red wine vinegar
salt

◆

Mix the ginger and vinegar in a small bowl, season with salt to taste and leave to stand for about 2 hours.

FRESH HERB SAUCE

Chicken and vegetables go particularly well with this tangy but slightly sweet dressing. Try it with Chicken Medallions, Steamed Tofu Hearts, or Bang-Bang Chicken.

◆

1 tablespoon (15 ml) corn oil
1 tablespoon (15 ml) Spanish onion, very finely sliced
½ fresh chilli, finely shredded
1½ teaspoons (7.5 ml) light soy sauce
juice of ½ lemon
½ teaspoon sugar
½ teaspoon cornflour mixed with 1 tablespoon (15 ml) water
salt and white pepper
1 tablespoon (15 ml) finely chopped coriander

◆

Heat the oil in a small saucepan over a moderate heat, add the onion and chilli and fry gently just to soften. Add the soy sauce, lemon juice, sugar and 1 tablespoon (15 ml) water and stir-fry briefly, then stir in the cornflour mixture and season to taste with salt and pepper. Turn off the heat and stir in the coriander.

SPICY SALT DIP

This is a simple but very classic dip for finger food and other titbits, such as Simple Baked Chicken, Smoked Quail and Frog's Legs with Plum Sauce.

◆

2 teaspoons (10 ml) salt
¼ teaspoon 5-spice powder
a pinch of freshly ground black pepper

◆

Fry the salt without any oil in a small frying pan over a moderate to high heat. Add the 5-spice powder and pepper and fry for a further 2 minutes, stirring.

❖

PEPPER AND SALT DIP

This may seem an obvious recipe, but a simple dip such as this is often put on the table for dishes like Crispy Crab Claws, Spinach and Seafood Rolls or Mange-tout and Cucumber Rolls.

◆

1½ teaspoons (7.5 ml) salt
½ teaspoon freshly ground black pepper

◆

Fry the salt without any oil in a small frying pan over a moderate to high heat for 2 minutes. Add the pepper and fry for a further 2 minutes, stirring.

❖

PEANUT SAUCE

This sauce has become identified with Malaysian cooking but is popular in China and other Oriental countries. It is used for dipping with Lamb Skewers, Bite-Size Chicken Wings and Korean Pork.

◆

6 oz (180 g) unshelled peanuts
3 oz (90 g) Spanish onion, finely chopped
1 large clove garlic, crushed
¾ tablespoon (12 ml) dark soy sauce
1 tablespoon (15 ml) Sweet and Chilli Sauce (p. 130)
1 tablespoon (15 ml) corn oil
pinch of salt
1½ teaspoons (7.5 ml) sugar
¼ teaspoon sesame oil

◆

Shell the peanuts and remove their skins, which will leave 4 oz (120 g) nuts. Roast then for 7–8 minutes on a baking tray in a hot oven 425°F (220°C, gas mark 7). Allow to cool, then blend to a slightly sticky paste in a food processor. Transfer the paste to a bowl. Blend the onions with the garlic and 1½ teaspoons (7.5 ml) water to a watery paste. Add to the peanut paste and mix well.

Transfer the mixture to a heated saucepan and cook over a moderate heat, stirring constantly, for 5 minutes, until most of the water has evaporated. Then add the soy sauce, sweet chilli sauce, corn oil, salt, sugar and ¼ pint (150 ml) hot water. Blend well, then add the sesame oil. Continue to cook over a low heat for about 20 minutes until the sauce is reduced to about ¼ pint (150 ml). If it seems rather thick, add a little more water.

❖

133

GARNISHES

6

7

8

9

10

11

12

13

14

15

16

135

PREPARATION TECHNIQUES

CUTTING INTO STRIPS

This takes the slicing process one stage further. The slices of food are cut crossways into smaller pieces of even thickness, as the recipe requires. Don't worry too much about very precise dimensions – they are not important, and measurements are only given as an indication of size relative to cooking time.

◆

DICING

Strips of food are cut crossways into small cubes of more or less uniform size.

◆

MINCING

Place the diced meat, poultry or fish on a board and chop it, using either a chopper or meat cleaver. Turn it over on the blade of the cleaver and chop again, until all the pieces are well separated. Repeat until you have a coarse mince. Firm meat, such as beef, will obviously require more chopping than chicken or fish. A mincer will not give satisfactory results for Chinese cooking, nor always will a food processor. See individual recipes for guidance on use of a food processor.

◆

SCORING

Scoring the surface of meat and fish enables it to cook more quickly and absorb flavour, particularly when its texture is dense, as in the case of squid or kidney, for instance. It can also have a decorative effect, enhancing the appearance of the finished dish. Score the meat or fish before it is cut into bite-sized pieces, making superficial parallel cuts at even intervals over the surface area. Hold the knife at an angle so it can be controlled more easily.

◆

SLICING

Since Chinese food is customarily eaten with chopsticks, it must be offered in small, manageable pieces. The method of slicing ingredients in preparation for cooking is very important, as it affects both flavour and texture. Beef, for example, must be cut *across* the grain so that it remains tender, while in some instances food is cut *along* the grain so that it holds its shape and remains firms after cooking. If meat is sliced at an angle, it can more easily be cut into thin, bite-sized pieces and will have a finer texture.

The Chinese use angled cuts for vegetables too, tapering them for elegance and to show them to best advantage. When meat and vegetables feature together in a dish, they should be cut into pieces of similar size; this is of particular importance in stir-frying, to ensure that they cook evenly, in the same length of time. A razor-sharp knife is essential for the preparation of meat and vegetables.

COOKING METHODS

Whereas much European cooking is done in the oven, Chinese dishes are usually cooked on top of the stove, where it is certainly easier to supervize their progress.

BRAISING

'Red' braising, involving the use Szechuan peppercorns and star anise, is common in Chinese cuisine, and is usually used for cooking meat. As in Western cooking, the ingredients are first fried in oil to seal in the juices, give flavour and colour to the meat and contribute to the rich, earthy appearance of the finished dish.

Long slow cooking ensures that meat is really tender and does not shrink too much. If the dish is cooked a day in advance, the meat will have time to absorb the flavour of the braising sauce. To achieve balance and texture, the Chinese like to serve braised dishes with something crisper or firmer, perhaps a dish of crunchy vegetables which would also provide colour contrast.

Braising is a highly convenient method for dinner party cooking, leaving the cook time to attend to other dishes requiring last minute attention.

◆

DEEP-FRYING

The wok or deep-fryer should be half full of oil, preheated to the specified temperature, so that it sizzles when a piece of food is added. Watch for changes in texture and colour as the food cooks, adjusting the heat and length of cooking time accordingly, if necessary. Test by tasting. Raw ingredients will of course need longer frying at a lower temperature than food that is already partly cooked. Deep frying will cause meat or fish to firm up and seal quickly as it makes contact with oil at the correct temperature, and the coating of the food will become attractively crisp. Thorough draining in a sieve and on absorbent paper is essential after deep-frying, to remove all traces of oiliness from the food.

The oil can become cloudy if it is not heated to a

136

sufficiently high temperature. Should this happen, it should be allowed to settle, then strained through muslin and skimmed, when it will be clear and ready for use again.

Various kinds of oil are suitable for deep-frying. I like to use corn oil, for its unobstrusive flavour, although many Chinese prefer peanut oil.

ROASTING

Oven-roasting is the method least practised by Chinese cooks; it is reserved for some Cantonese and Pekinese dishes. In Chinese cuisine the meat or poultry is either marinated or brushed with a coating sauce before roasting, then hung from a hook in the top of the oven, or roasted on a rack. Sometimes the roasting method is used just to finish a dish that has already been cooked. Unlike Western roasting the food is not put into pan of fat, indeed there is no contact with fat or oil and consequently no basting to be done.

Chinese roast poultry is chopped through the bones into smallish pieces and other roast meat is carved into slices before being served with accompanying dishes.

RUNNING THROUGH THE OIL

Commercially-prepared Chinese food is almost invariably cooked in two stages, and this is often done at home too. The initial brief deep-frying is known as 'running through the oil', involving 30 seconds' cooking at a temperature of 300–350°F (120–180°C). This seals the ingredients, preventing them from breaking up, and giving a clean, neat finish to the dish, with no seeping juices to spoil its appearance. This preliminary brief frying also reduces the length of stir-frying in the second stage. No additional oil is needed in the second stage and although the food has been fried twice, it will not be at all greasy. You may find it easier to use a deep fryer for the first stage, and a wok for the second, to avoid having to pour away the hot oil used for the preliminary frying, which can be awkward and messy. After frying, the food must be drained in a wire sieve, then on absorbent paper if necessary.

SMOKING

In the West, smoking is associated with drying and curing food, and can take a long time. In Chinese cuisine ingredients to be smoked will usually have been pre-cooked; a very brief smoking gives a final touch in terms of additional flavour and aroma to food which is already dark in colour. The food to be smoked is set on a rack in a covered wok at the bottom of which are placed 2

tablespoons of tea leaves and a teaspoon of sugar. The wok is heated for 1–2 minutes over a high temperature and the smoking process is then completed.

STEAMING

Steaming is not only comparatively speedy, but ensures that food retains its natural colour and flavour and is moist, delicate-textured and easily digested. Steamed dishes make a good contrast with richer fried, braised or roast dishes. Steaming is a particularly suitable method for cooking vegetables, fish, seafood and dumplings.

Steamed food is cooked at a constant high temperature, either in a bamboo steamer or on a dish placed over a steaming rack in a wok covered with a lid. Apart from checking that the water level remains just beneath that of the rack or bamboo steamer, the actual steaming process requires no attention, in contrast to stir-frying.

STIR-FRYING

This method, characteristically Chinese, is the one perhaps most often associated with Chinese cuisine. There are 4 distinct stages. First the flavouring (e.g. garlic and ginger) is fried in hot oil. Next the vegetables are briefly fried, then removed and set aside. Then the meat or seafood is added to the pan and fried quickly. Finally the vegetables are returned to the pan and all the ingredients stir-fried together briefly. Since the ingredients are cut into bite-sized pieces, only this very short cooking time is needed. All the ingredients should be stirred constantly, maintaining an even contact with the heat. Stirring is, of course, made easier by the wok's curved shape. The oil must be very hot to prevent the food from sticking to the pan and to ensure that the outside of meat is sealed.

Exact timing is difficult to determine. I have given general indications, as even regulating the heat can vary. Many stir-fry dishes can be cooked in 3–4 minutes. Be guided by changes in colour and texture, and test by tasting. Gas, which has the advantage of virtually instant control, is undoubtedly more convenient for stir-frying. If you are using electricity, remove the pan from contact with the heat while you adjust the temperature. In some cases, whether you cook by gas or electricity, you may need to place the wok on a stand (see Cooking Utensils).

Stir-fried food should be immediately transferred to a heated serving dish and served at once, or kept warm briefly in a hot oven. Reheating stir-fried food is possible in a microwave oven, but this would take too long in a conventional oven and would result in overcooking.

137

UTENSILS

BAMBOO STEAMER

This traditional piece of Chinese kitchen equipment comes in various sizes, with room for a dish inside. A steaming rack in a wok with a lid serves the same purpose, but the steamer is both more attractive and authentic.

◆

CHOPSTICKS

Made of plastic, plain or lacquered wood, ivory or bamboo. The bamboo type are useful in cooking as well as for eating, particularly in deep-frying.

◆

CLEAVER

These come in different sizes, the largest being three times the size of the smallest. Ideally the largest are best for chopping, the smaller for slicing. If you are buying just one, compromise on an all-purpose medium cleaver.

◆

STRAINER

Traditional Chinese strainers are flatter than the European variety and are attractive objects in themselves. They are used to remove food that is deep-fried or boiled.

◆

WOK

The wok performs many functions – stir-frying, boiling, braising, deep-frying – and even steaming, in the absence of a bamboo steamer. It can be used for either large or small amounts. The bottom of the wok is traditionally rounded, and the edges curved to make stirring easier. This also allows plenty of room for the hot oil, minimizing the danger of spillage. Some woks are made of stainless steel and some are non-stick, but the most common variety is made of mild steel and needs light oiling when not in use to prevent rusting. Generally a wok comes with a lid, but, if not, it is advisable to buy one.

If your hob will not accommodate a wok happily, buy an open wire ring to stand it on. Avoid solid rings, even perforated ones, as air cannot circulate freely round them, and damage may result.

Seasoning a wok is rather like a launching! In the case of the steel type, wash off the protective sealing, but avoid using an abrasive pad as this will damage the surface. Heat the wok to a high temperature, then add a little oil, put in 2 pieces of garlic and ginger and swirl the oil around so that it covers the entire surface. Turn off the heat, discard the flavourings and wipe the wok with absorbent kitchen paper, leaving a film of grease. Wash before use.

138

MENU SUGGESTIONS

BUFFET FOR 30

Entertaining on this scale requires considerable planning and advance work. You should allow 2–3 days for shopping and preparation. Serve a fruity, crisp white wine, such as a Sancerre from the Loire region, or a well-chilled, good-quality rosé.

You should aim to give your guests a choice of 5–6 dishes, or limit the range of choice and increase the quantities – up to 3 times if they are gourmands as well as gourmets.

Spare Ribs
Prawn Balls with Mock Seaweed
Chicken Medallions
Coral and Pearl Butterfly Prawns

Mixed Seafood and Vegetables with Shar-Shiu Pork
Beribboned Beef
Stuffed Okra with Cucumber and Mange-tout
Shell Pasta with Chicken
Fried Rice with Mushrooms

Melon and Ginger Sorbet Plus
Nectarines with Poached Meringue and Blackberry
Sauce

Bite-sized Chicken Wings
Spicy Mussels

Crunchy Vegetables
Grilled Mackerel with Black Soya Beans
Lamb Balls with Mint
Crabmeat with Lettuce
Eight Jewel Rice

Lattice Layers with Fruit

SUNDAY LUNCH FOR 20

Like the larger buffet, this occasion will demand advance planning. I have kept the number of first courses to two or three and the main courses to three or four dishes. After one of these Sunday treats, a simple dessert of fresh fruit would refresh the guests.

Onion Circlets. To serve with aperitifs

Spinach Fish Soup (in double quantity)
Crispy Crab Claws (at least 1 per person)

Lobster with Monkfish (in double quantity)
Beef Noodles with Chilli Bean Sauce (in triple quantity)
Stir-fried Vegetables (such as French beans, mange-
tout, broccoli, allowing 1 lb (480 g) of each)

◆

Chicken Parcels
Crabmeat and Rice Balls
Coral and Pearl Butterfly Prawns

Stuffed Baby Squids (one per person)
Beribboned Spicy Beef (double the given amount)
Aubergine and Pork Muffins (one per person)
Simple Fried Rice (double the given amount)

DINNER FOR 8

*Some work during the dinner itself is unavoidable, but
with planning it can be kept to a minimum, and most
of it can be done in advance. Any marinating should be
done earlier and vegetables may be prepared
beforehand, then kept wrapped in clingfilm in the
refrigerator. Rice may be cooked ahead and reheated.
Two of the suggested menus are for non-meat eaters.*

Shell Pasta with Chicken
Crunchy Vegetable Stir-fry

Tofu with Vegetables
Beef in Oyster Sauce
Peking Duck and Mandarin Pancakes

◆

Mock Squid Decked with Seaweed
Chicken Medallions

Braised Shin of Beef
Bean Sprouts with Fresh Herbs
Salted Prawns with Chilli
Fried Rice with Mushrooms

◆

Bang Bang Chicken
Deep-Fried Wun Tun

Half Moons and Butterflies

Pomegranate Duck
Sizzling Prawns with Crisped Rice
Beef Noodles with Bean Sprouts

◆

Lamb Balls with Mint
Frogs' Legs with Plum Sauce
Prawn Fingers

Lobster with Monkfish
Stir-fried Chicken, Prawns and Broad Beans

Fried Noodles Singapore Style

Vegetarian Menus

Hot and Sour Soup
Cucumber Egg Cups (substitute vegetable stock)
Tofu with Vegetables (omit streaky bacon; use
vegetable)

Fried Rice with Celery
Shell Pasta (omit chicken)

◆

Tofu Triangles (omit bacon)
Onion Circlets
Carrot Hearts

Tofu and Spinach Island (vegetable stock; omit ham
from garnish)
Bean Sprouts with Fresh Herbs
Fried Rice with Mushrooms

INFORMAL SUPPER FOR 4–6

*These suggested menus can be prepared at relatively
short notice. When time is short, cut down on the
number of dishes and increase the quantities instead.*

Sesame Prawn Toast

Chicken with Almonds
Bean Sprouts and Fresh Herbs
Beef and Spring Onion Fried Rice

◆

Chicken or Lamb Skewers

Braised Duck with Chestnuts
Fried Rice with Celery

139

INGREDIENTS

Many Chinese cooking and serving sauces will keep indefinitely at room temperature. Tinned ingredients, once opened, should be transferred to screwtop jars for storing, in the refrigerator if necessary.

140

BA-CHOY

A popular Chinese leafy vegetable with white stems and green leaves. The size of the plant determines the leaf colour, the larger ones being darker, stronger and more fibrous. Ba-choy can be stir-fried, steamed or braised.

CELLOPHANE TRANSPARENT NOODLES

Made from mung beans and water, these fine white noodles have a very light texture which surpasses any other type. They come in tied bundles of various sizes and require soaking before cooking, unless they are to be deep-fried.

CHILLI BEAN SAUCE

Also known as Szechuan chilli paste, this is made from chillies, salted black beans, soy sauce, garlic and peanut oil. It is medium to dark brown, thick and coarse-textured, with a hot, slightly nutty taste. It can be used as a dipping sauce or in cooking and is sold in screwtop jars.

CHINESE CHIVES

This larger version of English chives has dark emerald green and straight – not tapering – leaves. They have a sweet, mild flavour and make a good garnish. If served as a vegetable they should be only lightly cooked so that they remain crunchy. Available in season from Chinese grocers or select greengrocers.

CHINESE FISH CAKE

This is sold in bars which are smooth and yellow, looking rather like gold ingots. It has a springy texture and is always cut into slices or strips for use in cooking. It freezes well.

CHINESE MUSHROOMS

This dried black edible fungus is expensive but has a pronounced, individual flavour. Thickness determines quality and those with mottled skins are to be preferred. They require presoaking and the stems must be discarded.

CHINESE RED VINEGAR

Dark reddish-brown, but not sharp, this is frequently used as a dip, and sometimes in cooking. It is sold bottled.

CHINESE SLAB SUGAR

This is made from unrefined sugar and has a slight aroma of coffee. It is sold in rectangles which must be broken into smaller pieces with a cleaver. It is used in braised dishes.

CHINESE WIND-DRIED SAUSAGE

The only kind of Chinese sausage, this is similar to salami, with a sweetish flavour, and is made of pork, pork liver or beef. As it is quite rich it should be used only in small quantities. It is best steamed before it is added to other ingredients. Steaming it over rice will give the rice flavour. It should be hung in an airy place or stored in the refrigerator.

CRUSHED YELLOW BEAN PASTE

This purée of fermented yellow beans, wheat flour, salt and water is used for cooking rather than as a serving sauce. It gives an authentic Chinese flavour to stir-fried dishes, but should be used sparingly as it is strong-flavoured. It is sold in tins.

DRY RICE STICKS

These are thin, white, wiry noodles made from rice flour and water. They are sold in long rectangular layers, and become semi-translucent when cooked. They are used in soups and fried dishes and require little cooking.

FIVE-SPICE POWDER

A mixture of ground star anise, Szechuan peppercorns, cloves, Chinese cinnamon and fennel seeds. It can be bought ready-made or prepared at home. It has a powerful aroma, with a hint of aniseed, and should be used sparingly in braising sauces.

FISH SAUCE DELICACY

Made from dried shrimps, onions, chillies and vegetable oil, this is a deep reddish-brown with a quite pronounced fishy taste. It is used as a serving or dipping sauce and is sold in bottles.

HOISIN SAUCE

Also known as barbecue sauce, hoisin sauce is made from soy sauce, garlic, sugar, salt, red bean paste and soya bean flour. It is dark brown and can be thinned with water and sesame oil to give a lighter texture. It is available in bottles and tins.

LOTUS ROOT, SEEDS AND LEAF

The *root* is beige-coloured, fibrous and full of holes. It is available fresh or tinned. The fresh variety is imported and infinitely preferable. It can be eaten raw or cut into chunks and used in soups, braised and stir-fried dishes, imparting a sweet taste.

The *seeds* are available dried (in which case they need presoaking) or tinned. When cooked they separate into 2 equal halves, with a central green core. They are used in savoury or sweet dishes.

The *leaf* is large and always sold dried, requiring pre-soaking. It is used as a wrapping for food and has a distinctive flavour.

OCEAN STICKS

Sometimes called crab sticks, these are made of sweet, stranded fish flesh tinted with red food colouring. They are sold frozen, individually wrapped and pre-cooked.

PLUM SAUCE

Made from yellow plums, sugar, water, garlic and chilli, plum sauce is translucent and thick, with a spicy but not sharp flavour. It is used for both cooking and serving.

◆

RED BEANS

These medium, dullish red beans, high in protein, are available dried. They are mostly used in desserts.

RED FERMENTED BEANCURD

Made from fermented fresh beancurd, salt and rice wine, with a strong flavour, this is used mostly in cooking. It comes in squares in tins or jars.

◆

RICE VINEGAR

Distilled from rice and water, this is pale golden, not unlike white wine vinegar. It is used in cooking and for adding to dips. It is sold in screwtop bottles.

◆

SHAOSHING WINE

Fermented from glutinous rice and yeast, with a rich golden colour, this is quite inexpensive and is widely used in Chinese cooking. It is not unlike medium dry sherry.

◆

SHARK FIN

This is cured from more than one species of shark, and is very expensive. It is virtually tasteless but is prized for its unique needle-like structure and gleaming, transparent appearance. A traditional whole fin requires 3 days' preparation and needs to be served to large numbers to justify its use. The dried processed variety is cheaper and easier to use.

◆

SNOW EAR OR SILVER EAR

This edible pale yellowish-white fungus is sold dried and must be soaked before use. It is virtually tasteless but is recommended for its texture. It can be used in savoury dishes, but features more often in Chinese desserts.

◆

SOY SAUCE (LIGHT AND DARK)

Soy sauce is made from soya beans, wheat, salt and sugar and is fermented with yeast. Both types are brown, with a pronounced salty taste. Dark soy sauce is thicker, more matured and less salty than the light variety. Soy sauce is used both in cooking and as a serving sauce. It is generally sold in bottles, sometimes in tins.

◆

SPRING ROLL PAPER

A paper-thin pastry made of flour and water, off-white in colour, this is available frozen from Chinese or Oriental grocers, in large or small sheets. It is best known for spring rolls, but can be used to wrap any food which is then deep-fried until crisp. It can be stored in the refrigerator, the wrapper well-sealed to prevent drying out.

STAR ANISE

This dark-brown spice is star-shaped with a pungent aniseed taste. It can be used ground or whole and is an essential ingredient in braising sauces.

◆

SWEET AND CHILLI SAUCE

Made from red chillies, sugar, vinegar and salt, sweet and chilli sauce is orange-red and attractively translucent. It is very hot and piquant and is good with hot or cold roast meat and as a dipping sauce for hors d'oeuvres. It should be used sparingly. It is sold in screwtop bottles.

◆

SWEET BEAN PASTE

Made from puréed sweet and red beans, this very dark red, thick, very sweet paste is used as a filling for pastries and traditional Chinese wedding cakes. It is sold in tins.

◆

SZECHUAN PEPPERCORNS

These small peppercorns are reddish-brown and have a spicy bouquet. They can be used ground or whole and are often combined with star anise.

◆

SZECHUAN PRESERVED CABBAGE

Misleadingly named, this is a brownish-green root vegetable, a type of mustard. It is sold in tins or earthenware jars, pickled in chilli powder and salt. It must be rinsed before use and has a strong flavour, popular in Chinese cooking. It is used mainly in stir-fried and steamed dishes.

◆

TAKA MIRIN

This Japanese flavouring is sweetish, syrupy and low in alcohol. It has a quite individual taste and is not to be confused with Chinese cooking wine.

◆

TARO

A dark greyish-brown root vegetable with a fibrous skin and off-white flesh, rather like a potato in texture. It is steamed, then eaten cold, dipped in syrup.

◆

WHITE RADISH OR CHINESE RADISH

A long white root vegetable, usually weighing 8 oz–1 lb (240–480 g) each. It is versatile and can be used in cooked dishes, in pickles and preserves, and as a garnish.

◆

WOOD EAR

This edible black fungus has a unique flavour and springy texture. It is sold dried and must be soaked before use.

141

INDEX

144

CW00346390

barbecue

barbecue

FROM SKEWERED PRAWNS TO HOT BEEF SATAYS

CLARE FERGUSON

jacqui
small

First published in 2007 by Jacqui Small,
an imprint of Aurum Press,
25 Bedford Avenue, London WC1B 3AT

Publisher   Jacqui Small
Editorial Manager Kate John
Art Director   Ashley Western
Photography   Jeremy Hopley and Martin Brigdale
Food Stylist   Clare Ferguson
Editor   Madeline Weston
Production   Peter Colley

ISBN: 978 1 903221 79 2

2009 2008 2007

10 9 8 7 6 5 4 3 2 1

Printed in China

contents

INTRODUCTION

Many of my happiest childhood memories involve food, drink and driftwood fires out of doors. Such activities still delight me: fresh air makes our eyes sparkle, gives edge to our appetites, gets our hearts racing.

Barbecues, by their very nature, involve primal sensations: heat, light, the gorgeous smell of sizzling snacks. While the charcoal progresses from sparks and flames to a steady ash-covered glow (the correct stage to barbecue) we can assemble ingredients, break bread, mix a dressing, pour drinks, hand out nibbles. Some people may admire the view, take a wander, bounce a ball, gather berries, paddle in the surf, or strum a guitar. Being away from our usual preoccupations means feeling part of a wider world than that of the kitchen and dining table ... enjoying intriguing hot, hissing sounds and the intense tastes of freshly cooked foods.

Picnicking and barbecuing are democratic activities. Tiny tots can gather flat stones, grandparents arrange driftwood piles, laconic teens and shy guests uncork wine, toss salads. Husbands or lovers may excel at mixing cocktails or marinating the chicken. Aunties can help by arranging umbrellas and cushions. Laughter, story-telling, charades, volleyball, are often enjoyable outcomes of time spent around the barbecue. Inhibitions vanish and we relax. Autumn or spring barbecues, perfect times for natural foraging (blackberries, watercress, fairy-ring or cep mushrooms, wild garlic leaves) may be just as successful as summer ones. Even winter barbecues can be exhilarating with tented shelters and vacuum flasks of hot soup or mulled wine.

Sand in the sandwiches, slugs in the salad, lukewarm champagne and charred sausages are a thing of the past: today's barbecue-givers and party-lovers enjoy simplicity and easy, often ethnic, foods as well as interesting drinks. Disasters can be avoided with a bit of clever planning.

Meat, fish or poultry brochettes in their basic state; ready-made marinades, dressings and toppings to add on site; crusty fresh bread, fresh fruits, seasonal fresh vegetables; local pastry specialities, regional cheeses: these typify a successful barbecue menu. And not everything needs to be cooked: raw can be best.

Now that multi-cultural weekday meals are the norm (tzatziki, crudités, chilli con carne, mousse) there's every reason to enjoy French-style radishes, bruschetta, game burgers then Munster cheese with pears. Throw away the rule book: let creativity flourish. Barbecues can provide real gaiety whether they take place in the back garden, on a roof terrace, beside river, lake or beach or during a school fête. Lift your spirits and have some convivial, *al fresco* fun with family and friends.

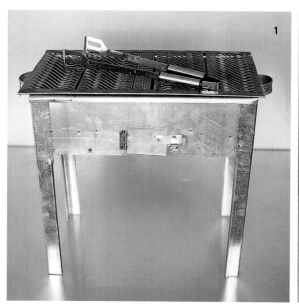
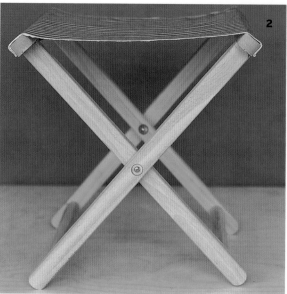

EQUIPMENT

Enjoyable barbecues don't necessarily require costly, complicated gear. Plastic hampers and insulated cool boxes work just as well as wicker-work hampers and silver ice buckets. Cardboard bottle carriers do the same job as the antique metal variety. Foil-tray disposables or a galvanised iron fold-up barbecue or a handsome French iron barbecue rack with legs and a handle can work just as efficiently as a glamorous domed chrome and enamel gas-fired contraption (though for certain ambitious events and situations, these barbecues are excellent too). Even a few stones or bricks and a grill rack can suffice. Absolute essentials are wood or metal barbecue skewers and some kitchen foil, kitchen scissors and a sharp serrated knife.

Methodical organisers often include umbrellas, waterproof groundsheets, rugs, cushions and insect-repellent candles or flares. They know that easy-to-operate gear - tongs, appropriate fuel, a corkscrew, bottle opener, well stacked china, cutlery and glasses and some kitchen paper on a roll - are essential needs. Take rubbish bags: littering is antisocial. Buy mineral water, bags of ice along with fresh juice, wines, beers and other temperature-sensitive items near to your destination if you have little in the way of insulated containers.

Supermarkets and petrol stations, home-supply stores, delicatessens, ethnic grocers, wayside stalls and farmers markets can provide food and drink essentials as well as useful tools.

1 A large galvanised metal barbecue can be found in Greek shops. The rack folds back to cook kebabs.
2 A lightweight camping stool can double up as a table and is easy to carry.
3 At dusk, a pressure lamp and lanterns will light your feast. Citronella candles will keep mosquitoes at bay.
4 A windproof camping gas stove and a lightweight kettle mean you can have a cup of tea anywhere.
5 Stainless steel cutlery may be heavier but it is a pleasure to use. Bowls and buckets are useful for salads and rice. **6** Other useful items include a penknife, can opener, tongs, oyster knife, corkscrew, camping plates and wooden spoons.

STARTERS & SOUPS

carrot, orange & cardamom soup

An exotic, vivid, colourful and fragrant soup that can be made in a flash. Serve it hot or iced. The harissa, a red, spicy North African condiment, is delicious when home made (see page 43) and is also available from French and African stores, and good delis and supermarkets.

1 Peel and thinly slice the carrots crosswise into a small saucepan. Add the hot stock, bring to boiling, and reduce to a lively simmer.

2 Add the salt, harissa and black cardamom seeds removed from their green pods. Stir to mix. Squeeze in the juice of the oranges. Use a grater or zester to remove 1/4-1/2 teaspoon of orange zest.

3 When the carrots are tender, 10-12 minutes, pour the pan contents plus the zest and shallot into a blender. Blend to a creamy soup.

4 Heat to boiling, or chill thoroughly. Pour the soup into a vacuum flask and seal. Wrap up the extra cardamom pods and take along as well.

5 Serve in bowls, cups, demitasse cups or glasses. Savour the aroma, scattering on some extra cardamom seeds for pleasure just before drinking.

Makes 1.2 litres (5 cups), Serves 4

Ingredients
500g (1¼ lb) large organic carrots
750ml (3 cups) chicken or vegetable stock, boiling
½ teaspoon sea salt flakes
1-2 teaspoons harissa (hot spicy) paste
20 green cardamom pods, crushed, plus 8 to garnish
2 oranges, scrubbed
1 small shallot, finely chopped

iced black bean soup with chipotle cream

A Mexican-style soup and a beauty - the perfect starter for a summer barbecue. If authentic dried black beans (not Chinese salted black beans) are hard to find, substitute several cans of good quality black beans: this saves hours. An ethnic grocer, deli or spice stall will stock essential ingredients.

1 Heat the oil, add the spring onions (scallions) and sauté 2-3 minutes. Add the garlic, green jalapeño, cumin, ground and fresh coriander (cilantro), tomato purée and beans. Pour in the boiling stock. Bring the pan contents back to boiling. Simmer, uncovered, for 15 minutes or so.

2 Blend the soup, in batches if necessary, until creamy. Return the soup to the pan. Stir, adjust seasonings and turn off the heat. Cool the soup over iced water. Chill in the refrigerator.

3 Make the chipotle cream: if using chipotles *en escabèche*, simply chop or mash. If using dried chipotles, dry roast them briefly in a hot frying pan then soak briefly in hot water, simmer until soft, then chop or mash.

4 Stir into the cream and pack separately. When the soup is cold, pour into one or two wide-mouthed vacuum flasks, adding 2 ice cubes to each. At serving time, stir the chipotle cream into the soup.

Makes 1.5 litres (6$^1/_4$ cups) , Serves 8

Ingredients
4 tablespoons corn oil
8 spring onions (scallions), chopped
4 garlic cloves, crushed
1 green jalapeño chilli, cored, deseeded, sliced
1 teaspoon ground cumin
2 teaspoons ground coriander
75g (3 oz) fresh coriander (cilantro), chopped
2 tablespoons tomato purée
750g (1 lb 10 oz) cooked or canned black beans
  (*frijoles negros*)
750ml (3 cups) boiling chicken stock
sea salt and freshly ground black pepper

To serve:
2 tablespoons chipotles *en escabèche*, or dried
  chipotles (smoked, dried jalapeños)
150ml ($^1/_2$ cup) thick (heavy) cream

parmesan & poppy seed palmiers

These pretty, curlicued pastries are a savoury version of the classic sweet ones. Paradoxically, they taste good dusted with icing sugar at serving time. To carry them, pack them into a napkin-lined box or shallow basket.

Makes 32–36

Ingredients
750g (1 lb 10 oz) bought puff pastry in the block (or pre-rolled)
4 tablespoons Dijon mustard
4 tablespoons blue poppy seeds
4 tablespoons grated Parmesan cheese (from the block)
2 tablespoons icing (confectioners') sugar

1 Roll out or unfold the chilled pastry into a rectangle about 20 x 70cm (8 x 28 in), and about 3mm ($^1/_8$ in) thick. Trim the edges. Spread the pastry first with mustard, then poppy seeds, then cheese. Starting from both short sides, roll each in tightly towards the centre so that they meet in a double roll with a 'ram's horn' appearance.

2 Turn the double roll over so that the flat side is up. Using a long, serrated knife and pressing firmly, slice down, crosswise, to give 32–36 slim palmiers.

3 Water spray, or wet by hand, 4 or more baking sheets and lay the palmiers on them, allowing space between each. Chill for 1 hour.

4 Bake 2 sheets at a time in an oven preheated to 230ºC (450ºF) for 6–7 minutes or until they start to caramelise underneath. With a fish slice, carefully turn each palmier over. Bake again for a further 4–5 minutes or until crispy and caramelised.

5 Repeat with the remaining palmiers until they are all cooked. Cool completely on wire racks. Store in an airtight container for up to 7 days.

6 At serving time, dust them lightly with icing (confectioners') sugar, using a fine sieve.

radishes, french style

Select beautiful radish specimens: crimson or pink and white, in fat bunches, leaves intact. Choose lovely butter, maybe French *Echiré* (which comes, conveniently, in tiny wooden pails containing 250g/9 oz) and Maldon sea salt.

Serves 4

Ingredients
2–3 bunches fresh, crisp radishes with leaves
unsalted or lightly salted butter, e.g. *Echiré*
50g ($^1/_4$ cup) Maldon sea salt flakes, *sel du mer* or kosher salt

To serve, have the washed, chilled radishes in a cloth-lined basket or box with the (room temperature) butter still in its pail, if possible, and a lidded small pot of salt. Encourage your companions to break off a radish, dunk in butter, dip in salt, eat.

Note:
Some Poilâne or other good sourdough bread might be a nice accompaniment.

hummus

Makes about 700g (1½ lb)

Ingredients
- 500g (1¼ lb) freshly cooked or canned chickpeas (about 225g/ 8 oz, if cooked from dry)
- 3 tablespoons tahini (toasted sesame seed paste)
- 4 tablespoons freshly squeezed lemon juice
- 4 garlic cloves, crushed
- ¾ teaspoon salt
- 125ml (½ cup) extra-virgin olive oil

To serve:
Paprika, flatleaf parsley, optional flatbreads

1 Drain the chickpeas but reserve some of the liquid. Put them into a food processor with the tahini, juice, garlic and salt. Process in several long bursts to a gritty paste.

2 With the machine running, drizzle in 110ml (7 tbsp) of the olive oil through the feed tube until you have a thick, creamy purée. Do not over-process – a little roughness is good. If it seems too dense, process again, in brief bursts, adding 6-8 tablespoons of cooking liquid.

3 Serve the hummus cool, straight away, or chill it if it is to be used at a later time: it keeps well, in the refrigerator, for up to 1 week.

4 Serve with the reserved olive oil drizzled over the hummus in its bowl, a pinch of paprika and some parsley sprigs, adding warmed torn flatbreads as needed.

rosita's guacamole

Makes 400g (14 oz) or 6-8 servings

Ingredients
- 1 medium white, or 1 small Spanish, onion, chopped
- 150g (5 oz) bunch fresh coriander (cilantro) leaves
- 2 teaspoons sea salt or kosher salt
- 4 garlic cloves, crushed
- 4 ripe Hass avocados
- 2 limes, halved, to garnish (optional)
- 2 green and 1 red chilli, sliced
- ½ teaspoon dried oregano (optional)
- 2 plum tomatoes, cut in 1cm cubes

To serve:
Tostaditas, tortilla crisps, warmed tortillas, torn

1 Using a big *molcahete* (Mexican mortar) or big mortar and pestle (or, less satisfactorily, a food-processor), combine the onion, coriander (cilantro), salt and garlic and pound and mash, or process in brief bursts, to a green aromatic paste.

2 Scoop in the avocado flesh. Add a squeeze of fresh lime, if you like and the green chillies. Stir, pound, mix or process briefly again.

3 Crumble the oregano on top, if using. Decorate with a tumble of red jewel-like tomato cubes and red chillies.

4 Serve in the *molcahete* or mortar or a bowl surrounded by the lime halves and the tostaditas, crisps and torn tortilla bits.

salsa

Makes about 400ml (1⅔ cups)

Ingredients
- 1 red onion, finely chopped
- 3 plum or vine tomatoes, finely cubed
- 2 hot fresh red or green chillies, deseeded, deveined and chopped
- juice of 2 limes or 1 lemon (5-6 tablespoons)
- 2 tablespoons stock or water
- sea salt flakes and crushed allspice, to taste
- 1 handful fresh coriander (cilantro), mint, parsley, chives or thyme, or a mix, chopped

Combine the ingredients in a non-reactive bowl, stirring. Taste, adjust seasonings as needed. Use the same day. Serve in small or large bowls.

Variations

Substitute 3 spring onions (scallions) for the red onion.

Substitute blanched, dehusked tomatillos, or green tomatoes, for the red tomatoes.

Add 1 teaspoon finely shredded fresh root ginger and black pepper instead of allspice and use all coriander (cilantro), for an Asian-style salsa.

Add 3-4 tablespoons of extra-virgin olive oil for a richer effect.

blini with taramasalata & 'saviar'

Blini are yeast-risen pancakes, Russian in origin. This recipe makes 48, so freeze what you don't need for another occasion. Taramasalata, a Greek classic, should be made using pressed, salted cod's roe from a Greek deli. Substitute some salted, smoked cod's roe if none can be found.

Blini method

1 Sift together the flours, yeast and salt in a large heatproof bowl. Add the milk, soured cream and egg yolks, and lightly beat together to make a thick batter. Cover using a large plastic bag. Set on a rack over hand-hot water, not touching the bowl, or in another warm place. Leave for 40–50 minutes or until risen.

2 Whisk the egg whites to a stiff foam and fold in carefully.

3 Preheat a large griddle, hot plate, non-stick or cast iron frying pan. Add 1 tablespoon butter or olive oil. Spoon 8 dessert-spoonfuls of batter, from the tip of a spoon, to make small pancakes. Once the batter sets and bubbles show on the upper surface, turn them over and cook again, briefly, until golden on the second side. Test one: it should be cooked right through.

4 Cook the remaining batter in batches in more hot butter or olive oil. Cool on wire racks.

Taramasalata method

1 Put the tarama or smoked cod's roe into a food-processor with the wet, crumbled bread, the garlic and juice of half the lemon. Process briefly until mixed.

2 With the machine running, drizzle in the oil, in a thin, fine stream until the mixture stiffens into a dense paste. Scrape down the sides as necessary.

3 Drizzle in 3–4 tablespoons of boiling water (or more as needed) with the machine running, to lighten the texture. Throw in the parsley and stop the machine.

4 Pack the taramasalata into a china or toughened glass jar with a lid. Wrap in plastic wrap or a wet cloth for transporting.

5 Pack the blini, in stacks, in a cloth- or napkin-lined little basket or box for transporting. To serve, set out the blini, opened taramasalata and the opened 'saviar' with the remaining lemon half. Have knives or spoons ready for scooping and spreading.

Makes 48

Allow 3–4 blini, 25g (1 oz) taramasalata and 1 large teaspoon 'saviar' per person for an appetiser; double this for a main course

Ingredients

Blini:

200g (1¾ cups) strong white bread flour
50g (½ cup) buckwheat flour
1 teaspoon or ½ sachet micronised, easyblend yeast
1 teaspoon sea salt flakes
275ml (1 cup) milk, warmed to blood heat
150ml (¾ cup) soured cream
2 eggs, separated
6 tablespoons butter or olive oil, for cooking

Taramasalata:

4 tablespoons tarama (salted, pressed, cod's roe), or 100g salted, smoked cod's roe, skinned, chopped
2 thick slices white bread, wetted and squeezed dry
2 garlic cloves, crushed
1 lemon
250ml (1 cup) extra-virgin olive oil
3–4 tablespoons boiling water
handful fresh parsley, chopped

To serve:
100g (4 oz) pot 'saviar' (salmon 'caviar')

pa am tomaquet

In Catalonia, Spain, this famous and delicious snack seems as usual as pizza does in Naples. It consists of chunky bread, grilled, rubbed with a smashed garlic clove then with a crushed ripe tomato. Salt is usually added, but the final flourish is a generous libation of good, fresh extra-virgin olive oil: a tomato sandwich that is a triumph of simplicity. Create it on site using a portable barbecue, bread, fresh toppings.

Serves 4

Ingredients

4 chunks bread from a crusty country loaf
4 garlic cloves, skin on
4 large ripe, juicy tomatoes
sea salt
estate-bottled, extra-virgin olive oil, for
    drizzling

1 Take the gear needed for a fire on the spot: portable barbecue, gas-fired element or aromatic wood. Get the relevant equipment to a high temperature or build the fire to hot and crackling. Toast the bread, both sides, over the heat.

2 Crush each garlic clove and use it to rub garlic all over one side of the toast. Now rub squashy tomato flesh over too; if it looks pink and messy: par for the course. Add salt to taste and a generous trickle of oil.

3 Eat each open sandwich while warm, aromatic and crusty. You may add more salt and oil to the tomato debris and eat that too.

ewe's milk cheese on bruschetta

Long before bruschetta became fashionable everywhere it was a peasant dish from the Abruzzi, in Italy, designed to maximise the pleasure of tasting the new season's olive oil. *Fettunta* is the Tuscan version. Chunks of homely bread are toasted or chargrilled briefly then rubbed with garlic and sprinkled lavishly with the best olive oil available. In this version, pecorino is added. Some wild greens – cress, rocket or wild garlic leaves – can also be added. A portable mini-feast, all of its own.

1 On site, fire up a portable barbecue, make a small wood fire (if it is safe) or heat a gas-fired element. Barbecue, toast or grill the bread on a rack over the heat.

2 Use the garlic to rub all over one side of the crusty bread, then drizzle on oil directly from the bottle, flask or can.

3 Add some slices of cheese and some wild herbs. (Note: Do rinse them thoroughly under some bottled spring water to clean them well.) Sprinkle with salt to taste.

4 To serve, hand around the ready-made open sandwiches.

Serves 4

Ingredients

4 thick slices Italian-style bread e.g. *pane integrale*
4 garlic cloves, squashed
cold, first-pressed extra-virgin olive oil, to taste
250g (9 oz) pecorino cheese or other ewe's milk cheese
wild, fresh herbs such as dandelion, radish, cress, rocket or wild garlic (optional)
sea salt

salmon-rice beignets in mini-romaine leaves

Smoked salmon, cooked rice and eggs combine to make 'beignets', golden and puffy, to eat in the fingers, and easy to transport in back-pack or pannier bag. They are good cool rather than chilled. Fold each in little leaves before eating. *Shichimi togarashi* is a kind of Japanese seven-spice mix: go to an Asian deli for this and for *wasabi* powder, an alternative.

Makes 24, Serves 8

Ingredients

125g (4$^1/_2$ oz) smoked salmon, scissor-chopped
125g (4$^1/_2$ oz) cooked white or brown long grain rice or wild rice
6 spring onions (scallions), chopped
2 teaspoons *shichimi togarashi* seasoning or $^1/_2$ teaspoon *wasabi* powder
3 tablespoons tomato juice
2 eggs, separated
sea salt and freshly ground black pepper
4 tablespoons extra-virgin olive oil
4 heads mini-romaine (Little Gem) lettuces
2 limes, quartered

1 Combine the smoked salmon, rice, spring onions (scallions), seasoning, tomato juice and egg yolks in a bowl, stirring with a fork. Do not mash.

2 In a small separate high-sided bowl, whisk the egg whites with a pinch of the salt to a stiff foam.

3 Fold this into the salmon-rice mixture with about 1 teaspoon of salt, and pepper to taste.

4 Heat 1 tablespoon of the oil in a non-stick or heavy-based frying pan. Spoon in 6 small portions (about a tablespoon each) of mixture. Reduce the heat to low. Cook until golden and crusty, 1$^1/_2$–2 minutes on each side. Test one: it must be cooked right through.

5 Repeat with more oil until you have finished the mixture (total of 4 batches). Cool the beignets to room temperature. Chill them if they are to travel far.

6 Pack the washed, whole lettuces separately, wrapped in wet kitchen paper with some ice cubes. Enclose in a plastic clip-top bag or box. Pack the cool beignets in another box.

7 To serve, wrap each beignet in a few lettuce leaves, squeeze a little lime juice over, and eat in your fingers.

mini game burgers with bacon

Delicious, gamey meat patties with juniper and Armagnac to accentuate the autumnal tastes. In France these are called *gaillettes* or *caillettes*, depending on the region. Just the thing for a day out!

1 Put the diced game into a non-reactive bowl. Reserve half the bacon; finely scissor-chop or mince (grind) the rest, and add to the bowl. Add the Armagnac and the herbs, onion and the seasonings. Marinate for 20 minutes, or several hours in the refrigerator.

2 Stir the minced (ground) meat, breadcrumbs, crushed juniper berries and the egg into the marinade. Mix well, kneading with clean hands to make a dense meat paste.

3 Stretch each reserved bacon slice using a knife blade and halve lengthwise. Divide the meat into 16 equal portions. Squeeze each portion tightly into a ball then flatten into a burger about 5cm (2 in) across. Wrap a bacon slice around the outer circumference. Hold it in place with a wooden cocktail stick (toothpick). Repeat until all are prepared.

4 Heat the oil in a large heavy-based or non-stick frying pan. Add the burgers and sauté over medium-high heat for 3–4 minutes on the first side, and 2–3 minutes on the second. The burgers should be slightly rosy inside, but if you prefer, cook them longer until *à point* (to your liking). Remove the cocktail sticks (toothpicks).

5 Serve hot, warm or cold (but not chilled) with spring onions (scallions) or salad leaves of the season. Eat using the fingers or with a knife and fork.

Makes 800g (1³/₄ lb), 16 burgers
Allow 2 burgers per serving as an appetiser

Ingredients

185g (6¹/₂ oz) boneless, skinless duck, boar or pheasant, in 1cm (¹/₂ in) cubes
250g (9 oz) smoked streaky bacon
4 tablespoons Armagnac
6 tablespoons chopped fresh herbs e.g. parsley, rosemary, thyme or oregano
1 small onion, finely chopped
salt and freshly ground black pepper
350g (12 oz) minced (ground) beef or veal
50g (1 cup) fresh breadcrumbs
2 teaspoons juniper berries, crushed
1 egg, beaten
2 tablespoons extra-virgin olive oil

MAIN COURSES

chicken fajitas with salad

Fajitas - traditionally made with strips of beef in a marinade - are made with wheat, not maize tortillas and are a favourite at any gathering. This cross-cultural version uses chicken. For a beach *parilla* (barbecue) for a crowd, make it simple. These fajitas are do-it-yourself: this makes it fun for all and not merely hard work for the cooks. The four-skewer system for holding the quickly-cooked chicken is foolproof: try it. There is no waiting as all the chicken is ready at the same time.

1 Mash the drained red beans in their can using a fork, either before you set out or on site, and adding the barbecue-tomato sauce to make a thick bean purée.

2 Put the mashed beans, guacamole, soured cream and the cheese in separate bowls or containers that can be passed around. Have the tortillas covered, in baskets or between cloths, near to the barbecue ready for being warmed and filled.

3 Make the coating for the chicken: mix the chopped fresh red chilli together with the tomato paste or tomatillo purée, mixing in the corn oil. Toss the chicken strips in the chilli mixture until coated. Line up 24 chicken strips in a parallel row. Using 2 long skewers, thread the strips on to the skewers like the rungs of a ladder: they can now be lifted as one unit.

4 Repeat with the remaining chicken strips and 2 more skewers. Set these 'chicken ladders' over the *parilla* (barbecue) and cook for 3-4 minutes on each side, until the chicken is firm and white inside.

5 To serve, pull out the skewers and let guests fill their tortillas with chicken, coriander and the accompaniments of their choice. Squeeze a little lime juice over.

Serves 8

Ingredients

450g (1 lb) can red beans, mashed
250ml (1 cup) barbecue-tomato sauce
500g (2$\frac{1}{2}$ cups) guacamole (see page 16) or bought guacamole
450ml (scant 2 cups) soured cream
450g (2 cups) low-fat soft cheese, crumbled or sliced
16 wheat flour tortillas
2 teaspoons fresh red chilli, sliced
6 tablespoons sun-dried tomato paste or tomatillo purée
4 tablespoons corn oil
8 boneless chicken breasts (breast halves), sliced lengthwise into 6
1 large handful fresh coriander (cilantro) leaves
4 fresh limes, in chunky pieces

roasted sweetcorn and spiced butter

Mexico taught me to appreciate sweetcorn and its potential. Roasting or barbecuing it directly over the heat, still in its wetted husks, then sizzling it with spices makes this homely vegetable seem delectable, new and exciting.

1 Mix together the garlic, butter and paprika and set aside.

2 Gently pull open the green husks and silks a little and drip some cold water inside each cob - about 1 tablespoon will be enough for each. Set them over a prepared barbecue, 5-7.5cm (2-3 in) from the embers or closer.

3 Cook them over the heat, turning them with tongs or fingers from time to time, for 10-20 minutes or until steamy and semi-tender. Remove from the heat and pull the dampened husks and silks back completely to reveal the kernels.

4 Replace the corn cobs on the barbecue. As the kernels char and darken, add about a teaspoon of the spiced butter in little dots along the length of each cob. Let it melt and drip.

5 Once the corn cobs look frizzled and charred dark in patches, remove them and add a share of the remaining spiced butter. Eat, in the fingers, while still hot, leaving on the husks for holding.

Serves 8

Ingredients
3-4 garlic cloves, crushed
50g ($1/4$ cup) salted butter, softened
2 teaspoons smoky paprika, Spanish-style
8 whole sweetcorn cobs, husks and silks still intact

skewered prawns with harissa

Harissa and herb butter make these king prawns (jumbo shrimp) on sticks very succulent and somewhat hot and spicy. If you cannot find raw prawns (shrimp) use ready-cooked ones instead: reheat rather than cook, using the same spicy butter, but for a shorter time.

1 Holding each prawn (shrimp) down flat on a cutting surface, use a sharp, serrated blade knife to cut the tail sections part-way through while leaving the head sections whole. The tail will divide into two, butterflying it. Discard the dark vein.

2 Mash the harissa with the flavoured butter. Use 1-2 teaspoons per prawn (shrimp) and coat the exposed tail surfaces of each. Thread the prawns (shrimp) in twos or fours on to long metal skewers, looping them round to fit as necessary.

3 Place the completed skewers over the glowing embers of the open fire, towards the cooler edge, or else rest them on a metal rack over the flames themselves. Once the shells turn rosy, brittle and aromatic and the flesh white and firm, they are cooked.

4 Serve the skewers with the remaining harissa butter in small pots, for individual use, and pass each diner a lemon half. Have lots of paper or cloth napkins for messy, spicy fingers. Toss the shells on to the fire with the lemon skins to burn to cinders. They continue to smell delicious and it also avoids messy clearing up at the end.

Serves 8

Ingredients
1-2kg (16) large raw (green) prawns (jumbo shrimp) in the shell (about 18cm/7 in long)
50g ($^1/_4$ cup) harissa spice paste (see page 43)
100g ($^1/_4$ cup) garlic butter or parsley butter, softened (bought or made)

To serve:
4 lemons, cut in half

pit-cooked lobsters, prawns & clams (clambake)

American summer clambakes are an old idea. The classic system, when at the beach, is to dig a pit in the sand, line it with stones, and build a fire in the pit. The food is placed on fine chicken-wire 'trays' which are lowered on to the hot stones, often between layers of wetted seaweed or samphire. The biggest foods go in first. As the steam works its way up it cooks the food to perfection. It does take some hours - this is all part of the fun. Have palmiers to nibble, soft drinks, beer, spritzers or white wine to drink until the main course is revealed. Get permission to build a fire if necessary.

1 Dig a pit 1 metre by 75cm (1 yard x 2¹/₂ ft) in area, and about 15-20cm (6-8 in) deep, in the sand. Line the base and sides of the pit with non-fracturing large stones. Make a fire with wooden kindling and charcoal in the pit and let it burn for 1-2 hours to heat the stones thoroughly. Have at least 2 pieces of fine chicken-wire cut slightly longer than the size of the pit, with the ends rolled to make 'handles' for lifting.

2 Kill each live lobster humanely: hold it down carefully, and pierce through the head with a sharp, heavy knife. Scrub the lobsters briefly in a bucket of sea or spring water.

3 When the stones are well heated and the fire has burned down, push the embers to one side. Place one chicken-wire 'tray' on the stones and cover with half the wetted samphire or seaweed. Place the lobsters on top with the sweet potatoes, onions (if used) and squash.

4 Add the second layer of chicken-wire then the clams, mussels and prawns (shrimp). Cover with the remaining wetted samphire or seaweed and a double layer of foil to act as a lid. Put large clean stones on top to keep the heat in.

5 Leave the clambake to cook for 2-3 hours or even longer. Uncover one side a little and test the food: it should be hot and cooked through.

6 Arrange the cooked food on several large platters, including the samphire, which is edible, and let the diners help themselves. Enjoy the foods dipped into the seasonings and then bowls of melted butter or olive oil. Lemons are an option.

Serves 8

Ingredients
8 x 500g (1¹/₄ lb) live lobsters
wetted samphire or seaweed, to cook
4 sweet potatoes, unpeeled
4 onions, unpeeled (optional)
2 x 500g (1¹/₄ lb) butternut squash, cut across into
    5cm (2 in) slices
2 quarts (5 pints) live clams, scrubbed
2 quarts (5 pints) fresh, live mussels, scrubbed
8 raw (green) jumbo prawns (shrimp)
salt and freshly ground black pepper

To serve:
500g (2¹/₂ cups) salted butter, melted or 500ml
    (2¹/₂ cups) extra-virgin olive oil
lemons (optional)

barbecued red mullet with orange

'Woodcock of the sea' is one description of this pretty, pink, Mediterranean fish: it has a sea-fresh taste. If necessary substitute small red snapper or red bream instead. The orange, olive oil and anchovy add a Mediterranean touch.

1 Make 2 parallel slashes on both sides of each fish, on the diagonal.

2 Zest the orange into fine shreds. Squeeze the juice separately. Mix 2 teaspoons of this juice into the zest and stir in the anchovy to make a paste. Use this to rub into the slashes. Foil-wrap the prepared fish to take to the barbecue.

3 Put the remaining juice, the salt, pepper and oil into a screw-topped jar, to take separately. Pack a portable barbecue, coals and tongs for handling the fish, and the brine-packed leaves, drained.

4 Get the barbecue to the correct temperature: no flames; a steady heat; an even layer of ash over all.

5 Shake the dressing. Rub or brush a little over the fish. Barbecue them for 2-3 minutes on the first side; 1-2 minutes on the second: too long and they'll fall apart.

6 To serve, wrap each fish in two vine leaves. Drizzle a share of the remaining dressing over. Eat hot, using your fingers, and enjoy the livers: an epicure's treat.

Serves 4

Ingredients
4 red mullet (about 900g/2 lb total weight) scaled, gutted but with livers left intact
1 orange, scrubbed, dried
1 teaspoon anchovy paste or sauce or 2 salted anchovy fillets, mashed
$1/2$ teaspoon sea salt flakes
$1/2$ teaspoon peppercorns
2 tablespoons extra-virgin olive oil

To serve:
8 brine packed, or fresh, vine leaves

fennel with pastis

Cooking accentuates the aniseedy sweetness of this vegetable. The aromatics are also boosted by the liquor: both suit seafood of many kinds, including the Barbecued red mullet with orange (above).

1 Halve the fennel bulbs, lengthwise, twice each to give 8 pieces.

2 Rub or brush these using the salt, pepper, oil and liquor mixed.

3 Cook the fennel over glowing charcoal for 4-5 minutes each side or until wilted, fragrant and caramelised.

4 Serve with leftover marinade and a sprinkle of the herbs.

Serves 4

Ingredients
2 large heads fennel, scrubbed
$1/2$ teaspoon sea salt flakes
freshly ground black pepper
3 tablespoons extra-virgin olive oil
1 tablespoon pastis (or aquavit or ouzo)
scissor-snipped fennel tops, dill or tarragon

flower pot chicken

A friend, whose city garden has no space for a formal barbecue, intrigued me by barbecuing on his front steps: cooking food on a metal grill set over glowing charcoal, arranged on broken bricks (or over earth) inside a large earthenware flower pot, about 45cm (18 in) across. Ingenious.

1 Pat the chicken dry. Make 2 shallow long cuts in the thickest parts of the chicken so it will cook evenly.

2 Mix together the sauce, olive oil, lemon zest, lemon juice and juniper berries. Rub this over the chicken in a shallow, non-reactive dish, turning the pieces to coat them.

3 Get the flower-pot barbecue to the right heat. Set the chicken, skin-side down, and cook over a moderate heat for 6–8 minutes each side or until the chicken is firm, white and the juices run clear and golden, not pink.

4 Serve hot. Eat in the fingers or using a knife and fork.

Serves 8

Ingredients

8 small boneless chicken breasts (breast halves)
1 tablespoon sweet chilli sauce (Chinese type)
2 tablespoons virgin olive oil
2 teaspoons finely shredded lemon zest
1 tablespoon freshly squeezed lemon juice
8 juniper berries, well crushed or chopped

chargrilled asparagus with gruyère cheese

A simply delicious way of cooking and serving asparagus in the open, this makes a great starter or an accompaniment to chicken or meat cooked over coals.

1 Snap off any tough stem bases and discard these. Using a sharp knife, make a criss-cross cut, 2.5cm (1 in) deep, up the base of each stem to let the heat penetrate better.

2 Drizzle enough of the infused oil over to lightly coat all the asparagus. Add seasonings which will stick to the oil.

3 Set the asparagus on a metal rack with a fine mesh so that the asparagus do not fall though. Barbecue or chargrill the asparagus for 3–5 minutes, turning it with tongs, or tipping the rack so that it rolls slightly.

4 Roll the spears close together and sprinkle over the cubed Gruyère. Cover the asparagus loosely with some foil or a pan lid. As soon as the cheese melts, serve the asparagus straight from the barbecue. Eat it using your fingers.

Serves 8

Ingredients

1kg (about 2 lb or 2 generous bunches) plump green asparagus
150ml ($^2/_3$ cup) basil-infused extra-virgin olive oil
sea salt flakes and freshly ground black pepper
250g (9 oz) Gruyère cheese, in 1cm ($^1/_2$ in) cubes

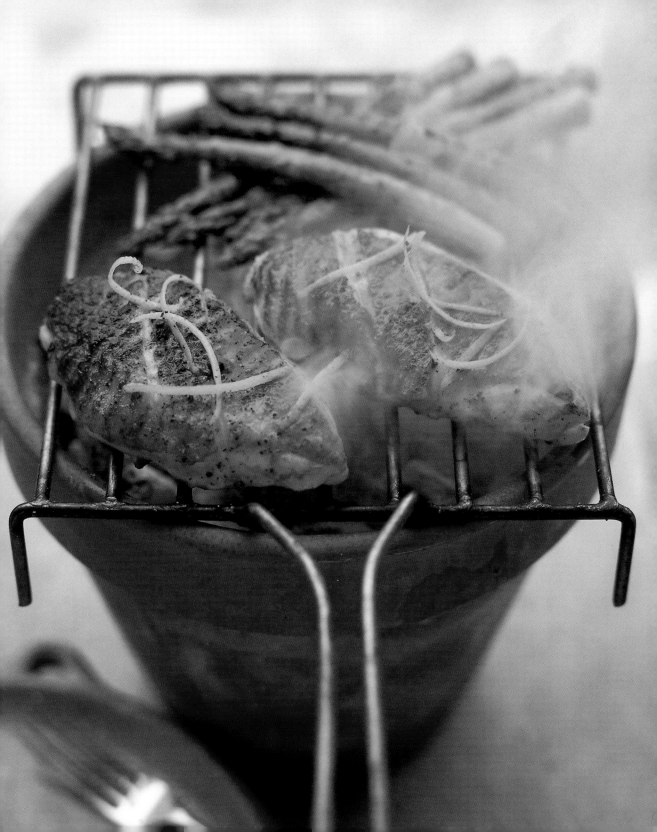

spatchcocked, barbecued quail with spiced plums

A perfect, crispy quail, cooked flat (spatchcocked) is easy to eat in the fingers at an informal barbecue. Spices, plums and a gamy glaze give distinctiveness to this easy game dish.

1 Scissor-snip up on each side of both birds' backbones then remove and discard the backbones.

2 Place the birds, skin sides up, each on its own sheet of heavy-duty aluminium foil. Pound hard to flatten the breast bones and turn both legs towards the centre. Cut a slash through both legs of each bird.

3 Mix the oil, garlic, salt, pepper, plum sauce (or jam) and half of the cinnamon. Pour some of this over each of the birds. Foil-wrap the quail, then plastic wrap as well.

4 Take the wrapped, marinated birds, the plums (sprinkled with the remaining spice), along with 6 skewers to the barbecue. Pack the salad leaves separately.

5 Prepare the barbecue: you should have ash-covered glowing coals. Skewer the plums into one row using 2 skewers.

6 Unwrap the birds. Push 2 metal skewers, right to left, across two flattened birds, as if using a needle. Repeat with the other two birds. Drizzle any remaining marinade over the plums.

7 Cook for 6-8 minutes on the skin side and 2-3 minutes on the second, until firm-cooked. Add the plums when you turn them over. Remove the skewers. Serve on some salad leaves with the barbecued plums alongside.

Serves 4

Ingredients
4 prepared quail (each 175g/6 oz)
2 tablespoons extra-virgin olive oil
2 garlic cloves, crushed to a paste
1/2 teaspoon each of salt flakes and cracked peppercorns
2 tablespoons plum sauce, plum jam or pomegranate molasses
1 teaspoon ground cinnamon
4 red-skinned plums, halved, pitted

To serve:
crisp lettuce or chicory (witloof) or red trevise or radicchio leaves, or mixed salad

hot beef satays with herbs

These quick beef satays have a subtly sweet Asian savour. They take moments to prepare – a brief time to cook. Garnish them with fresh herbs at serving time, such as Thai basil or European basil.

1 Soak 16 short satay sticks or bamboo or wood skewers in water while the satay ingredients are prepared.

2 Mix together the first 7 ingredients to make the marinade. Reserve half to use as a dipping sauce. Thread equal amounts of beef cubes on the skewers. Set on a shallow, non-reactive plate. Pour the marinade over. Turn the satays and leave for 5 minutes.

3 Barbecue over glowing embers for about 2 minutes each side, basting with the marinade, until golden outside but still slightly rosy inside. Dip into the sauce and eat hot or cool, scattered with basil.

Variation
Substitute chicken breast for the steak, if you like; add $1/2$ teaspoon turmeric (optional) and use light soy sauce instead of dark.

Serves 8

Ingredients
8 tablespoons canned coconut cream
2 tablespoons dark soy sauce
1 tablespoon dark soft brown sugar
10cm (4 in) fresh lemongrass, thinly sliced crosswise
4 red or green bird's eye chillies, sliced
2 teaspoons freshly puréed garlic
2 teaspoons grated fresh root ginger
675g ($1^{1}/_2$ lb) rump, sirloin or blade steak, in 1cm ($1/2$ in) cubes
1 handful Thai basil or European basil, torn

skewered potatoes

An easy, tasty idea made simpler by having the baby new potatoes part-cooked before they are barbecued. The crusty, crunchy outsides are really tempting. If you can, cook the new season potatoes for this dish the day before the barbecue and refrigerate them.

1 Boil or steam the baby potatoes until barely cooked and still firm. Drain. Have at least 8 flat metal skewers ready. Push an equal number of potatoes on to each skewer.

2 Mix together the butter, oil, honey and half the spring onions (scallions). Dab or brush this all over the skewered potatoes. Cook them, at a reasonable distance from the heat source, for 3-5 minutes each side or until golden and crusty. It may take a little longer.

3 Sprinkle the remaining spring onions (scallions), the sea salt and pepper on top or around, and serve.

Serves 8

Ingredients
2kg ($4^{1}/_2$ lb) new season baby potatoes, scrubbed
75g (6 tbsp) salted butter, softened
2 tablespoons extra-virgin olive oil
2 tablespoons clear honey
4 spring onions (scallions), finely chopped
sea salt flakes and roughly crushed black pepper

barbecued beefsteaks

Charcoal and beef steaks go together like bread and butter. The trick is to barely cook the meat at all: just sear and caramelise the exterior and keep the interior juicy, pink (or even 'blue') and wonderfully tender. Cook one steak per person or else buy a very large, thick steak then slice it into pieces for the guests. Using rubs, marinades and seasoning pastes adds lots of interesting tastes; apply them at cooking time or up to one hour before: too long and valuable juices will be leached out and lost. Buy the best steak you can afford: matured steaks from beef (not dairy) cattle.

1 Rub, brush or spread some of the selected flavouring on both sides of each steak. Ideally this is best done 10-20 minutes before cooking.

2 Enclose steaks in some oiled foil and twist ends up to create a package. Take them to the barbecue in this pack. Take some extra foil.

3 Have the barbecue prepared: glowing coals with grey ash on top, and set the rack about 3-4 cm (1^1/$_4$-1^1/$_2$ in) above the heat source.

4 Remove each steak, using tongs, and set on the rack. Cook for 2 minutes or until dark and aromatic; turn and cook on the second side for the same time. Cook the large steak for 3-4 minutes each side.

5 Move the steaks to one side away from the heat. Cover them with fresh foil and leave to stand for 2 minutes.

6 Serve the steak with a drizzle of oil, salt and pepper and some scissor-snipped fresh herbs.

7 Some cold potato salad and baby salad leaves are great accompaniments, as is robust red wine.

Serves 4

Ingredients

2-4 tablespoons chosen rub, marinade or sprinkle (see page 42)
4 x 250-300g (9-10 oz) beef steaks cut 2cm (^{3}/$_4$ in) thick; such as sirloin, rump or fillet or 1 x 1.2 kilo/ 2^3/$_4$ lb rump steak cut 3cm/1^1/$_4$ in thick
cold, first-pressed extra-virgin olive oil, for drizzling
sea salt flakes and freshly ground black pepper
1 bunch fresh parsley, chervil or basil

marinades

Dry mixes, semi-dry pastes, sprinkles, rubs, or liquid flavourants can add huge appeal to quickly-cooked meats, game, poultry or seafood. Even certain cheeses, vegetables and fruits can benefit. Since such concentrated mixtures may draw out too much natural juiciness, apply 10 minutes before - or up to 1 hour ahead - for best results. Some can be sprinkled or drizzled over after cooking.

bombay spice rub

Makes about 125g (4½ oz)

Ingredients

2 cinnamon sticks, crushed
2 tablespoons coriander seeds
1 tablespoon fenugreek seeds
15g (½ oz) dried crushed hot red chillies
1 tablespoon cloves
6-8 dried bay leaves, crumbled
50g (¼ cup) coarse salt crystals
2 teaspoons asafoetida powder (optional)
1 tablespoon nigella or black cumin seeds

1 Combine the first 6 ingredients in a *karai*, heavy iron pan or wok. Dry roast until aromatic, then cool.

2 Using a large pestle and mortar or an electric spice grinder, grind these to a powder, adding the salt towards the end.

3 Stir in the asafoetida powder and nigella seeds. (The asafoetida is optional but lends pungency.) Store in a stoppered jar or pot.

Use in Indian dishes as a coating, a seasoning or a dry marinade. Also on lamb, chicken, veal, pork, or beef grills, kebabs and meatballs.

peri peri wet mix

Makes about 150ml (²⁄₃ cup)

Ingredients

2 tablespoons dried, or
4 tablespoons fresh red bird's eye chillies, half crumbled or chopped, half left whole
4 garlic cloves, chopped
shredded zest and juice of 2 limes
100ml (7 tbsp) peanut (groundnut) or corn oil
1 teaspoon sea salt flakes

Pierce the whole chillies with a pin. Shake up all the ingredients in a pretty, stoppered glass jar or flask, ideally with a non-metal lid. Use as a marinade, to baste, or as a salad dressing. This adds a powerful hotness so use with care.

Baste prawns, white fish steaks or cutlets, kebabs or whole small fish, slashed with this spicy liquid dressing. Drizzle it over cooked cutlets, fillets or steaks of salmon, tuna or swordfish. Sardines, herrings and smoked or plain mackerel also benefit from it.

provençal wet mix

Makes about 150ml (²⁄₃ cup)

Ingredients

2 teaspoons sea salt flakes
3 garlic cloves, crushed, but left whole
100ml (7 tbsp) first cold-pressed extra-virgin olive oil
30ml (2 tbsp) red wine vinegar
2 stems (about 15cm/6 in total) fresh rosemary, bruised
8 fresh heads lavender, crumbled (or ½ teaspoon, dried)
7.5cm (3 in) strip fresh orange zest, crushed
8 fresh basil leaves, torn or chopped

Pound the garlic and salt together using a pestle and mortar to make a paste. Combine this with the remaining ingredients in a large sealable glass jar or a flask with a cork stopper. Shake well. Leave in a warm place. Use within 1 day.

Great for salads, for tenderising red meats and for use with roasted, cold chicken. Useful for pouring over grilled goat's cheese in a salad. Try also over grilled tomato halves, barbecued red and yellow (bell) peppers, chargrilled *gaillettes* (page 23) or lamb kebabs.

'ali berberé' mix

Makes about 125g (4½ oz)

Ingredients

2 tablespoons dried black peppercorns
2 tablespoons allspice berries
1 tablespoon whole cloves
2 tablespoons dried hot red chillies
5cm (2 in) piece cinnamon, crumbled
1 tablespoon coriander seeds
1 nutmeg, grated
20 green cardamom pods, crushed
2 teaspoons turmeric powder
2 teaspoons dried ginger

1 Put the peppercorns, allspice, cloves, chillies, cinnamon and coriander into a dry frying pan or *karai* or wok. Heat briefly, stirring, until they begin to smell aromatic. Do not let them darken and scorch or they will be bitter.

2 Tip them out of the pan and cool them. Add the grated nutmeg, the cardamoms, the turmeric and ginger.

3 Using a big mortar and pestle or an electric spice grinder, pound or grind the mixture to a coarse dry powder. Cool.

Store in jars and use at an *al fresco* meal - sprinkle it over barbecued quails and poussins, spatchcocked pigeons or guinea fowl joints. Use on barbecued aubergine (eggplant) chunks, carrot and parsnip halves or fennel chunks. Add to couscous and bulgur salads.

mexicana mix

Makes about 100g (4 oz)

Ingredients

2 tablespoons allspice berries
1 teaspoon dried oregano
2 teaspoons annatto powder or 1 teaspoon saffron stigma
15g (½ oz) dried chipotle flesh (smoked, dried jalapeño), torn into tiny pieces
4 tablespoons mild or hot paprika
4 tablespoons piloncillo or soft dark brown sugar
1 tablespoon coarse salt crystals or kosher salt
1 teaspoon lemon pepper

1 Combine the allspice, oregano, annatto powder and chipotle pieces in a dry pan and dry roast briefly over a gas flame or a barbecue. Do not let them scorch, merely become aromatic. Cool these.

2 Put the roasted spices, the paprika, half of the sugar, all of the salt and the lemon pepper into a mortar and pestle (in Mexico it's a basalt *molcahete* - perfect for this) or electric spice grinder and pound or grind to a gritty powder. Stir in the remaining sugar.

3 Store in a stoppered bottle or screw-top jar.

Try this with tortilla-wrapped barbecued pumpkin, chicken, lamb or some white cheeses. Sprinkle it over avocado, red bean, chickpea or blue cheese dips. Stir it into butter as a baste.

harissa

Makes 450ml (scant 2 cups)

Ingredients

30g (1 oz) large, dried hot red chillies, crumbled
1 carrot, sliced
2 large red (bell) peppers, cored, deseeded, cubed
8 garlic cloves, crushed
1 teaspoon salt, or more to taste
2 tablespoons green cardamom pods to yield ½ teaspoon seeds
2 tablespoons each of cumin and coriander seeds
1 tablespoon black peppercorns
75ml (5 tbsp) extra-virgin olive oil

1 Cover the chillies, carrot and red (bell) peppers in a medium saucepan, with about 5cm (2 in) of boiling water. Bring back to boiling, cover, reduce to a simmer and cook for 15 minutes or until tender. Drain and put the solids into a food processor.

2 In a mortar and pestle, pound the garlic, salt, black cardamom seeds (having discarded the seed pods), the cumin and coriander seeds and black peppercorns.

3 Add to the food processor with ⅔ of the olive oil and process to a rough paste. Taste and add more salt if necessary.

4 Pour the harissa into small, ideally sterilised, jars, leaving 1cm (½ in) headroom. Pour on the remaining olive oil as a seal. Refrigerate.

Use to accompany barbecued meats, fish, seafood or vegetables, also pasta, bean or grain dishes.

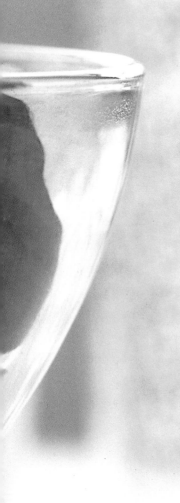

SALADS

potato & cheese salad

Easy, versatile, delicious: this salad can be served warm or cold made using whichever potatoes you choose. Some lively green leaves are added, as an edible garnish, at serving time.

Serves 8

Ingredients

900g (2 lb) smallish potatoes, scrubbed
salt
2 garlic cloves, crushed
200g (1 ½ cups) soft blue cheese, such as Dolcelatte or Bleu de Bresse, cubed
100g (½ cup) fromage frais
4 tablespoons extra-virgin olive oil
2 tablespoons tarragon vinegar
crushed black peppercorns (optional)
handful salad leaves, e.g. red chard, nasturtium, spinach, dandelion or frisée, to garnish

1 Place the potatoes in a pan and barely cover with boiling water; add salt to taste. Cook, covered, for 16-20 minutes or until tender but still firm. Drain them well.

2 Turn off the heat and return them to the empty, dry pan. Cover the pan with a cloth and leave them for several minutes to dry out.

3 Meanwhile make the dressing: put the garlic, blue cheese, fromage frais, oil and vinegar into a blender or food processor. Blend or process to a creamy dressing, adding a splash of cold water if the consistency is too thick.

4 Cut the cooled potatoes into halves or quarters. Pack them into a portable container or clip-top bowl; sprinkle with some pepper, if you like. Pour the dressing over the top and seal the container.

5 Take the washed salad leaves separately in a sealed container. On site, mix the dressing in well or leave it as a topping. Toss the salad leaves on top. Serve the salad warm, or cool but not chilled.

pink, green and gold salad

Crisp beetroot and apple contrast with the cabbage, spinach and sultanas. The sweet-sour effect is emphasised by a creamy dressing which turns pink when the salad is tossed.

Serves 4-6

Ingredients

4 raw beetroot (beets), scrubbed
½ head red cabbage, thinly sliced
2 red-skinned dessert apples, quartered, cored and sliced
100g golden sultanas
2 handfuls baby spinach leaves, washed, not dried

Dressing:
4 tablespoons freshly squeezed lemon juice
4 tablespoons extra-virgin olive oil
2 tablespoons clear, flower-scented honey
2 teaspoons caraway seeds, pan-toasted briefly
1 teaspoon sea salt flakes
½ teaspoon black peppercorns
2 garlic cloves, crushed
4 tablespoons strained Greek yogurt

1 Use a vegetable peeler to peel the raw beetroot (beets). Slice them into rounds, crosswise. Stack these and slice into batons. Put them into a portable salad bowl and add the sliced cabbage, sliced apples and sultanas.

2 Drizzle over 2 tablespoons of the lemon juice and 2 tablespoons of the oil. Toss until coated.

3 Put the remaining juice and oil, and all of the honey and the seeds into a dressing container like a screw-top jar.

4 Grind together the salt, pepper and garlic using a pestle and mortar. Stir this paste and the Greek yogurt into the dressing: it will turn creamy when shaken.

5 Take the spinach leaves in a sealed bag, along with the salad bowl and separate dressing, to the barbecue.

6 Toss the dressing into the salad until it turns pink, top with the spinach leaves, and serve.

rice noodle salad

A fresh, flavourful salad with both Thai and Vietnamese influences. Add the separately-cooked rare beef for avid omnivores and use fish sauce, but leave the salad free of meat and use light soy sauce for vegetarians: this salad works splendidly well both ways.

1 Pour boiling water over the dried rice noodles in a colander set in a large heatproof bowl. Leave for 3-4 minutes or until the noodles feel pliable. Drain.

2 Pour cold water over the noodles; leave 3-4 minutes or until cool but do not let them become soft. Drain well and return them to the empty bowl.

3 Add the next 6 ingredients; stir gently to mix.

4 Put 1 tablespoon of the peanut oil into a non-stick frying pan. Heat until very hot; add the steak, if using. Cook for 1-1$\frac{1}{2}$ minutes, turning, or until the outside is brown, the inside rare. Cool. Slice the steak into fine, ribbon-like, strips.

5 Combine the remaining peanut oil with the remaining ingredients. Shake well, pour over the salad and toss gently. Cover and leave to stand.

6 Take the salad in a snap-top container; wrap the beef and its juices in foil or plastic wrap. On site, divide the salad between the serving bowls; add strips of rare beef for those who like it, adding some of the juices as well. Serve cool.

Serves 8

Ingredients

250g (9 oz) dried wide rice noodles
$\frac{1}{2}$ cucumber, in julienne strips
1 mango, in 1cm ($\frac{1}{2}$ in) cubes or strips
2-3 birds' eye chillies, finely sliced
100g (2 cups) fresh coriander (cilantro) leaves, coarsely chopped
100g (2 cups) fresh mint leaves, coarsely chopped
5cm (2 in) chunk fresh root ginger, shredded
4 tablespoons peanut oil
400g (14 oz) slice rump steak, cut at least 2cm thick (optional)
4 garlic cloves, chopped or shredded
12 spring onions (scallions) or 1 red onion, sliced
1 tablespoon caster (superfine) sugar
2 tablespoons dark sesame oil
2 tablespoons fish sauce or light soy sauce
3-4 tablespoons rice vinegar
2 tablespoons roasted sesame seeds (optional)

DESSERTS

mixed fruits salad with passion fruit

A luscious, fresh fruit dessert that is vividly scented and colourful. Substitute seasonal fruits for any of those suggested. The essential, however, is the fresh passion fruit. Without these this is just a fruit salad. Remember that passion fruit – in their hard wrinkly shells – will keep for weeks in your refrigerator. Pomegranate molasses is a sharp, sweet, scented Middle Eastern condiment: look for it in ethnic grocers.

1 Scoop the flesh out of half of the passion fruit. Combine the flesh in a blender with the flower water and the pomegranate molasses or cassis. Give 8 or 10 short, sharp blitzes: you want to separate the seeds from the pulp to obtain an intense syrup.

2 Strain the pulp through a non-metal sieve and discard the seeds.

3 Select a beautiful, but portable deep dish or glass jug. Add the syrup, the remaining passion fruit, halved but otherwise intact, the peaches, figs, nectarines, cherries and the melon. Stir. Add the citrus juice. Stir gently.

4 Transport to the site and, to serve, let people help themselves.

Serves 8

Ingredients
12 fresh passion fruit (about 400–650g/14oz–
    1 lb 7 oz), washed and halved
½ teaspoon orange flower, geranium or rose water
2 tablespoons pomegranate molasses or crème de
    cassis
500g (5 medium) fresh peaches, white- or yellow-
    fleshed, pitted and in chunks
4 fresh, ripe figs, green or black, halved lengthwise
4 ripe nectarines or red-fleshed plums, pitted and in
    chunks
250g (1–1½ cups) cherries, still on the stalk
250g (2 cups) orange- or green-fleshed melon,
    seeded, in 5cm (2 in) chunks
juice of 4 minneolas, tangelos, tangerines or
    satsumas

munster with pears

Though unctuous and silky to eat and deceptively mild, the strong aroma of Munster is often enough to deter many a diner. It combines blissfully with ripe pears.

1 If your Munster is a little underripe, be bold: heat it, still paper-wrapped, in an oven preheated to 230°C (450°F) for 5 minutes or else use a microwave (700-850 watts) on High for 2 minutes. This acts as an accelerated ripening process. The effect is intense. Take the cheese to the barbecue just as it is. It will begin to trickle and run before too long.

2 Leave the stalks on the pears. Using an apple corer, push upwards from the base of each pear almost to the top stem area. Do not sever nor twist. At serving time, push down on the stem area and remove the core.

3 Unwrap the cheese just as you begin to eat. Leave the pears whole. Let your guests use knives or fingers to eat their 100% edible pear.

Serves 8

Ingredients

small Munster cheese (a washed-rind cheese from Alsace), about 225g (8 oz)

8 ripe but firm dessert pears

raspberry fool with meringues

This is an ingenious recipe. The 'impossible' meringue idea, from my sister Alison, works brilliantly and makes quick, foolproof meringues: 80-100 or so. These are small, crisp and can be stored, in airtight jars, for months. But if you'd prefer to use purchased meringues, this too is an option. The actual dessert is assembled pretty much on the spot: its crunch, softness, sweetness and sharpness is a pleasant paradox.

1 Combine the 5 meringue ingredients, in order, in a heatproof bowl standing in 2.5cm (1 in) of near-boiling water. Using an electric whisk or rotary beater, whisk continuously until the unpromising-looking mix forms a dense, glossy, stiff meringue which will keep its shape. Remove the bowl from the water.

2 Set some wetted non-stick paper on 2 large oven trays. Wet the surface of these again. Put the meringue into a piping-bag with a 1cm ($^1/_2$ in) star nozzle (tube). Pipe 80-100 small, neat meringues. Bake at 130-140°C (250-275°F) for 1-1$^1/_4$ hours or until crisp.

3 Take half, or as many as you want, to the barbecue along with the berries, sugar and cream, in insulated containers. Take a bowl, too, in which to mash everything together.

4 On site, mash the berries and sugar roughly with a fork and trickle this purée into the cream, adding whole or smashed meringues at will. Dust with a little icing (confectioners') sugar and serve in glasses, cups or platefuls.

Serves 8

Ingredients

'Impossible' meringues:
325g (1$^1/_2$ cups) caster (superfine) sugar
2 egg whites
1 teaspoon vanilla essence
1 teaspoon malt vinegar
60ml (4 tbsp) boiling water
Note: Makes 80-100 tiny meringues. Substitution: 200g (8 oz) bought meringues

Berry fool:
350g (2 cups) fresh raspberries
50g (1 cup) icing (confectioners') sugar, plus extra for dusting
450ml (2 cups) double (heavy) cream, whipped or 600ml (2$^1/_2$ cups) extra-thick, double (heavy) cream

chocolate cream pots

Chocolate is a favourite with young and old and these are luxurious, indulgent desserts to finish off a perfect meal. Use chocolate with a high percentage of cocoa solids - the difference is amazing.

1 Put the cream and the chocolate into a large heatproof bowl and microwave (700–850 watts) on High for 2–2$^1/_2$ minutes, stirring occasionally, until melted. Alternatively, set it in a heatproof bowl over a pan of boiling water and stir until melted.

2 Fold in the mascarpone to obtain a marbled effect. Sift the icing (confectioners') sugar and cinnamon together and stir into the chocolate mixture, then stir in the liqueur. Mix until creamy.

3 Spoon, pipe or smooth the chocolate cream into 8 small china or glass pots to be taken to the barbecue. Do not overfill them. Firm them up by placing them in the freezer for 20 minutes, or chill for several hours or overnight.

4 Pack the pots into a larger box with a lid, or wrap them securely in foil into one large packet. To serve, unwrap the pots, and put a little stack of fine wafers such as *crêpes à dentelles* or chocolate matchsticks beside each dessert.

Serves 8

Ingredients
2 tablespoons double (heavy) cream
200g (7 oz) bitter (dark) chocolate, broken into bits
50g ($^1/_3$ cup) icing (confectioners') sugar
2 teaspoons ground cinnamon
4 tablespoons Amaretto di Saronno or Cointreau liqueur
400g (1$^3/_4$ cups) mascarpone

To serve:
1 box crisp wafers or chocolate matchsticks

flambéed peaches with cognac and cointreau

This delicious dessert complements a bonfire banquet perfectly. Use peaches that are bought fully ripe or - if not - ripen them in a warm place. This is a bold but messy dish but well worth the effort.

1 Halve the peaches by scoring around the circumference, twisting them and removing the pits. Heat the peach halves in 2 large frying pans over a corner of the fire (you may want to use old frying pans for this as the flames may discolour them slightly).

2 Tear or cut the oranges in half and squeeze the juice over the peaches; trickle the honey over. Add the orange halves to the pan, if you like, for extra flavour.

3 When the peaches are warmed through and juicy, warm a large metal ladle and half fill with cognac, then top up with Cointreau. Stir to mix. Hold the ladle near the heat and carefully ignite the contents with a long match or taper. Pour it, still flaming, over the peaches. Spoon the peaches and their liquid into pretty dishes and eat them warm.

Serves 8

Ingredients
16 small or 8 large ripe, scented peaches (2-3kg/ 4$^1/_2$-6$^1/_2$ lb)
2 oranges
4-8 tablespoons clear honey
250ml (1 cup) cognac, or more to taste
250ml (1 cup) Cointreau (triple sec), or more to taste

DRINKS

elderflower tea

Ready-made elderflower syrup is available from delis, good grocers and even some supermarkets. Use it along with a delicate China tea and, if real elderflower is blooming, add some washed heads of flowers too.

Serves 8

Ingredients

1 litre (4 cups) boiling water
10g (¼ oz) China tea, e.g. jasmine
2 tablespoons elderflower syrup or cordial
2 fresh elderflower heads, if in season

Use a heatproof glass jug, vacuum flask, whatever pleases you and suits the occasion. Pour the water over the tea, tied up in muslin or in a tea infuser, and leave to infuse for 5 minutes. Remove the tea 'bag' or infuser and pour in the syrup or cordial. To serve, push the flowerheads (rinsed in spring water) into the tea at serving time. Serve in small cups, goblets or tumblers.

Note:
If made double strength (using only 500ml/2 cups of boiling water) and poured over 500ml (2 cups) of ice cubes, this can become a chilled drink instead of a hot one.

scented tea with rum

Tea made with aromatics is very alluring. Use China, Indian or an exotic tea from Sri Lanka or Nepal. Vary the additions according to taste.

Serves 4-6

Ingredients

1 litre (4 cups) boiling water
1 cinnamon stick, crushed
4 cloves
6 green cardamom pods, crushed
7.5cm (3 in) strip of orange zest or 2.5cm (1 in) piece of fresh root ginger, bruised
15g (¼ oz) tea leaves
150ml (⅔ cup) dark rum, ideally Stroh type
1 orange, pith removed, sliced into rounds

Pour the boiling water over the cinnamon, cloves, cardamom pods; bring back to the boil, cover, reduce heat to simmering. Simmer for 3-4 minutes. Put the zest and tea, in a tie of muslin with a string attached, or in a tea infuser, into a vacuum flask. Pour in the boiling spiced liquid, including all spices. Stopper the flask. Infuse for 5 minutes then remove the tea and zest. If taking to a barbecue, take along another flask of plain boiling water, and the rum in a separate bottle. To serve, pour the tea, and add slices of orange and a dash of rum to each serving of the hot spiced tea.

mint tea

Tunisian tea houses taught me how refreshing this hot, sweet tea can be. Don't stint on the fresh mint: it is crucial to its success.

Serves 8

Ingredients

1 litre (4 cups) boiling water
15g (½ oz) green (unfermented) tea
150g (5 oz) bunch fresh mint, ideally spearmint, lower stems discarded
16-24 sugar lumps (cubes) or 8 tablespoons caster (superfine) sugar
sliced lemon or lime, to decorate

Pour the boiling water over the tea, tied up in muslin or in a tea infuser, in a jug or vacuum flask, adding half of the mint. Crush and press the mint then seal and leave to infuse. To serve, add sugar to each cup, glass or goblet, and a share of the remaining mint. Crush the mint and pour the hot tea over. Decorate with sliced lemon or lime.

sun tea

This can be made in a jug of water, sitting in a sunny spot with some fragrant tea bags suspended in it. Result - a thirst-quencher, alcohol-free, of simplicity and merit.

Serves 8

Ingredients

6 good quality tea bags or 15g ($^1/_2$ oz) loose tea (tied in muslin or in a tea infuser) e.g. China or Indian, mixed red fruits or Japanese green tea

1 litre (4 cups) spring water, tap water or filtered water, at room temperature

ice cubes

handful of fresh mint, lovage, bergamot or lemon balm leaves

2-3 tablespoons lemonade, undiluted

1 lemon, 2 limes or 1 orange, sliced iced sparkling water, ginger ale, tonic or even lemonade, to top up

Leave the tea to infuse in the water. This may take 30 minutes or 2 hours depending on the temperature, the type of tea and the situation. Stir occasionally. Strain. Pour into a flask or bottle. Take along the ice, fresh herbs, lemonade, citrus fruits, and the top-up liquid of your choice. To serve, on site, crush the herbs and sliced citrus in a big glass jug with the ice. Pour the sun tea over. Add the top-up liquid to taste. Drink cold.

coffee with calvados

'Calva' with or in coffee is a delightful French idea. Add sugar - or not - to this fragrant coffee, depending on your taste buds.

Serves 8

Ingredients

520ml ($2^1/_2$ cups) freshly made, hot coffee

8 sugar lumps (optional)

120ml ($^1/_2$ cup) Calvados, apple brandy or apple jack

Transport the hot coffee in a vacuum jug or flask. Combine a share of hot coffee, some sugar, if liked, and some of Calvados in each demitasse coffee cup. Stir, sip and enjoy. Alternatively, serve the coffee as is, taking along 8 tiny shot glasses. Serve a shot of Calvados per person in each glass, as an additional pleasure.

This indulgent drink is delicious when poured over scoops of frozen vanilla ice cream - a sort of frothy *affogato* is the result: a lovely dessert. (Keep ice cream cold by wrapping in in five or six layers of newspaper, then some heavy cloth. It will stay solid for 1 hour or so. Ideally, buy it near to the barbecue site, just before you start your meal.)

vanilla coffee

In Mexico, Café de Olla, an after-dinner drink, is sometimes served in big countrified earthenware pitchers. Adapt this idea for your own celebrations.

Serves 8

Ingredients

4 vanilla pods, sliced almost into halves, lengthwise

1 litre (4 cups) boiling water

4 teaspoons cloves, bruised

4 teaspoons allspice berries

200g ($1^1/_3$ cups) dark muscovado sugar

5cm (2 in) strip orange zest, bruised

2 litres (8 cups) freshly made cafétière coffee, e.g. Brazilian

1 Scrape out the seeds from the vanilla pods. In a saucepan, heat together the water, vanilla seeds, cloves, allspice and muscovado sugar for 5 minutes, stirring. Add the orange zest, crushing it well. Turn off the heat. Let it infuse 2 minutes. Remove the orange zest, and take this syrup to the barbecue in a vacuum flask, or in a heatproof jug that can be set on the grill.

2 To serve, reheat the syrup over the fire if necessary. Pour out some hot coffee into cups, mugs or glasses. Add a top-up of hot syrup. Pass around to your friends. Add half a cinnamon stick per person, too, if you like.

margaritas by the jugful

This Mexican creation is one of the world's most successful cocktails. More ice means more dilution; crushed ice will give a 'frozen margarita' – like a slush. Drunk *al fresco* it's usually easiest to shake the cocktail up with ice cubes. The salt rim is an essential.

Serves 8

Ingredients
350ml (1½ cups) gold or white tequila
250ml (1 cup) Cointreau or Grand Marnier
350ml (1½ cups) freshly squeezed lime juice
fine sea salt, to decorate
8 lime wedges (optional)
500ml (2 cups) ice cubes or crushed ice

Pour the tequila, liqueur and lime juice into a large jug, shaker or flask. Seal. Shake vigorously. To serve, put the salt into a shallow saucer. Rub a lime wedge around each glass rim. Invert each glass in the salt to crust it. Shake off the excess. Drop these lime wedges into the glasses. Stir or shake the margarita up with the measured volume of ice cubes until very cold. (If using crushed ice, process in a blender.) Pour the cocktail into the jug; serve in the prepared glasses.

mint julep

To 'muddle' two ingredients means to gently mash and crush them, using a long-handled spoon, to extract the maximum flavour and aroma. Any long-handled, blunt implement will do.

Serves 4

Ingredients
about 16 large, fresh mint sprigs
4 teaspoons caster (superfine) sugar
300ml (1¼ cups) crushed ice
300ml (1¼ cups) rye whiskey (bourbon)

Make these in 4 tall glasses. Put 3 sprigs of mint into the base of each. Add the sugar. 'Muddle' these well together to extract the flavours. Stir in some crushed ice and 'muddle' again. Pour in the rye whiskey (bourbon). Stir. Top up with extra crushed ice. Add the remaining mint to the glasses and serve.

Variations

mint-lime julep
Add a thick wedge of lime to the mint-sugar mix. Continue as above.

bitter mint-lime julep
To either of the drinks mentioned above add 2 shakes of Peychaud's or Angostura bitters to each glass. Do not stir. Leave as a 'blush'. Drink through straws.

applejack julep
Use applejack, Calvados or apple brandy in place of the rye whiskey (bourbon).

grown-up martini

Some martini aficionados merely pass the vermouth bottle, closed, over the top of the glass! Here is a recipe, rather stronger than usual, which is stirred, not shaken.

Serves 8

Ingredients
360ml (1½ cups) London dry gin
60ml (4 tbsp) dry vermouth
12–16 ice cubes
8 green olives (optional)
8 x 7.5cm (3 in) strips of lemon zest (optional)

Have the 8 glasses ready chilled: put them in the freezer for at least an hour or pack in an insulated bag full of ice. Stir the gin and vermouth together in a large jug over the ice cubes. Into each glass pour some martini. Drop in an olive or a lemon twist. Alternatively twist the lemon above each drink or rub the zest around the glass rim.

Variation

gin & it
Substitute dry red vermouth for the dry vermouth, but use equal quantities of gin and vermouth.

frozen vodka

To make this decorative ice jacket, take a large empty plastic bottle and cut off the top just below the shoulders. Place the vodka bottle centrally in the plastic sleeve, and fill the cylinder with water. Push bay sprigs, pretty leaves or flowers, colourful berries or lemon slices into the water around the vodka bottle and place the whole - upright - in a freezer for at least 24 hours. Take it to your barbecue complete. The outer plastic will slide off when slightly warmed - either after the travelling time, or after a little warm hand pressure. The vodka will pour thickly. Enjoy its opulent cold texture and taste!

SUPPLIERS

For accessories such as plates, napkins and containers:

The Conran Shop
Michelin House
81 Fulham Road
London SW3 6RD
Tel: 020 7589 7401
www.conran.com

Divertimenti
33-34 Marylebone High Street
London W1U 4PT
www.divertimenti.co.uk

Habitat
Branches throughout the UK
Tel: 0845 601 0740
www.habitat.net

Harvey Nichols
109-125 Knightsbridge
London SW1X 7RJ
Tel: 020 7235 5000
www.harveynichols.com

Heal's
196 Tottenham Court Road
London W1P 9LD
Tel: 020 7636 1666
www.heals.com

Ikea
2 Drury Way
North Circular Road
London NW10 0TH
Tel: 020 8208 5600
Branches throughout the UK
www.ikea.com

John Lewis Partnership
Oxford Street
London W1A 1EX
Tel: 020 7629 7711
Branches throughout the UK
www.johnlewis.com

Liberty
210-220 Regent Street
London W1B 5AH
Tel: 020 7734 1234
www.liberty.co.uk

Lombok
142 Notting Hill Gate
London W11 3QG
0870 240 7380
www.lombok.co.uk

Muji
6-17 Tottenham Court Road
London W1P 9DP
and branches
Tel: for stockists 020 8323 2208
www.muji.co.jp

Purves & Purves, Head Office
20 Europa Studios, Victoria Road
London NW10 6ND
Tel: 020 8838 0200
www.purves.co.uk

Super Green Thumb dot Com
A superb range of barbecues and
barbecue equipment.
0845 241 7413
www.supergreenthumb.com

For rugs and other decorative items:

Designers Guild
267 Kings Road
London SW3 5EN
Tel: 020 7351 5775
www.designersguild.com

Earth Tones
36 Trent Avenue
London W5 4TL
Tel: 020 7221 9300
www.earthtones.co.uk

Egg
36 Kinnerton Street
London SW1 8ES
Tel: 020 7235 9315

Nicole Farhi
202 Westbourne Grove, Notting Hill
London W11 2RH
020 7792 6888
www.nicolefarhi.com

For delicacies to pop into your picnic basket, try:

Selfridges & Co
400 Oxford Street
London W1A 1AB
www.selfridges.com

Borough Market, 8 Southwark Street
London SE1 1TL
Tel: 020 7407 1002
www.boroughmarket.org.uk
Opening hours: Friday 12 noon - 6pm
Saturday 9am - 4pm

The Grocer on Elgin
6 Elgin Crescent
London W11 2HX
Tel: 020 7221 3844
www.thegroceron.com

ACKNOWLEDGEMENTS

The publisher wishes to thank Rhona Nuttall and Kathryn Dighton at Muji for the items they loaned for photography. Muji's containers are superbly practical, and are aesthetically beautiful as well. To Earth Tones, thanks for all the lovely rugs and throws which even kept the crew warm on a few gale-force days. Also we would like to thank John Lewis Partnership, YHA Adventure Shops and Habitat for their help.

Photography by Jeremy Hopley except for: half title page, pages 17, 32, 35, 36-37, 38, 40-41, 47 and endpapers: photography by Martin Brigdale.

AUTHOR'S ACKNOWLEDGEMENTS

Thanks to my husband Ian Ferguson for research, word-processing and moral support: all were invaluable.

Thanks to Christine Blane and Liz Spicer for their word processing skills.

Additional photography: thanks to Martin Brigdale for his superb photography.

The following food and wine suppliers and specialist shops have helped immeasurably in the evolution of this book:

James Knight of Mayfair Ltd., 67 Notting Hill Gate, London W11 3JS   020 7221 6177

R. Garcia and Sons, Spanish Delicatessen, 248-250 Portobello Road, London W11 1LL

Jeroboams Cheese and Wine, 96 Holland Park Avenue, London W11 3RB

David Lidgate of C. Lidgate, Butchers and Charcutiers, 110 Holland Park Avenue, London W11 4AU

Speck, Italian Delicatessen, 2 Holland Park Terrace, Portland Road, Holland Park, London W11 4ND

Michanicou Brothers, Greengrocers, 2 Clarendon Road, Holland Park, London W11 3AA

Mr Christian's Delicatessen, 11 Elgin Crescent, Notting Hill, London W11 2JA

Kingsland, The Edwardian Butchers, 140 Portobello Road, London W11 2DZ

Portobello Road stallholders and shopkeepers, of London W11, whose vivacity is a constant inspiration.